The Face of the Earth and Other Imaginings

Those who are acquainted with Blackwood's work will know that he did not write simple ghost stories. From his childhood Blackwood had a love for the natural world and for much of his life, whenever he could, he would escape the city and the town and take himself into the remotest corners of the world, there to commune not simply with Nature, but with the very Spirit of the Earth.

Blackwood firmly believed that the human race had become too civilized, its senses and its soul dulled by the modern world, with all its conveniences and technological progress. It was only by returning to Nature that our senses would be reawakened and become more aware of the full scale of the world about us.

The stories and essays included in this book are the products of his most imaginative years. And so this collection came together, a blend of eighteen short stories, most of them previously uncollected, and twelve essays, none of which has been reprinted—the whole seeking to show the range of Blackwood's early work and the source of his inspiration: just what it was that made his imagination awake.

—from "Introduction: Imagination Inspired" by Mike Ashley

"[Blackwood] was one of the most influential supernatural writers of his time."
Storm Constantine, author of
The Wraeththu Chronicles

The Face of the Earth & Other Imaginings
by Algernon Blackwood

compiled and edited by
Mike Ashley

STARK HOUSE

Stark House Press • Eureka California

THE FACE OF THE EARTH & OTHER IMAGININGS

Published by Stark House Press
1315 H Street
Eureka, CA 95501, USA
griffinskye3@sbcglobal.net
www.starkhousepress.com

ISBN: 1-933586-70-2
ISBN-13: 978-1-933586-70-0

Book design by Mark Shepard, shepgraphics.com
Cover illustration by C. B. Williams
Proofreading by Rick Ollerman

First Stark House Press Edition: March 2015
FIRST EDITION

CONTENTS

INTRODUCTION: IMAGINATION INSPIRED

by Mike Ashley

This book has been compiled to achieve two aims. One was to bring back into print many of the early writings of Algernon Blackwood that have hitherto been uncollected and secondly, by doing that, to show what Blackwood drew upon for his inspiration.

Algernon Blackwood was one of the twentieth century's masters of supernatural fiction. His short (and not-so-short) fiction is held in high regard, especially "The Willows" and "The Wendigo," and some of his novels, such as *The Centaur* and *Julius Le Vallon*, are at last receiving the critical and popular recognition they deserve.

Most of Blackwood's fiction was originally published in magazines and newspapers and then assembled in one of a number of original collections running from *The Empty House* in 1906 to *The Doll and One Other* in 1946. In 1989 I had the privilege of compiling a selection of Blackwood's lesser known material, *The Magic Mirror*, most of which had not previously been collected. Since then I have unearthed several more of his early stories and though I don't profess to having discovered all of his published material—I quite expect there to be further undiscovered gems—I do feel I am getting close. At least as regards his fiction.

There weren't enough new discoveries to make a whole new collection, but I have always been aware that in addition to his fiction Blackwood wrote a significant amount of non-fiction, and virtually none of that has been reprinted, apart from a few mood pieces which were included in *Ten Minute Stories* and *Tongues of Fire*. It seemed to me there was scope to reprint these newly discovered stories, alongside some of the other early fiction, and link it to some of Blackwood's other writings, especially those that showed from where he drew his inspiration.

Those who are acquainted with Blackwood's work will know that he did not write simple ghost stories. Sure, some of his earliest work does fall into that category, but he soon moved beyond that. From his childhood Blackwood had a love for the natural world and for much of his life, whenever he could, he would escape the city and the town and take himself into the remotest corners of the world, there to commune not simply with Nature, but with the very Spirit of the Earth. Blackwood firmly believed that the human race had become too civilized, its senses and its soul dulled by the modern world, with all its conveniences and technological progress. It was only by returning to Nature that our senses would be reawakened and become more aware of the full scale of the world about us. This became evident in his fiction with "The Willows," in his second collection *The Listener* in 1907, and in more stories that made up the volumes *The Lost Valley* (1910) and *Pan's Garden* (1912). But what is easily overlooked is that Blackwood had been writing about his passion for the wild world long before these stories came to fruition. His essay "Thoughts on Nature," which is included in this volume, was written as early as 1890 and expresses vividly how his soul is inspired by the moods of Nature.

Throughout his life Blackwood would write about the places he had visited and how these brought alive thoughts and ideas which later found their way into his stories. Two such essays included here, "Down the Danube in a Canadian Canoe" and "The Psychology of Places," describe both the physical adventure that Blackwood had that inspired "The Willows," and the spiritual experiences that fed into that story. There are similar studies reflecting upon his experiences in Canada, the Jura mountains, the Caucasus and Egypt, all of which imprinted themselves deeply in his psyche and led to an outpouring of intensely passionate fiction.

Blackwood also wanted to stimulate that same mood in others. His stories could convey some of that to adults, but he found the greatest joy was in seeking to free the imagination of children whose minds had yet to be burdened by everyday life. It is not too surprising that Blackwood wrote books and stories both for children and about children, using a child's-eye view of the world to help adults free their own imagination. Some of these stories he later worked into his novels, but the original stories have not themselves been reprinted. I have included here one such example, "The Night-Wind," which was later revised to form a key chapter, "Imagination Wakes," in *The Extra Day*. It is an ideal example of how Blackwood would encourage children to use their imagination in games and at the same time gain a wider view of the natural world.

In due course, Blackwood became affected by the First World War in which he served as an Intelligence Agent and then as a Red Cross Searcher. What he did and what he witnessed severely damaged his sensitive soul and it required all his spiritual power to recover. During the War he was involved in propaganda writing but, as you can imagine, his approach was not the tub-thumping call to recruitment but rather to help rebuild people's spirits by reminding them of the beauty of the world, and the wonder of the collective spirit. Even here, though, you can sense how Blackwood's spirit was itself being suffocated. The same person who wrote "The Miracle" and "The Memory of Beauty" also wrote "The Paper Man" and "Onanonanon," two quite surreal and almost dislocated stories which show how the War affected the mind and people's attitudes to each other.

The War changed Blackwood and although he recovered to some degree and continued to write for over thirty more years, it was a different Blackwood. The stories and essays included in this book are the products of his most imaginative years. And so this collection came together, a blend of eighteen short stories, most of them previously uncollected (except for a few revived from *The Magic Mirror*) and twelve essays, none of which has been reprinted—the whole seeking to show the range of Blackwood's early work and the source of his inspiration: just what it was that made his imagination awake.

At the end of the book I have provided a complete bibliography of Blackwood's published fiction and essays, in chronological order. I hope this will help devotees follow through his material in the order in which it was published, and perhaps also provide an opportunity to see what may be missing—just in case!

The Face of the Earth
and Other Imaginings
by Algernon Blackwood

SECTION 1: EARLY TALES

Blackwood's first published short story, so far as we know, was "A Mysterious House" in the July 1889 *Belgravia*, which leads off this section. Prior to this he had appeared with three short satirical poems in *Judy*, the serio-comic rival to *Punch*, edited by Charles H. Ross, the creator of the first comic-strip character, Ally Sloper. Blackwood won a pound for each of the three poems which were written to highlight (or lampoon) a political issue of some significance. His first, "A Grand Old Nightmare," in the issue for 19 December 1888, related to the Irish Home Rule Bill, which Blackwood clearly did not favour. This was written while Blackwood was at Edinburgh University and was probably composed *after* "A Mysterious House," which would have taken a few months before it appeared in print.

"A Mysterious House" is much more the fare we would have expected from Blackwood. At the time, before he went to university, Blackwood undertook the investigation of purportedly haunted houses on behalf of the Society for Psychical Research. He was not himself a member, but knew Frank Podmore, who was a leading member in the Society and worked with Blackwood's father. I have no idea whether the house in this story relates to any of Blackwood's investigations, but it must, at least, have been drawn from his experiences.

"A Strange Adventure in the Black Forest" has never previously been reprinted. I was delighted to stumble across it in the November 1889 issue of *The Blackfriar's Magazine*, which was the official organ of the Post Office, published at St. Martins-le-Grand in London where Blackwood's father served as Secretary, a position second only to the Postmaster General. The story, which relates to Blackwood's early years in the Black Forest, where he was a pupil at the School of the Moravian Brotherhood at Königsfeld, shows that "A Mysterious House" was not a one off. Although Blackwood later maintained that he had never thought to submit any stories for publication, this shows that he had, and that his first two stories were both ghost stories. Although writing fiction would go on hiatus while he struggled to make a living in Canada and New York in the 1890s, Blackwood's roots as a writer of weird fiction were clearly planted seventeen years before his first book was published.

While Blackwood was in Canada and New York he wrote some non-fiction, discussed later, but very little fiction. There was one piece which was not supernatural but a tale of unrequited love, "The Story of Karl Ott," published in *Pall Mall Magazine* in 1896. I have not reprinted that here because my focus has been on his strange stories. He did not turn to fiction in earnest until he had returned to England in 1899 and, interestingly, his first sale then, "A Haunted Island," was both supernatural and inspired by his years in Canada.

Blackwood continued to write, mostly essays at this time, but such fiction as he did produce tended to end up in a cupboard rather than be sold to a magazine. It was only when a reporter friend, Angus Hamilton, asked to see some, borrowed them and, unbeknown to Blackwood, submitted them to a publisher, that his first book *The Empty House*, saw print in 1906. It was followed a year later by *The Listener* and the year after that by the blockbuster *John Silence*, which sold so well that Blackwood realised he could earn a living by writing, with sufficient income to allow him to travel to his favourite places in Europe and beyond.

Blackwood now started to submit stories to magazines in earnest. There had been a few prior to 1906, but after *The Listener*, he began to see this as a career and took it seriously. The first of these that I know of, and another recent discovery, was "The Farmhouse on the Hill." I have yet to find the British source for this story and only learned of it because it was reprinted in the *Adelaide Chronicle* in Australia in December 1907. This leaves me pondering that there may have been a few other stories around this time that appeared in as yet unknown publications. "The Farmhouse on the Hill" was included in the omnibus volume of *Ten Minute Stories* and *Day and Night Stories* which Stark House published in 2013 as an example of one of the stories Blackwood may have left out of *Ten Minute Stories* when he was in a sudden panic about the contents (see the introduction to that volume for the full story). I've decided to include it here as well in order to present the full picture of Blackwood's emerging work.

After the success of *John Silence*, though, Blackwood went into overdrive. He found he could write stories anywhere and would often pen short pieces for newspapers, such as the *Westminster Gazette*, which would pay enough for his day-to-day expenses, and then save the longer, more detailed stories for the higher paying magazines which his newly acquired literary agent, A. P. Watt, handled on his behalf.

Some of these early stories were not supernatural, such as "The Secret," the first of his contributions to the *Westminster Gazette*, which nevertheless found its way into *Ten Minute Stories*. But at the same time he was producing further strange stories, starting with "The Kit-Bag." A surprising number of these early stories did not reappear in Blackwood's later collections and those are included in these first two sections. Amongst them is "The Face of the Earth" which, along with "The Man Who Found Out" (published in 1909 but uncollected until *The Wolves of God* in 1921), were amongst the earliest of Blackwood's writings to consider the concept of animism, particularly as expressed in the works of Gustav Fechner, who believed that all of Creation, including the Earth itself, had a spirit or soul—literally Mother Earth. This belief saw its full expression in *The Centaur*, but "The Face of the Earth," unreprinted until now, shows Blackwood's earliest exploration of the idea. Interestingly, "The Face of the Earth" includes a character called Arthur Spinrobin, a surname that Blackwood used again for Robert Spinrobin in *The Human Chord*. It is fairly evident that

Spinrobin is Blackwood's projection of himself.

These early stories, therefore, show Blackwood experimenting with themes and ideas that would later develop into his larger stories and novels. They show his imagination starting to grow.

—*Mike Ashley*

A Mysterious House

Explanations are usually very tedious, and so without any introduction or pre-ambulation I will plunge right into the midst of this uncanny story I am about to tell.... When, some fifteen years before the time of which I write, I was a schoolboy at Eton I made close friends with a fellow above me in the school, named Pellham. We were very great chums, and later on we went to Cambridge together, where my friend spent money and time in wasting both, while I read for holy orders, though I never actually entered the Church. Since that time I had completely lost sight of him and he of me, and, with the exception of see-ing his marriage in the papers, had no news at all of his whereabouts. One morn-ing, however, towards the close of September 1857, I received a letter from him, short, precise, and evidently written in a great hurry, asking me to go down and see him at his family seat just outside Norwich. I packed my bag and went that very same evening. He met me himself at the station and drove me home. We hardly recognized each other at first sight, so much had we changed in ap-pearance, both being on the dark side of thirty-five, but our individual char-acters had remained much the same and we were still to all appearances the best of friends. My friend was not very talkatively disposed, and I kept up a fire of questions until we drew up at the park gates. Going up the drive to the house he brightened up considerably, and gave me plenty of information about him-self and family. He was quite alone, I was surprised to hear, his wife and two daughters with an uncle of his having left for the Continent two days previously. After dinner he seemed quite the old "Cambridge Undergrad" again, and once settled round the old-fashioned hearth, with cheroots and coffee, we talked on over the days spent at Eton and Cambridge. We were just discussing our third edition of tobacco, when Pellham suddenly changed the subject, and said he would tell me now why he had written so shortly to me to pay him this unexpected visit. His face grew grave as he began by asking me if I was still a sceptic as regards ghostly manifestations.

"Indeed I am," was my answer; "I have had no reason to change my views on the subject, and think exactly as I used to at Cambridge, when we so strongly differed; but I remember you then saying that, if ever in after years you should come across an opportunity of proving to me your ideas on the subject, you would write to me at once, and I also recollect giving my word that, if possible, I would come. But during the fifteen years that have since passed by I have be-stowed little, if any, thought on the subject."

"Exactly," answered Pellham, with a grave smile that did not please me; "but now I have at last heard of a case which will satisfy us both, I think, so I wrote to you to come down and fulfil your old promise by investigating it."

"Well! Let me hear all about it first," I said cautiously. I certainly was not over-joyed to hear this news, for, though a sceptic to all intents and purposes, still "ghosts" was a subject for which I had a certain fear, and the highest ambition of my life was not to investigate haunted houses and the like just because I had years ago promised I would should a chance occur. But I repressed my feelings and tried to look interested, which I was, and delighted, which I certainly was not. Pellham then gave me a long account—thrilling enough too it was—of the case, which I have somewhat condensed in the following form. Some three or four years before, my friend had bought up a house which stood on the moor-land about eight miles off. One morning before breakfast the tenant of the house, a Mr. Sherleigh (who was there with his family), suddenly burst into my friend's study without any ceremony, and, in great heat and excitement, shouted out the following words:

"You shall suffer for it, Lord Pellham, my wife mad, and the little boy killed with fright, because you didn't choose to warn us of the room next to the drawing-room, but you shall—" Here the footman entered, and at a sign from his master led the excited and evidently cracked old man from the room, but not before he had crashed down some gold pieces on the table, with: "That's the last rent you'll get for that house, as sure as I am the last tenant."

"Well," continued my friend, "that very day, now two years ago, I rode over there myself and the house was empty. The Sherleighs had left it, and since that day I have never been able to let it to anyone. Mr. Sherleigh, who was quite mad, poor fellow, threw himself before a train, and was cut to pieces, and Mrs. Sher-leigh spread a report that it was haunted, and now no one will take it or even go near it, though it stands high and is in a very healthy position. Two nights ago," he went on gravely, "I was riding past the road which leads up to it, and through the trees I could see light in one of the upper rooms, and figures, or rather shadows, of a woman's figure, with something in her arms, kept cross-ing to and fro before the window-blind. I determined to go in and see what on earth it was, and tying my horse just outside I went in. In a minute or two I was close underneath the window where the light was still visible, and the shadow still moving to and fro with a horrible regularity. As I stood there, undecided, a feeling within warned me not to enter the house, so vivid, it was almost a soft voice that whispered in my ear. I heard no noise inside, the night air was moan-ing gently through the fir trees which surrounded the house on one side and nearly obscured the upper part of the window from view. I stooped down and picked up a large stone—it was a sharp-edged flint—and without any hesita-tion hurled it with all my might at the window pane, some eight or ten feet from the ground. The stone went straight and struck the window on one of the wooden partitions, smashing the whole framework, glass and all, into a thou-sand splinters, many of which struck me where I stood. The result was awful and unexpected. The moment the stone touched the glass the lights quite dis-appeared, and in the blackness in which I was shrouded, the next minute, I could see hiding behind the broken corners of glass a dark face and form for a short instant, and then it went and all was pitch dark again. There I was among those gloomy pine trees hardly knowing which way to turn. The face I had caught a momentary glimpse of was the face of Mr. Sherleigh, whom I knew to be dead! My knees trembled. I tried to grope my way out of the wood, and stumbled from tree to tree, often striking my head against the low branches. In vain. With the weird light in the window as a guide, I had taken but a few minutes to come, but now all was dark and I could not find my way back again. I felt as if the dismal tree trunks were living things, which seemed to move. Suddenly I heard a noise on my left. I stopped and listened. Horror! I was still close to the window, and what I heard was a cracking and splintering of broken glass, as if some one from inside were slowly forcing their way out through the hole made by my stone! Was it he? The fir tree next to me suddenly shook violently, as if agitated by a powerful gust of wind, and then in a gleam of weird light I saw a long dark body hanging half-way out of the window, with black hair streaming down the shoulders. It raised one arm and slammed down something at my feet which fell with a rattle, and then hissed out: 'There's the last rent you'll ever have for this house.' I stood literally stupefied with horror, then a cold numb sensation came over me and I fell fainting on my face, but not until I had heard my horse give a prolonged neigh and then his footsteps dying away in the distance on the hard moorland road.

"...When I recovered consciousness it was broad daylight. I was cold and damp; all night I had lain where I fell. I rose and limped, stiff and tired, to the place where I had tied my horse the night before, but no horse was there. And the horrible sound of his hoofs echoing away in the distance came back to me, and I shuddered as I thought of what I had seen. After a terrible trudge of three hours I reached home. A tremendous search had been made for me, of course, but no one dreamt of looking for me where I really was. The horse had found his way home, and I have never found out what frightened him so."

My friend's account was over. He lit his cigar, which had gone out during the narrative, and settling himself comfortably in his chair, said, "Well, old boy, that's a case I don't feel at all inclined to investigate by myself, but I'll do it with your aid. You know, a genuine sceptic is a great addition in such things, so we'll get to the bottom of it somehow."

My feelings at that moment were not difficult to describe. I disliked the whole affair, and wanted heartily to get out of it; and yet something urged me to go through with it and show my friend that the house was all right, that imagination did it all, that the horse may have taken fright at anything, and that very possibly there really was someone in the house all the time, and imagination had done the rest. Such were the somewhat mixed thoughts in my mind at the time. However, in a few moments all was settled and we had agreed to go the following night, search the house first, and then sit up all night in the room next to the drawing-room. Then we both went to our separate bedrooms to think the

matter over and get a long sleep, as we neither expected to get any the following night.

Next morning at breakfast we both talked cheerfully about the coming night
and how best to meet its requirements as regards food, etc. We agreed to take
pistols for weapons, horses as a means of conveyance, and abundant food
wherewith to fortify ourselves against a possible attack of ghosts.

The day drew on towards its close. It was very hot and sultry weather, and not
a breath of wind stirred the murky atmosphere, as at 4:30 p.m. we bestrode our
horses and made off in the direction of the "White House." A long gravel road,
lonely in the extreme, led us across the wild uncultivated moorland for six or
seven miles, then we saw a copse of fir trees which, my friend informed me, were
the trees which sheltered one side of the house. In a few minutes we had passed
through the front garden gate and were among the dark fir trees, and then as
we turned a sharp corner the house burst full upon us. It was square and ugly.
Great staring windows in regular rows met our eyes and conveyed an unpleasant impression to the brain—at least, they did to mine. From the very moment we had passed the front gate till I left the house next morning, I felt a nasty
sick sensation creep over me, a feeling of numbness and torpor which seemed
to make the blood run thick and sluggish in my veins. The events of that night
have remained engraven on my brain as with fire, and, though they happened
years ago, I can see them now as vividly as then. Only an eye-witness can possibly describe them, should he wish to do justice to them, and so my feeble pen
shall make the attempt.

It was about 6:30, and we had settled our horses in a barn outside for the night.
There were only two walls to keep the barn in position, and these were simply
a row of rotten posts, half-decayed in places, so we securely tied the horses and,
with a good supply of hay, left them for the night. We then approached the door
and, after fumbling in the lock for some time, Pellham succeeded in opening
it. A sickly, musty odour pervaded the hall, and the first thing we did after a
thorough search, which revealed nothing, was to open all the doors and windows all over the house, so as to let in what little air there was. Then we went
upstairs into the little room next to the drawing-room, where, according to Sherleigh, strange things had occurred. But the window was in pieces, and hardly
an entire pane of glass was left, and we were forced to select another room on
the same floor (i.e., the second) and looking out on the same copse of pine trees,
whose branches almost touched the glass, so close were they. It was a very ordinary room; a fireplace, no furniture but a rickety table and three chairs, one
of which was broken. The only disagreeable feature we noticed about the room
was its gloominess; it was so very dark. The trees outside, as I have already said,
were so close that the slightest breath of wind rustled their twigs against the window. We soon had six candles fixed and burning in different parts of the little
room, and the blaze of light was still further increased by a roaring fire, on which
a kettle was singing for tea, and eggs boiling in a saucepan, and at half-past seven

we were in the middle of our first tea in a haunted house. It was, indeed, less luxurious than the dinners I had been used to lately, but otherwise there was nothing to find fault with, and a little later the tea things were cleared away in a heap in a corner (where, by-the-by, they are to this day), and we were sitting round an empty table, smoking in silence. The door out into the passage was fast shut, but the window was wide open. The sun had sunk out of sight in a beautiful sky of wonderful colouring. Small fleecy clouds floating about caught the soft after-glow and looked unearthly as seen through the thick fir branches. The faint red hue of the western sky looked like the reflection of some huge and distant conflagration, growing dimmer and fainter as the dark engines of the night played upon it, extinguishing the leaping flames and suffusing the sky with a red reflected glow. Not a breath of air stirred the trees. My friend had left the window and was poking and arranging the fire, with his back turned towards me. I was standing close to the window, looking at the fast-fading colours, when it seemed to me that the window sash was moving. I looked closer. Yes! I was not mistaken. The lower half was gradually sinking; gradually and very quietly it went down. At first I thought the weight had slipped and gone wrong, and the window was slipping down of its own accord; but when I saw the bolt pulled across and fastened as by an invisible hand, I thought differently. My first impulse was to immediately undo the bolt again and open the window, but on trying to move—good heavens! I found I had lost all power of motion and could not move a muscle of my body. I was literally rooted to the ground. Neither could I move the muscles of my tongue or mouth; I could not speak or utter a sound. Pellham was still doing something to the fire, and I could hear him muttering to himself, though I could not distinguish any words. Suddenly, then, I felt the power of motion returning to me; my muscles were relaxing, and turning, though not without a considerable effort, I walked to the fireplace. Pellham, then, for the first time noticed that the window was shut, and he made a remark about the closeness of the night, asking me why I had closed it.

"Hulloa," he went on, before I had time to answer, "by the gods above! What is happening to that window? Look—why it's moving!"

I turned. *The window was slowly being opened again.*

Yes, sure enough it was. Slowly and steadily it moved or was pushed up.

We could but believe our eyes; in half a minute the window was wide open again. I turned and looked at Pellham and he looked at me, and in dead silence we stared at one another, neither knowing what to say or wishing to break the silence. But at length my friend spoke.

"I wish I were a sceptic, old man, like you are; sceptics are always safer in a place like this."

"Yes," I said, as cheerfully as I could, "I feel safe enough, and what's more, I am convinced that the window was opened by human agency from outside."

Pellham smiled, he knew as well as I that no human fingers could have fastened the bolt from outside. "Well," he said briskly, "perhaps you are right;

come, let's examine the window."

We rose and approached it, and my friend put his head and shoulders out into the air. It was very dark, and a strange oppressive stillness reigned outside, only broken by the gentle moaning sound of the night wind as it rustled through the trees and swept their branches like the strings of a lyre. I followed my friend's example, and together we peered out into the night. Soon my eyes rested on the ground below us, and at the base of one of the nearer pines I thought I could distinguish a black form, clinging, as it seemed, to the tree. I pointed it out to Pellham, who failed to see anything, or at least said so; anyhow, I was glad to believe that my excited imagination was the real cause. We were still leaning out of the window in silence, when several of the trees, especially the one where I imagined I had seen the shape, were most violently agitated, as though by a mighty wind; but we felt not the slightest breath on our faces. At the same instant we heard a subdued shuffling sound in the room behind us, which seemed to come from the direction of the chimney. But neither of us referred to it as we slowly walked back to the fire and took up our places on either side on the two chairs, which were at the best very rickety.

"It isn't wise to leave the window open," said my friend, suddenly, "for if there really is anyone outside, they can see all and everything we do; while we, for our part, can see absolutely nothing of what goes on outside."

I agreed, and walked up to the window, shutting it with a bang and firmly drawing the bolt.

"I've brought a book," he went on, "which I thought we might read out aloud in turn to relieve the dullness and the silence."

He stopped speaking and looked at me, and at the same moment I raised my eyes to his face. To my intense horror and surprise I noticed for the first time a long smear of blood, wet and crimson, across his forehead. My horror was so great that for some seconds I could not find my tongue, and sat stupidly staring at him. At last I gasped out:

"My dear fellow, what has happened to you, have you cut yourself?"

"Where? What do you mean?" he replied, looking round him with surprise.

For answer I took out my handkerchief, and wiping his brow, showed him the red stains. But as I stood there showing him this proof and as he was expressing his utter astonishment, I distinctly saw something that for the moment made the blood rush from the extremities and crowd into my head. Something seemed to tighten round my heart. I saw a large, gleaming knife and hand disappear into the air in the direction of the window. It was too much; my nerves failed me, and I dropped fainting to the floor.

When I came to myself I was lying where I fell by the fireplace. Pellham was sitting beside me.

"I thought you were dead," he said, "you've been unconscious for over an hour." He said this in such a queer manner and laughed so fiendishly that I

wondered what had happened to him during the interval. Had he seen something awful and gone mad? There was a strange light in his dark eyes and a leer
on his lips. Just then he took up his book quite naturally and began to read aloud,
every now and then he made a comment on what he was reading, quite sensi-
bly too, and soon I began to think, as I sipped my brandy out of our flask, that
I must have had a frightful dream. But there at my feet lay the bloodstained
handkerchief, and I could not get over that. I glanced at his face; the smear had
disappeared, and no scratch or wound was visible.

Pellham had not been reading long, perhaps some five or ten minutes, when
we heard a strange noise outside among the trees, just audible above the death-
like stillness of the autumn night. It was a confused voice like the low whispering
of several persons, and as I listened, still weak from the last shock, the blood
stood still in my veins. Pellham went on reading as usual. This struck me as very
curious, for he must have heard the noise plainly; but I said nothing, and
glancing at him I saw the same light in his eyes and the evil leer on his mouth,
looking ugly in the flickering glare of the candles and firelight.

Suddenly we heard a tremendous noise outside, altogether drowning the
first. The horses had broken loose and were tearing wildly past the house. Long
and wild neighs rang out and died away, and we knew our horses were gone.
Pellham was still reading, and as I looked at him a sudden and horrid thought
flashed through my brain. It was this: had he anything to do with this? Was it
possible? Before I had time to answer my question Pellham threw down the
book and made for the door, locked it, drew out the key, and opening the window threw it far away among the trees. I then recognized the awful fact that I
was alone with a madman. I glanced at my watch, it was a quarter to one. Instead of one hour I must have been unconscious two at least. This was terrible
in the extreme. He was a man of far more powerful physique than I. What was
to be done? Pellham strode grinning up to the fire, went down on both knees
and commenced blowing between the bars with all his might. I saw my chance,
and quietly walking to the window, without a word I climbed out, and letting
myself as far down as my arms would allow I then let go and dropped. It was a
distance of four or five feet, but in the darkness I tumbled forward on my face.
As I rose, uninjured, I distinctly heard the sound of running feet close to me,
but in my bewilderment I could not make out clearly in which direction they
were going; they only lasted a moment or two. But what a terrific sight met my
gaze as I turned the corner of the house, and saw volumes of smoke pouring
steadily out of the windows and roof of the back portion of the house. Now and
again a long flame, too, shot up to heaven.

"Good God!" I cried, "the house is on fire."

No wonder the horses had taken flight. But my poor friend, what could I do
for him? The window was too high for me to climb in again, and the doors were
locked. In a few minutes the flames would spread to this side of the house and
the poor fellow would be burnt to death unless he had enough sense left to jump

out of the window.

I hurried back to the spot where I had let myself down from the window, just in time to see the last scene of the most ghastly experience I have ever witnessed. Pellham was standing at the window. In his hand was a red-hot poker, and it was pointed at his throat, but the strain was too great for my nervous system and with a violent start *I woke up!*

After our heavy tea we had both fallen asleep, just as we were in our chairs. Pellham was still snoring opposite me, and the light was stealing in through the window. It was morning, about half-past six. All the candles had burnt themselves out, and it was a wonder they had not set fire to the dry wood near them.

Twenty minutes later we had re-lit the fire and were discussing the remnant of eggs and coffee. Half an hour later we were riding home in the bright, crisp, morning air, and an hour and a half later we were in the middle of a second and far superior breakfast, during which I did not tell my dream, but during which we did agree that it had been the dullest and most uncomfortable night we had ever spent away from home.

A Strange Adventure in the Black Forest

In the southern portion of the Duchy of Baden, situated in the darkest depths of the Black Forest, lies the primitive village of Königseld. For some little distance round this lonely collection of houses the land has been considerably cleared of trees, and from certain points of vantage—the village stands 30,000 feet above the sea—one gazes round on the flowing curves of the Black Forest range, ever clothed in the sombre garments of the pines, which give the hills a soft appearance of velvet. On every side hundreds and hundreds of tall pine trees stretch away over hill and vale, until at length, in the far distance, the eye fails to distinguish them, as the sky seems to come down and mingle with their gloomy tints.

This little village of Königsfeld, far away from the world on these wild heights, is a Moravian settlement, and a model one of its kind. Built in a square, with fresh green gardens, and a fountain in the centre, it is complete in itself. On one side rises the church, facing which, on the opposite side of the square, stands a large, ugly building of stone, a little out of keeping, perhaps, with the modest size of the surrounding wooden houses. This is nothing else than the school—the "Knaben-Anstalt." One of those simple, strict, and striking establishments known as "Moravian schools."

It was to this school that, one morning in May, 187—, my father packed me off, for better, for worse, and it was in this lonely hamlet, and among its unsophisticated inhabitants, that I had my first experience of Continental life. But of that I intend to say nothing; it can be of little interest, and, beyond the novelty of living with French, Italian, Russian, and Brazilian youths, all struggling with the German tongue, and the excitement connected with strange customs, fierce winters, hot summers, and wonderfully beautiful surroundings—beyond this, there would be, indeed, little of interest to relate. But what I propose to record is an event that occurred to me before I had been there very long, an event that to me was, and always has been, totally inexplicable on natural grounds.

When I had been an inmate of the said establishment for nearly three months, having sufficiently mastered the language to be able to peer into its deeper mysteries, I was one morning suddenly summoned from my work-table, where I had been poring over a German version of Euclid, half asleep in the heat of the midday sun—summoned to the august presence of the Herr Direktor. There he stood behind his high desk, covered with papers, vigorously smoking a long cigar and staring fixedly at me through his strong spectacles, which made his eyes look as big as saucers. In his hand he held a letter, and, before he spoke, I remember puzzling my sleepy brain as to his object in sending for me. Could he have known that my "Euclid" had been upside down, and that I was thinking sadly of my home in Kent? Could he possibly have been aware that, for the half-hour preceding his summons for me, I had slyly been producing from my pocket one fat cherry after another, and, under the pretence of scratching my nose, had introduced them in slow succession to the inside of my cavernous mouth? Impossible! I thought, but my surmises were cut short by his stentorian voice, which woke me once more into life, in spite of the heat of the day. "Blackvood," he began, and then, looking for something on his desk, he paused a moment. "Ja," I gasped, fearing he was hunting for a stick, and then, without rhyme or reason, I added "Ja, bitte!" Though thoroughly accustomed to hear the words of his native tongue put to any use, and made to serve any purpose that might seem fit to the "user," still he smiled a gentle smile at my inane "Ja bitte," and having found what he was looking for, namely, a letter, he proceeded to inform me that my father had written to him to say that my sister, C—, was on a visit to Nüremberg, and that, if his son had been well-behaved, could he—the Herr Direktor—see his way to letting me go to see her for a few days in that town.

I was so delighted at this news, that, forgetting in whose presence I was, I ejaculated "Hurrah!" and, at the same time, gave a sort of jump for joy—modified somewhat by the size of the room I was in. But hardly had I done this iniquitous act when I remembered where I was, and seeing the saucer eyes upon me, I shuffled meekly and again said "Ja bitte," adding this time a modest "Ach! Ach!" But the "Herr Director" was in a good mood, and saying that as I had been working well (I thought of the Euclid still lying upside down and I murmured "Jawohl") and the holidays were near, he had no objection to my going and hoped that I should enjoy myself.

So it was all settled, and before evening the whole school knew that "Blackvood" was going. But I kept my counsel and told no one where or wherefore I was going. The consequence was that various reports were spread about. One was that I was expelled, another that I had received bad news, while a third said that I had complained of the living, and having given the Herr Direktor a bit of my mind, I was leaving of my own accord; and this was the version that, by sundry signs and winks, I induced the school to believe.

However, the following morning, before the rest of the place was awake, I was rolling along in a cart, down the broad, white road that led to our nearest station, some five or six miles distant. It was a lovely morning, and as my driver took me along at a brisk pace through the fresh, sweet air I simply revelled in the thought that I was really free from supervision for a whole week. The road lay mostly through the deepest part of the forest. On either side a wall of stately pines shot up to heaven, and their summits gleamed bright in the first rays of the rising sun. The air, redolent of pines and moss, was life itself, and now and then was mingled with it that delicious odour of newly-sawn wood, as we passed the stacks near the roadside.

I was thus taking in the sweet scents and scenery, and forming plans for my visit to Nüremberg, when suddenly the horse reared up as high as the cart would allow it, and began to kick and plunge violently. To my surprise I noticed, on looking round me, that there was nothing that could possibly have frightened the animal. The road was just the same there as it had been for the last two miles, except that on our right a clearing of some fifty yards square, had been made. The ground of this clearing was soft and marshy and a small stream ran through it and under the road. Across this stream, dividing the clearing into two halves, ran a high bank, evidently an old mill-dam of some sort.

Meanwhile the driver had left his seat by my side, and was leading his horse, still frightened, past the spot. When he had taken his seat again, I asked him at what the horse could possibly have shied, and he answered mysteriously, in his half dialect I could only just understand, that he never knew a horse that did not take fright on passing that spot, since the "Rothe Mühle" had disappeared. I was by no means superstitiously inclined in those days, but thinking I might hear a genuine Black Forest legend, I further questioned the man, and, after some time, induced him to tell me the following story, which I have since confirmed, and now condense somewhat as follows:—

A good many years previous to the time of which I write, there had stood in that clearing, described above, a tall reddish building of wood, called the Red Mill. It was owned and worked by a peasant, one Hans Binschedler, a man of an evil reputation, which he thoroughly deserved. A slave to drink and a man of frightful passions, he was much feared by the neighbouring peasantry, and few cared to pass his way at night-time alone. Many stories were afloat concerning him, but no one took any steps to stop the man in his supposed course of crime. However, at length the climax was reached. One morning, when the winter's snow lay thick upon the ground, a body was found lying on the road just opposite the Red Mill. It was the corpse of a traveller, and on his neck were marks of violence, whilst all round the snow was much disturbed by the signs of an awful struggle, and down the road for some distance tracks of long strides told of a terrible chase—a chase ending in murder. Before the tracks began to lengthen by running, the traces of a second man came out of the forest; so that it was pretty clear the murderer had followed, or waited for his victim in the shades of the forest, and then rushed out suddenly upon him and accomplished the act. The guilt of the grim deed was easily brought home to the door of Binschedler, for he was discovered two days afterwards at the bottom of his mill pool. So the neighbourhood was freed from his evil presence, but soon a report spread that the mill had disappeared, and on investigation this proved to be the case, the whole structure appearing to have been engulfed by the swampy land on which it had stood.

But, besides this, other reports soon spread far and wide. One man passing there at night—alone of course—had seen the gaunt, red form of the mill standing there in the darkness, as of old. A second man swore he had heard a muffled scream; while a third averred on his life that, while driving past there in the dusk, he had heard footsteps in the forest, keeping even with his trap, at a pace no man could possibly maintain in the dense forest, and what was more, that his horse had heard it and bolted, and had not stopped for miles. Such were the stories afloat, and, at length, things grew to such a pass, that a body of the villagers, with the "Prediger" of the brotherhood at their head, set out to exorcise the unclean spirit that haunted the fatal spot. Having reached the spot, the preacher opened his bible *three times in succession*, it having, on all three occasions, been shut by an invisible hand. After this they returned home discomfited, and ever since the evil reputation has stuck to the place, with a determination that will take long to dispute.

Such was the story my driver told me, and when he had finished, the old gateway of Villingen was in sight, and, the forest once left behind us, I soon forgot the story, which at the time had amused and interested me, in the bustle of getting into the train and the excitement of gleaning what information I could concerning my journey from the railway officials. In due course Nüremberg was reached, that

"Quaint old town of toil and traffic;
Quaint old town of art, and song;
Memories haunt thy pointed gables,
Like the rooks that round them throng;
Memories of the middle ages,
When the emperors, rough and bold,
Had their dwelling in thy
Time defying, centuries old."

Oh! What a happy week I spent there, within the precincts of those ancient and massive walls. Each day a blazing sun shone in a deep blue sky and a delicious breeze kept cool the narrow old streets. I was, perhaps, scarcely old enough to fully appreciate the artistic beauties of the wonderful old city, but my sister, who was no tyro with her brush, and who had the eye and soul of a true artist, was enthusiastic to a degree, and certainly I shared her delight. Of course, she had not been staying alone in the town, but had with her a companion—a travelling companion, a female companion! A beautiful female companion!! And, must I own it?—the society of this beautiful female companion was much sought by me and served in no little way to heighten my enjoyment. True, I was always glad to carry my sister's painting stool and box, when in the calm eventide we would go and sit on the bridge over the Pegnitz to catch some lovely sunset tint, or mount the hill, and from the grim old bastions of the fortress, strive to put faithfully on canvas the shade and form of the "Blue Franconian Mountains," I was only too pleased to do this, but I was much more pleased when, my sister once settled on her stool I would stroll off to a little distance with the "beautiful travelling companion," and in that most romantic spot talk of the past and of the future, for I was not afraid to confide anything to—to go to any length with—even to kissing—one who, although a beautiful travelling companion, could never be anything to me but an elderly and very favourite *"Aunt"*! But we were a happy trio and we passed a happy week. Only too quickly the days sped by, and I scarcely realised that one of the pleasantest visits of my early days was over, until I suddenly woke up in the railway carriage, as the train drew up at Villingen station, just about the time when my sister and aunt were arriving at Prague. The delightful dream of the quaint old city had fled, and as I stood on the platform and watched the train grow smaller and smaller, till it at length turned a corner and disappeared into the depths of the forest, I remembered that I had omitted to send word for a conveyance to meet me. At first I was extremely annoyed and muttered a good deal about "echte Deutsche Dumheit," when really it was "echte Englische Dumheit." But on second thoughts, the prospect of a walk seemed to me not so unpleasant as I had at first imagined; the distance was nothing, only some five or six miles, a lovely country, too, to be seen on the way and there was a good chance of getting a lift *en route* from some peasant's cart returning late to his home. So leaving word that my bag would be sent for in the course of the next day, I started off on my lonely trudge with nothing to carry but a walking stick of English holly.

It was about half-past seven, and the sun was just sinking behind the distant ridge of tall pines which, clearly and sharply defined, stood out against the golden sky. It was very beautiful indeed; where the forest was less dense the slanting rays found their way in between the straight, dark trunks, and lit up the carpet of bright mosses, throwing long and curious shadows across the road, which, however, were soon lost in the deep gloom of the closer and denser forest on the other side. The colours of the sky, and the sweet fresh air soon took my memory back to Nuremberg, and I walked on and on, going over again in my mind our various deeds during the past week. At one time my fancy took me back to the hot street glaring beneath our feet and above the deep blue sky. In front of us rose Albrecht Dürer's house, where that evangelist of art lived and laboured. At another time we were slowly pacing the cool aisles of Sainte Lawrence's Church or looking from the height of the walls, across the valley of the Pegnitz, with the blue background of mountains in the far distance.

But though I was little thinking of my actual surroundings there was no fear of my losing the way or taking a wrong path, for there was but one in those days, and that one I was following straight enough and the least deviation from it would have been sufficient warning, for I should have charged the pine tree stems in so doing.

But after some time my thoughts were called back from roving the streets of Nüremberg, as I became aware that it had grown very dark. I abruptly stood still in the middle of the road and looked around me. The sun had long since disappeared and though in the open country it would still have been fairly light, yet here, where the narrow road was walled in on either side by closely-packed tall pine trees, the remaining light of day could not so easily find its way, and the result was that, except straight overhead, where a narrow streak of daylight still remained, it was very dark indeed, and beneath the trees the gloom was so deep that it was with very great difficulty I could distinguish even the nearest trunks from the surrounding darkness. I glanced at my watch and found that it was considerably past eight, so I knew that I must have covered at least three miles, or about half of my distance.

I was in a happy state of mind and in no hurry to get back to the grim establishment of learning, to mix once more with somewhat grimy specimens of other nations, so I started off again at a rather slow pace, thinking that I might possibly get a lift later, though I knew this was only a chance, and a very remote one at that. My mind was now less employed than before, and as I walked lazily along, thinking how far I still had to go, what distance I had come and so forth, for the first time the extreme loneliness of the road struck me. There was not a sign of another living being beside myself, nor even of animal life. There are but few birds in the Black Forest, I mean singing birds, and these had gone to rest. There were no rabbits to dart suddenly across the road, no squirrels to be frightened and seen scuttling up the trees. Not even a moth flew across my path, and, if any had, I should scarcely have been able to see them, unless they had been white ones. Everything was hushed and still; nature was breathing her very gentlest. Only from time to time a large night-beetle would whirr round me, with his metallic buzz, and then whirr heavily away in the darkness. The night wind had risen and gently stirred the topmost branches of the tall trees, but the moaning murmur of that sound, at such an hour and in such a place, was to my mind worse than absolute and awful silence. On I tramped, a little faster than before, and the clack of my boots rang out hard on the dusty road. But there was no echo; the thick trees deadened the sound to such an extent that one might stand and scream, and even if people were near, which is not the case, one's shouts would be sucked in by the hundreds and myriads of trees long before the sound could travel any distance. Still I walked on, but without the confidence of my starting moments. The gloomy surroundings had their effect on me, and my thoughts took a gloomy turn. The fantastic depths of a somewhat morbid, though powerful, imagination were stirred within me. I grasped my stick more firmly and went a little faster. Now and then I glanced behind me, but there, as in front, the white glimmer of the road was soon lost in the all-pervading darkness. I began to long for the friendly lights of Königsfeld village, but I knew that I had at least two miles to go before I could possibly see them.

I earnestly wished that I had a cheery companion with me, and even a rough old woodcutter, with his terrible dialect, would still have been to me pleasant company. But there was no one, neither behind, nor coming to meet me. I was quite alone with trees, hundreds and thousands of them, all alike, all tall, straight, grim and gaunt, and black as ink. Nothing but trees, tree, trees! Their crests, like the plumes on a hearse, swayed mournfully in the moaning breeze, as I passed them in never-ending succession. Suddenly another sound rose sharply on the still night air! It was the sound of a footstep in the forest, as the dry fir needles crackled underneath its tread. A footstep close to me, on my right side, unmistakably. I stopped short, and my heart beat loudly and my breath came short and thick. The sound was not repeated for a second, and as I stood there waiting in suspense, the silence was so deep and awful that I felt I must break it, and in a loud voice, that seemed to rise above the trees and escape their deadening effect, I shouted:

"Wer ist's? Wer geht da?"

Not a sound followed my question! The blood rushed from my heart and an indescribable sensation of fear crept over me. I could stand it no longer and firmly seizing my stout holly stick, I dashed off at a pace that made the road seem to fly past my feet like a flash of light, and the trees seem like a dark paling with a level top. But what was my intense horror to hear, as I madly tore along, the accompanying steps of some one in the forest on my right hand, ever keeping even pace with me, a feat I knew *no man* could accomplish in amongst so dense a growth of trees. I had not been mistaken, then, before, when I imagined I had heard a footfall on the pine needles. These thoughts flashed through my brain in less than a second, and at the same time I suddenly remembered the horrible story that the driver had told me, when a week before I had driven through this way to the station, and which I had since completely forgotten. But now with frightful force it came back to my mind, and maddened with fear I dashed on at a pace I should have thought myself incapable of. But, horror! The terrible steps ever kept even with me. Now sounding heavy and dead on the thick moss, now sharp and clear on the pine needles, they never for a moment slackened, as we gradually drew nearer the scene of the murder—the clearing where the Rothe Mühle once stood. The easy pace I had taken at first now stood me in good stead, and without a sign of failing wind or strength I flew on. But it was useless; in vain I tried to outstrip the sickening thud of the other runner. Suddenly, and before I was fully aware of it, I reached—or, must I say we reached?—the dreaded clearing. I knew, or rather I *felt*, that something would happen here, that either I must fail and give in, that the other steps would cease, or else that something, of which I had no idea, would occur to stop the awful flight. I cannot say why I thought this, but I did, and I was not mistaken in my notion. The clearing was on my left, while the "steps" ever sounded on my right. As, faster than ever, I clashed passed the bared spot of the crime, the "steps" suddenly left the softer ground of the forest and, sounding hard and clear on the road, seemed to *pass in front of me*, and crossing the road, I heard a splash, as of a heavy body falling on to the soft marshy ground—and all was still! Still as death! At the same instant a cold puff of wind swept across my face, and as I leapt on faster still in my agony of fear, my stick in some unaccountable manner caught between my legs, and tripping, I was thrown forward several feet along the road and fell heavily on my face and hands.

When I came to myself again I was still lying where I had fallen, namely a little to one side of the dusty road. It was darker than ever, and, for a few minutes, I lay there totally unable to think where I was or to recollect what had happened. I made a slight movement, and a sudden pain shot up my leg from my knee-joint. That shock brought back to my scattered senses the earlier events of the evening, and I shuddered to myself as I thought of the chase I had had. But I was neither frightened nor badly hurt. I sat up and found that beyond a bruised knee and torn trowsers, and a few ugly scratches on my hands, I was unhurt; and by an effort—for I was very stiff—I rose to my feet. The blood rushed to my head tumultuously, and, in trying to steady myself, I missed the familiar support of my stick. But it was useless to hunt for it in the dark, so, striking a match, I glanced quickly round me. The match went out almost instantaneously, but not before the flickering light had enabled me to see the straight white line of my holly stick a few feet in front of me on the roadside. After groping a little, I laid my hand on it and slowly resumed my walk.

After twenty minutes' trudge, I suddenly passed out from between the dismal walls of pines and saw the lights of the village before me, and in my whole life, neither before or since, have I been so glad to see and welcome houses and signs of life. Once out of the forest I was able to see clearly; there was no moon, but myriads of stars studded the vault of heaven, and, after inspecting for some seconds the white face of my watch, I discovered that it was only twenty minutes past nine, so that I could not have been insensible for more than half-an-hour, if so long. As I drew nearer the village and the school building, I reflected that reasons for my late arrival would have to be forthcoming, and, after some little thought on the subject, I determined that, at all costs, I would conceal the real cause of my delay, for though, undoubtedly, I had received a terrible scare, yet I felt that I should only look ridiculous before the eyes of my schoolfellows, and, to tell the plain truth, I owned to myself that I felt somewhat foolish. The consequence was that, when I did at last arrive within the prison walls of that severe establishment, I somewhat dissembled by saying and repeating with great eagerness that I had spent over half-an-hour in Villingen town, in a vain search after a vehicle.

But the Herr Direktor did not discover my prevarication and lack of moral courage, and only expressed his pleasure on hearing how I had enjoyed my visit to Nüremberg.

But, whenever I passed that clearing in the forest—which I often did, though never again alone—and heard an ignorant or sceptical remark or a breathless question about the ghost of Binschedler and the haunted mill, I smiled quietly a very superior smile, for, although I might not know the mysteries of German syntax, I had at least been acquainted with a genuine German ghost!

The Farmhouse on the Hill: A Ghost Story

William Beach, surveyor, arrived about midday at the small station of a
south Dorchester village and shouldered his bag and instruments to walk
across to the inn, where he had already telegraphed earlier in the day for a room.
His surveying, having little to do with the account of his distressing subsequent
adventures, may be left at once out of the story; but the fact that the inn was in
the throes of temporary building operations is important to mention, since it
led to the landlord's directing him to the only place in all the length and breadth
of the scattered hamlet where accommodation was likely or even possible, the
farmhouse half-way up the hill.

"That dark old house where you see the smoke 'anging about the trees," he
pointed. "Garfit's away, but his missus'll find you a bed, no doubt, if you care
for that kind of a place. That is," he added quickly, by way of correction, "if you
ain't too particular."

"Anything wrong with it, d'you mean?" asked the surveyor.

"Oh, I don't say there's nothing wrong with it," said the man, emphasising
a word in every phrase. "I'm not one to criticise my neighbors at any time, and
I've known of other gentlemen sleepin' there quite comfortable. Any'ow there's
no other house to take you!" And he looked savagely at his own dilapidated hotel as though it cut him to the heart to send a customer elsewhere.

Now there was something in the tone of the disappointed innkeeper and in
his curiously suggestive choice of words that combined to affect the surveyor
disagreeably and make him vaguely conscious of a certain depression of spirits. He slipped at once into a minor key and when he turned a corner of the sandy
path and found himself suddenly face to face with the old grey-stoned Tudor
house, massive of wall and irregular of shape, its forbidding aspect produced
so marked an impression on him that he instinctively hesitated, trying to seize
the actual definite quality that caused gloom to hang about it like a cloud; and
wondering rather uncomfortably how, and why, so picturesque a building, back-
ing against a whole hill-side of heather—there in the full flood of mid-day sunshine—should contrive to present so dolorous and lugubrious an appearance.
For this first view at close quarters struck the dominant note of the place with
undeniable vividness; the impression it conveyed was unpleasant, but "sinister" was the word that at once leaped to his mind.

With the weakness peculiar to impressionable persons, Beach would probably have retired there and then, but while his purpose was still an instinct
merely, he became suddenly aware that a figure with fixed gaze had been staring at him for some time from the pillars of the deep porch where the yew trees
that lined the approach threw their darkest shadow. A second glance showed

him that it was a woman, a woman dressed in black. Clearly this was Mrs. Garfit; and he advanced to meet her.

She was, he saw, a big strong-faced woman, yet with a cast of features somewhat melancholy, and she gave him a formal smile of welcome, which, if not over cordial at first, changed to something a little more pleasant as soon as she learned his errand.

"We can manage something, perhaps," she said in a flat colorless sort of voice, cutting short his explanations about the inn and turning slowly to enter the house.

"I'm willing to pay the ordinary inn charges," he added, noticing her want of alacrity and smiling to observe the changes produced by his words.

"Oh, of course, if you pay in advance," she said—which he had not exactly offered to do—and signing him to follow her in.

The surveyor no longer was puzzled by the innkeeper's description. Plainly the farmer's wife was a grasping woman; she bled her occasional customers more successfully than he did, that was, no doubt, where the poison lay!

He followed her through the cold hall, stone-flagged, and up the broad wooden stairs to the landing, noting the dark beams across the ceiling and the curious sudden slopings of the floors; for the odor of great age breathed everywhere about him and the interior of the building was as charming as the exterior was sinister.

Then Mrs. Garfit opened a door, moving aside for him to pass, and he saw a small room with a skylight window in the sloping ceiling, a cramped brass bed in the far corner and hooks in the wall from which a number of faded old dresses hung in a dingy row. The air smelt musty and there was no fireplace.

The surveyor's heart sank appreciably.

"If you have a somewhat larger room—" he began, turning to her, "one with a fire place, too, as I shall be working a bit in the evenings—"

Mrs. Garfit looked blankly at him, screwing up her eyes a little, while she weighed the possibility.

"The fire would be a shillin' extra," she said presently, "and I could let you 'ave this room for another two shillin' more than the small room." She crossed the landing and showed him the room referred to; it was large, with two windows, an arm-chair and a deep fireplace.

"Only I recommends the other," she added somewhat inconsequently.

"I prefer the larger one, thank you," said Beach shortly, and then and there clinched the bargain, making the best terms he could with her for breakfast and supper as well.

"Then you holds to the big one," repeated the woman, after counting over the silver in her big bony hands, "because my 'usband—and he'll be back ter-morrer, 'e says the little one sleeps in best."

Beach ordered his fire to be lit immediately and then went out to catch the short hour of light still available, glad to escape for the moment from both house and woman. His work took him out upon the open hilltops, where the sight of the sea, dull crimson under the wintry sunset, and the beauty of the hilly country did so much towards further dissipating the original impression of gloom that when he returned about six o'clock, with a roaring appetite, he had passed into a more vigorous and cheerful state of mind, and paid little attention to the dour-faced farmer's wife or to sensations of uneasiness and dismay which had at first oppressed him.

He had a high-tea before the kitchen fire, shared—both tea and fire—by a black cat of huge proportions, which insisted upon rubbing against his knees, jumping up on his lap, and at last even putting her velvet paws into the very middle of his jam and butter.

The general servant clattered about the place, waiting upon him, under occasional orders from the mistress; and a young man, presumably a Garfit, lumbered once or twice through the kitchen with noisy nailed boots and a curiosity to inspect the stranger within his gates. But the food was excellent; he had done a good bit of work; and the friendly attentions of the black cat soothed him so pleasantly that he passed gradually into a happy state of indifference to everything but the seductions of a good pipe and the prospect later of a refreshing sleep.

Then, midway in a stream of most pleasantly flowing reflections, his nerves answered to a startling shock, and his sensations of content were scattered suddenly to the winds of heaven. There, at the end of the room, Mrs. Garfit was bending over an open drawer and, through the smoke curling upwards from his pipe, he had caught sight unexpectedly of her face reflected in the mirror that hung upon the cupboard door. She was evidently not aware of being inspected, and her visage, sombre at any time, now wore an aspect so malefic that the sudden revelation positively horrified him. He saw it, dark and hard, with eyes at once terrible yet haunted, the mouth set, and a deep settled gloom upon the features that was quite dreadful. A flicker of fear, like the faint passing of a light, showed itself for a moment there, and was gone as swiftly as it came.

The surveyor gave a sudden start that sent the cat flying from his knee, and when the woman turned again to face the kitchen she had resumed the mask of her normal expression of countenance.

"I'll take my candle and go up to read a bit," he stammered, as though surprised in an unauthorised or guilty act. "And please let me have breakfast at eight o'clock."

He was disturbed and not a little alarmed, by the sight of that changed and evil face, and as he slowly went upstairs he could not help connecting it in his mind with the pain of a tormenting conscience. It seemed to turn the face black—black, with mental pain—and the pallor of the skin had made the contrast truly horrible. It lived vividly in his imagination, unpleasantly alive.

A blazing fire in his bed-room, a good novel, and a tolerably comfortable arm chair, he hoped, would soon put to flight, however, the distressing effects of the vision. Yet, somehow, when he closed the door, it did not keep the woman out. That face came into the room with him. It perched on the table beside his book and seemed to watch him as he read. The picture persisted in his mind; it kept rising before his eyes and the printed page. A sense of presentiment and apprehension began to gather heavily about his heart.

Then, as he sat there, half reading, half listening to the sounds below stairs, his thoughts took another turn. He thought of his brother Hubert.

Now, Hubert was the antithesis of himself; practical and keen-minded. They had formerly known great arguments—visionary versus materialist—in which Hubert's cool and logical mind invariably gained the victory, and William, with what dignity he could muster, always fell back upon the quotation that has often helped others in a similar predicament, "There are more things in heaven and earth, Hubert,"—the lines need not be completed, but he wished Hubert were with him now. Hubert might have argued things away perhaps, certain feelings and trepidations, a strangely persistent inner trembling—a slowly growing fear....

Then, with a fresh start, he recognised that it was this very sense of alarm that had suggested Hubert to his mind at all, and that in his sub-consciousness he was already groping for help! Plainly this was the reason of his brother's appearance upon the scene. The sinister setting of his night's lodging, the desolate hills, and above all that revelation of the woman's changed face had combined to touch his imagination with unholy suggestion. The idea of companionship became uncommonly pleasant.

His thoughts dwelt a good deal upon these things, but, after all, the strong Dorsetshire air was not to be denied; the fire, moreover, was comforting, and his limbs ached. By degrees he persuaded the novel to possess him more and more, until at length he found relief from his inquietudes in the exciting adventures of others.

The coals dropped softly into the grate and the winter wind came mournfully over the hills and sighed round the walls of the house; there was no other sound; down stairs everyone seemed to have gone to bed. He would read one more chapter and turn in himself. Good sleep would chase the phantoms effectually. But the new chapter began with wearisome description and his thoughts wandered again—theodolite—black cat—Hubert—the woman's face....

His eyes were travelling heavily through a big paragraph when a faint sound made itself audible in the room behind him, and he turned with a quick start to look over the back of his chair. The candle threw his head and shoulders, greatly magnified, upon wall and ceiling; but the room was empty; nothing seemed to stir. Yet the moment he looked down again upon his book the sound was repeated.

Instantly, he was in the whirl of a genuine nervous flurry, confused a little, and thinking of a dozen things at once. Perhaps, the friendly black cat had followed him up and was hiding in the room; he would get up and search. But before he could actually leave his chair a slight movement close beside him caught the corner of his eye. The brass knob of the door-handle at his left was turning. That was where the sounds came from. There was someone at the door.

Beach caught his breath with a rush. His first instinct was to dash forward and turn the key; his second, to seize the poker; yet he found no strength to do either, the one or the other. He glued his eyes to the knob, watching it slowly turn. It stopped for a moment, and then the door pushed gently open and he saw the figure of Mrs. Garfit partially concealed by a black shawl over the head, and wearing the very expression that he had seen reflected in the mirror downstairs a few hours before. She was staring intently into the empty room behind him. Encircled by both arms and grasped by her great muscular hands, she carried a kind of loose bundle which she held pressed closely into her body.

The woman, thus drawn in patches of black and white, standing erect in the doorway with darkness at her back, and that face of set evil dominating the picture, presented an appearance so appalling that at once the fear in the surveyor's heart passed into terror, pure and simple, and he found himself unable to utter a sound or make the smallest movement.

Without taking the slightest notice of him she tiptoed softly forward into the room, and Beach then became aware for the first time that she was not alone. A man crouched behind her in the darkness of the landing, holding a lantern beneath the folds of a cloak. He was kneeling; and his face, with red hair and beard, and half-opened mouth showing the teeth, was just distinguishable in the faint glimmer of the shrouded light.

Looking neither to the right hand nor to the left the woman passed almost soundlessly beside him, brushing the arm of the chair with her black gown, and making obviously for the end of the room. And when Beach, fearing that any moment she might face about and come towards himself, turned his head by a supreme effort and saw that she was already at the far end beside the bed, he made at the same time the further startling discovery—a cold sweat bursting through his skin—that the bed was occupied!

For one second he saw on the pillow the face of a young girl, sleeping peacefully, with masses of light hair about her, and then the black outline of that terrible woman bent double over her, and the loose bundle she carried in her hands descended full upon the pillow with her great weight above it, and remained there motionless, like a tiger upon its prey, for the space of what seemed to him many minutes.

There was no struggle and no sound; nothing but a little convulsive movement beneath the bed-clothes lower down; and then the surveyor still powerless to move or cry in the grip of a real terror, was aware that the man had left his post of observation in the passage and was already half way across the floor. He, too, went past him, as though unaware of his presence, but the woman, hearing the stealthy approach, straightened herself up beside the bed and turned to meet him. The lantern carried by the man, who was short and humpbacked, shed a faint upward light upon her features, and the slow smile it revealed coming into being on her fixed white face was so ghastly that it gave Beach that little extra twist of terror needed to release the frozen will and make speech and movement possible.

With a loud cry he leaped out of his chair and dashed forward upon the fiendish couple still standing beside the bed of murder—and woke with a violent start in his arm-chair before an extinguished fire in a room that was pitch dark and miserably cold.

Whew! A nightmare after all! But the chill in his blood was due to more, he could swear, than a cold room and a blackened grate. With trembling fingers he lit the second candle and saw to his immense relief that the room was untenanted, the bed smooth and empty. The other candle had long ago guttered out, and his watch showed him that he had slept three hours. It was one o'clock in the morning.

He examined the bed, that awful bed where he had seen a young girl smothered in her sleep, and the horror of the nightmare remained so vividly with him that he gave up trying to persuade himself that it had been nothing more than a dream, and that two evil persons, and a third, had not vacated the room. One thing was certain—he could never sleep in such a bed. He would slip across to the other room. The dread of perhaps meeting the woman in the passage gave him pause for a moment, but after all it was a lesser terror, and he softly opened the door and crept, candle in hand, over the cold boards to the other side of the landing. He stood and listened for a moment—the house was utterly still—and then quietly turned the knob. But the door was locked. He was obliged to return to his own room, where he passed the remainder of a troubled night in what sleep he could snatch upon an arm-chair and two others.

The late daylight, cold and grey, brought no such balm to his imagination as the bright sunshine of a spring morning might have done, and the horror of his dream possessed him so painfully that he realised he could not spend another night in that room unless—yes, that was a splendid idea—unless he could get his brother, Hubert, down for the week-end to share it with him. Hubert's cold logic would work wonders. Ah, and another thought! It would be interesting to see if he felt anything odd about the house or room. He would say nothing about his own impressions, or his own experience, and would see what Hubert felt. The idea possessed him at once and he decided to telegraph the moment he had finished breakfast. Then, having arranged for another bed to be moved into the room he took some bread and cheese with him and spent the entire day surveying the hills until the darkness fell over the country, and it was time to meet the train.

And Hubert came; glad of the prospects of walks and talks with his brother, and seduced by the telegraphic description of the "jolly old farmhouse" among the hills. He appeared delighted, too, with the Tudor building.

"You ought to advertise, ma'am, and take in summer boarders," he said briskly to Mrs. Garfit.

"You better tell my 'usband that," she replied with something like a sigh mixed up in her sullen voice. "He'll be here to-night or to-morrer mornin'."

"Surly old cat," said Hubert, when they were alone at bed-time in their room; "she'd have to wear a veil to keep her boarders. Her face is like some of those women in the Chamber of Horrors." He laughed cheerfully, and plunged into the details of his week's work—he was a stockbroker—and of family matters that were of interest between them. William avoided all reference to his own feelings and kept the talk purposely on the most matter-of-fact subjects possible. He had carefully maneuvered that Hubert should occupy the large bed, but he could not repress a creeping sense of horror when the time for sleep came and he saw his brother snuggling down under the sheets and blankets and putting his head upon that haunted pillow.

All through the night, as long as the fire light lasted, he lay awake and watched to see if anything would happen. But up to the late hour when he finally fell asleep nothing did happen. It must have been very early in the morning when he woke with a start and saw someone standing beside his bed in the darkness, and heard his name called softly. It was Hubert.

"I say, Billy, is that cursed woman in the room, or what—who is calling?"

His brother jumped up and struck a light. Hubert's face was blanched. This was the first thing he noticed.

"What's up?" he stammered, still dazed with sleep. "The door's locked; there's no one here—is there?"

Hubert stood there shivering. Then he took the candle, and walked round the room, poking into corners and cupboards, and even looking under the beds. He went back to his own bed again and pulled the sheets about savagely.

"What did you hear?" asked William nervously.

"I'm not sure I heard anything. Something woke me—I couldn't breathe properly—felt suffocated—and I thought I heard that woman calling to 'hurry up.' Been dreaming, I suppose—"

He hesitated a moment. William saw that he had only told half, and wanted to say something else that rather stuck in his gorge.

"You'll get your death of cold standing there," he whispered.

Hubert ceased fumbling at his own bed and crossed the floor; his face was white as chalk.

"I say, old Billy, do you mind very much if I sleep with you? I think, perhaps, my sheets seem a bit damp," he whispered at length.

And when he had crawled into bed William felt that he was shaking all over, and for a long time before sleep again overtook them he kept giving little nervous starts of fear. He knew his brother too well to ask him just then what had really happened, but next morning, when the sunshine was in the room, he pressed him for an explanation, and Hubert admitted that he had never felt so frightened in his life; horrible dreams of being stifled had haunted his sleep, and finally someone had come stealthily up to the bed and tried to suffocate him by putting a blanket over his face. For a wonder, too, when, he heard his brother's story, he neither argued nor scoffed, but merely remarked that it would be interesting to find out the history of the house and also to see if Mr. Garfit resembled the man with the lantern.

And the first person they met on going down to a belated breakfast was the farmer himself coming in from a gig standing in the yard. He was humpbacked and very short. Moreover he had red hair and beard, and a trick of leaving his mouth open so that the teeth showed.

The landlord of the Purbeck Arm, when suitably urged, furnished something of the required "history" of the house by stating that, some years before, Garfit's step daughter had been found suffocated in her bed, and that the couple of them, man and wife, had only escaped the gallows because the circumstantial evidence was weak.

"It was long before I came to these parts," he said, "but you'll find the whole story in the newspapers of that date."

"I remember the Garfit case when I was a boy, now you mention it," the surveyor said.

"You see," interrupted the man significantly, "the girl had money of her own from her mother. The Garfits, of course, got that."

The Sunday trains were very bad, but they were preferable, the brothers thought, to another night in such a house.

"And such damp sheets too!" explained Hubert with a shudder.

"There are more things in heaven and earth, Hubert," began his brother gravely. "You felt the presence of the dead, and I, being more psychic, was impressed by the vivid thoughts of the living—the haunted living."

"Ah!" said Hubert, looking straight ahead. "We might have a chat about it some day. By the way," he added, "have you got tuppence for the porter, Billy?"

But a thorough search of the newspaper files at the club when they got back to London corroborated all that the innkeeper had told them of the Garfit murder. The surveyor, moreover, prepared a careful report of the case for the Psychical Research Society and when it was published, sent a copy to his brother with various annotations down the margins in red ink.

The Kit-Bag

When the words "Not Guilty" sounded through the crowded courtroom that dark December afternoon, Arthur Wilbraham, the great criminal KC, and leader for the triumphant defence, was represented by his junior; but Johnson, his private secretary, carried the verdict across to his chambers like lightning.

"It's what we expected, I think," said the barrister, without emotion; "and, personally, I am glad the case is over." There was no particular sign of pleasure that his defence of John Turk, the murderer, on a plea of insanity, had been successful, for no doubt he felt, as everybody who had watched the case felt, that no man had ever better deserved the gallows.

"I'm glad too," said Johnson. He had sat in the court for ten days watching the face of the man who had carried out with callous detail one of the most brutal and cold-blooded murders of recent years.

The counsel glanced up at his secretary. They were more than employer and employed; for family and other reasons, they were friends. "Ah, I remember; yes," he said with a kind smile, "and you want to get away for Christmas? You're going to skate and ski in the Alps, aren't you? If I was your age I'd come with you."

Johnson laughed shortly. He was a young man of twenty-six, with a delicate face like a girl's. "I can catch the morning boat now," he said; "but that's not the reason I'm glad the trial is over. I'm glad it's over because I've seen the last of that man's dreadful face. It positively haunted me. That white skin, with the black hair brushed low over the forehead, is a thing I shall never forget, and the description of the way the dismembered body was crammed and packed with lime into that—"

"Don't dwell on it, my dear fellow," interrupted the other, looking at him curiously out of his keen eyes, "don't think about it. Such pictures have a trick of coming back when one least wants them." He paused a moment. "Now go," he added presently, "and enjoy your holiday. I shall want all your energy for my Parliamentary work when you get back. And don't break your neck skiing."

Johnson shook hands and took his leave. At the door he turned suddenly.

"I knew there was something I wanted to ask you," he said. "Would you mind lending me one of your kit-bags? It's too late to get one tonight, and I leave in the morning before the shops are open."

"Of course; I'll send Henry over with it to your rooms. You shall have it the moment I get home."

"I promise to take great care of it," said Johnson gratefully, delighted to think that within thirty hours he would be nearing the brilliant sunshine of the high Alps in winter. The thought of that criminal court was like an evil dream in his mind.

He dined at his club and went on to Bloomsbury, where he occupied the top floor in one of those old, gaunt houses in which the rooms are large and lofty. The floor below his own was vacant and unfurnished, and below that were other lodgers whom he did not know. It was cheerless, and he looked forward heartily to a change. The night was even more cheerless: it was miserable, and few people were about. A cold, sleety rain was driving down the streets before the keenest east wind he had ever felt. It howled dismally among the big, gloomy houses of the great squares, and when he reached his rooms he heard it whistling and shouting over the world of black roofs beyond his windows.

In the hall he met his landlady, shading a candle from the draughts with her thin hand. "This come by a man from Mr. Wilbr'im's, sir."

She pointed to what was evidently the kit-bag, and Johnson thanked her and took it upstairs with him. "I shall be going abroad in the morning for ten days, Mrs. Monks," he said. "I'll leave an address for letters."

"And I hope you'll 'ave a merry Christmas, sir," she said, in a raucous, wheezy voice that suggested spirits, "and better weather than this."

"I hope so too," replied her lodger, shuddering a little as the wind went roaring down the street outside.

When he got upstairs he heard the sleet volleying against the window panes. He put his kettle on to make a cup of hot coffee, and then set about putting a few things in order for his absence. "And now I must pack—such as my packing is," he laughed to himself, and set to work at once.

He liked the packing, for it brought the snow mountains so vividly before him, and made him forget the unpleasant scenes of the past ten days. Besides, it was not elaborate in nature. His friend had lent him the very thing—a stout canvas kit-bag, sack-shaped, with holes round the neck for the brass bar and padlock. It was a bit shapeless, true, and not much to look at, but its capacity was unlimited, and there was no need to pack carefully. He shoved in his waterproof coat, his fur cap and gloves, his skates and climbing boots, his sweaters, snow-boots, and ear-caps; and then on the top of these he piled his woollen shirts and underwear, his thick socks, puttees, and knickerbockers. The dress suit came next, in case the hotel people dressed for dinner, and then, thinking of the best way to pack his white shirts, he paused a moment to reflect. "That's the worst of these kit-bags," he mused vaguely, standing in the centre of the sitting-room, where he had come to fetch some string.

It was after ten o'clock. A furious gust of wind rattled the windows as though to hurry him up, and he thought with pity of the poor Londoners whose Christmas would be spent in such a climate, whilst he was skimming over snowy slopes in bright sunshine, and dancing in the evening with rosy-cheeked girls— Ah! That reminded him; he must put in his dancing-pumps and evening socks. He crossed over from his sitting-room to the cupboard on the landing where he kept his linen.

And as he did so he heard someone coming softly up the stairs. He stood still a moment on the landing to listen. It was Mrs. Monks's step, he thought; she must be coming up with the last post. But then the steps ceased suddenly, and he heard no more. They were at least two flights down, and he came to the conclusion they were too heavy to be those of his bibulous landlady. No doubt they belonged to a late lodger who had mistaken his floor. He went into his bedroom and packed his pumps and dress-shirts as best he could.

The kit-bag by this time was two-thirds full, and stood upright on its own base like a sack of flour. For the first time he noticed that it was old and dirty, the canvas faded and worn, and that it had obviously been subjected to rather rough treatment. It was not a very nice bag to have sent him—certainly not a new one, or one that his chief valued. He gave the matter a passing thought, and went on with his packing. Once or twice, however, he caught himself wondering who it could have been wandering down below, for Mrs. Monks had not come up with letters, and the floor was empty and unfurnished. From time to time, moreover, he was almost certain he heard a soft tread of someone padding about over the bare boards—cautiously, stealthily, as silently as possible—and, further, that the sounds had been lately coming distinctly nearer.

For the first time in his life he began to feel a little creepy. Then, as though to emphasize this feeling, an odd thing happened: as he left the bedroom, having just packed his recalcitrant white shirts, he noticed that the top of the kit-bag lopped over towards him with an extraordinary resemblance to a human face. The canvas fell into a fold like a nose and forehead, and the brass rings for the padlock just filled the position of the eyes. A shadow—or was it a travel stain? For he could not tell exactly—looked like hair. It gave him rather a turn, for it was so absurdly, so outrageously, like the face of John Turk, the murderer.

He laughed, and went into the front room, where the light was stronger.

"That horrid case has got on my mind," he thought; "I shall be glad of a change of scene and air." In the sitting-room, however, he was not pleased to hear again that stealthy tread upon the stairs, and to realize that it was much closer than before, as well as unmistakably real. And this time he got up and went out to see who it could be creeping about on the upper staircase at so late an hour.

But the sound ceased; there was no one visible on the stairs. He went to the floor below, not without trepidation, and turned on the electric light to make sure that no one was hiding in the empty rooms of the unoccupied suite. There was not a stick of furniture large enough to hide a dog. Then he called over the banisters to Mrs. Monks, but there was no answer, and his voice echoed down into the dark vault of the house, and was lost in the roar of the gale that howled outside. Everyone was in bed and asleep—everyone except himself and the owner of this soft and stealthy tread.

"My absurd imagination, I suppose," he thought. "It must have been the wind after all, although—it seemed so *very* real and close, I thought." He went back to his packing. It was by this time getting on towards midnight. He drank his coffee up and lit another pipe—the last before turning in.

It is difficult to say exactly at what point fear begins, when the causes of that fear are not plainly before the eyes. Impressions gather on the surface of the mind, film by film, as ice gathers upon the surface of still water, but often so lightly that they claim no definite recognition from the consciousness. Then a point is reached where the accumulated impressions become a definite emotion, and the mind realizes that something has happened. With something of a start, Johnson suddenly recognized that he felt nervous—oddly nervous; also, that for some time past the causes of this feeling had been gathering slowly in his mind, but that he had only just reached the point where he was forced to acknowledge them.

It was a singular and curious malaise that had come over him, and he hardly knew what to make of it. He felt as though he were doing something that was strongly objected to by another person, another person, moreover, who had some right to object. It was a most disturbing and disagreeable feeling, not unlike the persistent promptings of conscience: almost, in fact, as if he were doing something he knew to be wrong. Yet, though he searched vigorously and honestly in his mind, he could nowhere lay his finger upon the secret of this growing uneasiness, and it perplexed him. More, it distressed and frightened him.

"Pure nerves, I suppose," he said aloud with a forced laugh. "Mountain air will cure all that! Ah," he added, still speaking to himself, "and that reminds me—my snow-glasses."

He was standing by the door of the bedroom during this brief soliloquy, and as he passed quickly towards the sitting-room to fetch them from the cupboard he saw out of the corner of his eye the indistinct outline of a figure standing on the stairs, a few feet from the top. It was someone in a stooping position, with one hand on the banisters, and the face peering up towards the landing. And at the same moment he heard a shuffling footstep. The person who had been creeping about below all this time had at last come up to his own floor. Who in the world could it be? And what in the name of Heaven did he want?

Johnson caught his breath sharply and stood stock still. Then, after a few seconds' hesitation, he found his courage, and turned to investigate. The stairs, he saw to his utter amazement, were empty; there was no one. He felt a series of cold shivers run over him, and something about the muscles of his legs gave a little and grew weak. For the space of several minutes he peered steadily into the shadows that congregated about the top of the staircase where he had seen the figure, and then he walked fast—almost ran, in fact—into the light of the front room; but hardly had he passed inside the doorway when he heard someone come up the stairs behind him with a quick bound and go swiftly into his bedroom. It was a heavy, but at the same time a stealthy footstep—the tread of somebody who did not wish to be seen. And it was at this precise moment that the nervousness he had hitherto experienced leaped the boundary line, and entered the state of fear, almost of acute, unreasoning fear. Before it turned into terror there was a further boundary to cross, and beyond that again lay the region of pure horror. Johnson's position was an unenviable one.

"By Jove! That was someone on the stairs, then," he muttered, his flesh crawling all over; "and whoever it was has now gone into my bedroom." His delicate, pale face turned absolutely white, and for some minutes he hardly knew what to think or do. Then he realized intuitively that delay only set a premium upon fear; and he crossed the landing boldly and went straight into the other room, where, a few seconds before, the steps had disappeared.

"Who's there? Is that you, Mrs. Monks?" he called aloud, as he went, and heard the first half of his words echo down the empty stairs, while the second half fell dead against the curtains in a room that apparently held no other human figure than his own.

"Who's there?" he called again, in a voice unnecessarily loud and that only just held firm. "What do you want here?"

The curtains swayed very slightly, and, as he saw it, his heart felt as if it almost missed a beat; yet he dashed forward and drew them aside with a rush. A window, streaming with rain, was all that met his gaze. He continued his search, but in vain; the cupboards held nothing but rows of clothes, hanging motionless; and under the bed there was no sign of anyone hiding. He stepped backwards into the middle of the room, and, as he did so, something all but tripped him up. Turning with a sudden spring of alarm he saw—the kit-bag.

"Odd!" he thought. "That's not where I left it!" A few moments before it had surely been on his right, between the bed and the bath; he did not remember having moved it. It was very curious. What in the world was the matter with everything? Were all his senses gone queer? A terrific gust of wind tore at the windows, dashing the sleet against the glass with the force of small gunshot, and then fled away howling dismally over the waste of Bloomsbury roofs. A sudden vision of the Channel next day rose in his mind and recalled him sharply to realities.

"There's no one here at any rate; that's quite clear!" he exclaimed aloud. Yet at the time he uttered them he knew perfectly well that his words were not true and that he did not believe them himself. He felt exactly as though someone was hiding close about him, watching all his movements, trying to hinder his packing in some way. "And two of my senses," he added, keeping up the pretence, "have played me the most absurd tricks: the steps I heard and the figure I saw were both entirely imaginary."

He went back to the front room, poked the fire into a blaze, and sat down before it to think. What impressed him more than anything else was the fact that the kit-bag was no longer where he had left it. It had been dragged nearer to the door.

What happened afterwards that night happened, of course, to a man already excited by fear, and was perceived by a mind that had not the full and proper control, therefore, of the senses. Outwardly, Johnson remained calm and master of himself to the end, pretending to the very last that everything he witnessed had a natural explanation, or was merely delusions of his tired nerves. But inwardly, in his very heart, he knew all along that someone had been hiding downstairs in the empty suite when he came in, that this person had watched his opportunity and then stealthily made his way up to the bedroom, and that all he saw and heard afterwards, from the moving of the kit-bag to—well, to the other things this story has to tell—were caused directly by the presence of this invisible person.

And it was here, just when he most desired to keep his mind and thoughts controlled, that the vivid pictures received day after day upon the mental plates exposed in the courtroom of the Old Bailey, came strongly to light and developed themselves in the dark room of his inner vision. Unpleasant, haunting memories have a way of coming to life again just when the mind least desires them—in the silent watches of the night, on sleepless pillows, during the lonely hours spent by sick and dying beds. And so now, in the same way, Johnson saw nothing but the dreadful face of John Turk, the murderer, lowering at him from every corner of his mental field of vision; the white skin, the evil eyes, and the fringe of black hair low over the forehead. All the pictures of those ten days in court crowded back into his mind unbidden, and very vivid.

"This is all rubbish and nerves," he exclaimed at length, springing with sudden energy from his chair. "I shall finish my packing and go to bed. I'm overwrought, overtired. No doubt, at this rate I shall hear steps and things all night!"

But his face was deadly white all the same. He snatched up his field-glasses and walked across to the bedroom, humming a music-hall song as he went—a trifle too loud to be natural; and the instant he crossed the threshold and stood within the room something turned cold about his heart, and he felt that every hair on his head stood up.

The kit-bag lay close in front of him, several feet nearer to the door than he had left it, and just over its crumpled top he saw a head and face slowly sinking down out of sight as though someone were crouching behind it to hide, and at the same moment a sound like a long-drawn sigh was distinctly audible in the still air about him between the gusts of the storm outside.

Johnson had more courage and will-power than the girlish indecision of his face indicated; but at first such a wave of terror came over him that for some seconds he could do nothing but stand and stare. A violent trembling ran down his back and legs, and he was conscious of a foolish, almost a hysterical, impulse to scream aloud. That sigh seemed in his very ear, and the air still quivered with it. It was unmistakably a human sigh.

"Who's there?" he said at length, finding his voice; but though he meant to speak with loud decision, the tones came out instead in a faint whisper, for he had partly lost the control of his tongue and lips.

He stepped forward, so that he could see all round and over the kitbag. Of course there was nothing there, nothing but the faded carpet and the bulging canvas sides. He put out his hands and threw open the mouth of the sack where it had fallen over, being only three parts full, and then he saw for the first time that round the inside, some six inches from the top, there ran a broad smear of dull crimson. It was an old and faded blood stain. He uttered a scream, and drew back his hands as if they had been burnt. At the same moment the kit-bag gave a faint, but unmistakable, lurch forward towards the door.

Johnson collapsed backwards, searching with his hands for the support of something solid, and the door, being farther behind him than he realized, received his weight just in time to prevent his falling, and shut to with a resounding bang. At the same moment the swinging of his left arm accidentally touched the electric switch, and the light in the room went out.

It was an awkward and disagreeable predicament, and if Johnson had not been possessed of real pluck he might have done all manner of foolish things. As it was, however, he pulled himself together, and groped furiously for the little brass knob to turn the light on again. But the rapid closing of the door had set the coats hanging on it a-swinging, and his fingers became entangled in a confusion of sleeves and pockets, so that it was some moments before he found the switch. And in those few moments of bewilderment and terror two things happened that sent him beyond recall over the boundary into the region of genuine horror—he distinctly heard the kit-bag shuffling heavily across the floor in jerks, and close in front of his face sounded once again the sigh of a human being.

In his anguished efforts to find the brass button on the wall he nearly scraped the nails from his fingers, but even then, in those frenzied moments of alarm— so swift and alert are the impressions of a mind keyed-up by a vivid emotion— he had time to realize that he dreaded the return of the light, and that it might be better for him to stay hidden in the merciful screen of darkness. It was but the impulse of a moment, however, and before he had time to act upon it he had yielded automatically to the original desire, and the room was flooded again with light.

But the second instinct had been right. It would have been better for him to have stayed in the shelter of the kind darkness. For there, close before him, bending over the half-packed kit-bag, clear as life in the merciless glare of the electric light, stood the figure of John Turk, the murderer. Not three feet from him the man stood, the fringe of black hair marked plainly against the pallor of the forehead, the whole horrible presentment of the scoundrel, as vivid as he had seen him day after day in the Old Bailey, when he stood there in the dock, cynical and callous, under the very shadow of the gallows.

In a flash Johnson realized what it all meant: the dirty and much-used bag; the smear of crimson within the top; the dreadful stretched condition of the bulging sides. He remembered how the victim's body had been stuffed into a canvas bag for burial, the ghastly, dismembered fragments forced with lime into this very bag; and the bag itself produced as evidence—it all came back to him as clear as day....

Very softly and stealthily his hand groped behind him for the handle of the door, but before he could actually turn it the very thing that he most of all dreaded came about, and John Turk lifted his devil's face and looked at him. At the same moment that heavy sigh passed through the air of the room, formulated somehow into words: "It's my bag. And I want it."

Johnson just remembered clawing the door open, and then falling in a heap upon the floor of the landing, as he tried frantically to make his way into the front room.

He remained unconscious for a long time, and it was still dark when he opened his eyes and realized that he was lying, stiff and bruised, on the cold boards. Then the memory of what he had seen rushed back into his mind, and he promptly fainted again. When he woke the second time the wintry dawn was just beginning to peep in at the windows, painting the stairs a cheerless, dismal grey, and he managed to crawl into the front room, and cover himself with an overcoat in the armchair, where at length he fell asleep.

A great clamour woke him. He recognized Mrs. Monks's voice, loud and voluble.

"What! You ain't been to bed, sir! Are you ill, or has anything 'appened? And there's an urgent gentleman to see you, though it ain't seven o'clock yet, and—"

"Who is it?" he stammered. "I'm all right, thanks. Fell asleep in my chair, I suppose."

"Someone from Mr. Wilb'rim's, and he says he ought to see you quick before you go abroad, and I told him—"

"Show him up, please, at once," said Johnson, whose head was whirling, and his mind was still full of dreadful visions.

Mr. Wilbraham's man came in with many apologies, and explained briefly and quickly that an absurd mistake had been made, and that the wrong kit-bag had been sent over the night before.

"Henry somehow got hold of the one that came over from the courtroom, and Mr. Wilbraham only discovered it when he saw his own lying in his room, and asked why it had not gone to you," the man said.

"Oh!" said Johnson stupidly.

"And he must have brought you the one from the murder case instead, sir, I'm afraid," the man continued, without the ghost of an expression on his face. "The one John Turk packed the dead body in. Mr. Wilbraham's awful upset about it, sir, and told me to come over first thing this morning with the right one, as you were leaving by the boat."

He pointed to a clean-looking kit-bag on the floor, which he had just brought. "And I was to bring the other one back, sir," he added casually.

For some minutes Johnson could not find his voice. At last he pointed in the direction of his bedroom. "Perhaps you would kindly unpack it for me. Just empty the things out on the floor."

The man disappeared into the other room, and was gone for five minutes. Johnson heard the shifting to and fro of the bag, and the rattle of the skates and boots being unpacked.

"Thank you, sir," the man said, returning with the bag folded over his arm. "And can I do anything more to help you, sir?"

"What is it?" asked Johnson, seeing that he still had something he wished to say.

The man shuffled and looked mysterious. "Beg pardon, sir, but knowing your interest in the Turk case, I thought you'd maybe like to know what's happened—"

"Yes."

"John Turk killed hisself last night with poison immediately on getting his release, and he left a note for Mr. Wilbraham saying as he'd be much obliged if they'd have him put away, same as the woman he murdered, in the old kit-bag."

"What time—did he do it?" asked Johnson.

"Ten o'clock last night, sir, the warder says."

The Boy Messenger

It was the afternoon of Christmas Eve.

Partly by train, partly on foot, they had come to a charming village, not much more than a dozen miles from London Bridge, and were sitting at tea looking out upon the garden of the inn. The dusk, like a thin veil, gathered silently about them, and a curtain of wintry mist, half moisture from the near woodlands, half smoke from the village, hung over the tumbled cottage roofs and shrouded the crests of the elm trees that circled the green.

A few children played near the well, a line of white geese straggled over from the pond, and a typical village dog strayed dangerously near the hoofs of a typical village donkey that was trying its best to nibble grass where grass there was none. For the rest, the hamlet seemed deserted, the street peopled by shadows only, and the dishevelled yew-tree in the churchyard spread vaguely through the gloom till it embraced the church and most of the gravestones into the compass of its aged arms.

They were an unimaginative party. It is doubtful if any one of them possessed sufficient insight to appreciate the feelings of an untipped waiter—surely the least of tests—and yet, before the eyes of three of them, two girls and a man, this thing plainly happened. True, their accounts varied curiously when they came later to compare notes; but then accounts of the simplest occurrence—say, a rabbit running across a road—will vary amazingly when half a dozen persons who saw it run come to relate their impressions. So that proves nothing; the important thing is that something happened, and the observers started even. The rest remains to be told.

They were waiting for the arrival of another friend, who was to bicycle over and meet them at the inn, and then return for the Christmas Eve party, when they realised that the cold had grown suddenly much greater, and one of them—it was the younger girl—made the suggestion that they should go part of the way to meet him. The proposal was welcomed, and instantly acted upon, and the man and the two girls were up and away in a twinkling, leaving the others behind to nurse the tea against their speedy return.

"The moment we hear the bicycle bell we'll make tea," they shouted from the inn porch, as the three forms scattered into the darkness, the voices and footsteps making an unusual clamour in the peaceful little hamlet.

The road, winding like a white stream, and slippery with occasional ice, ran downhill out of the nest of cottages, and the trio followed its course headlong through the gloom, regardless of ruts or loose stones. A couple of villagers, walking briskly by, turned their heads to stare; a dog made a sudden run, barking shrilly; a cat shot silently across the road in front of them; and then, quite suddenly the village was left behind and the broad highway dwindled into a country lane. As they ran, the hedgerows flew past like palings with a level top, and the frosty evening air, keen with odours of ploughed fields and dead leaves, stung their cheeks sharply and whistled in their ears.

They had gone perhaps half a mile in this way, still urging the pace downhill, and they were running abreast along a clear stretch with nothing to obstruct, so that all had the same point of view, when suddenly—and this is where the accounts first begin to vary—they realised that something stood immediately in the road before them, something that brought them all up instinctively with a dead halt.

How they managed it, going at that pace downhill, is hard to understand—some things apparently possess the curious power of compelling a stop—for they came to a full halt as completely as though they had charged an invisible iron barrier breast-high across the road. Panting and speechless they drew up in line as by common instinct—drew up in presence of a fourth.

So far at least, they were all agreed—that it was a fourth.

Outlined against the white road where a moment before had been empty dusk, of indefinite shape in the mingling of the lights, stock still and bang in the centre of their path—the slang alone describes the uncompromising attitude of the thing—stood this fourth figure, facing them with a deliberate calmness of survey that seemed a little more than insolence, and only a little less than menace. Another second and their headlong rush would have sent them ploughing over it as an ocean liner ploughs over a fishing smack in the night. Moreover, so sudden was the appearance, and so abrupt the halt, that for more than a whole minute they merely stood in silence facing it, and staring back with no thought of doing anything. To each of them the idea came that it was not possible to get past it, that there was no available space. Though actually diminutive, it seemed to fill the entire road just as a mail cart might have done. And, quite apart from this singular deception of sight, each member confessed afterwards to an uncommon emotion, which warned them that to force a way past was somehow not exactly the right, or proper, or safe thing to do.

So at first they stood and stared rather helplessly—till at length their startled vision focussed itself better and the man of the party, finding his senses, expressed the relieved conviction of them all with a loud exclamation:

"Why, I declare, it's only a boy after all!" he cried, with a laugh.

Yet the words, as soon as uttered, had a false ring about them, for there was that about the figure of this little boy—this diminutive person dressed in clothes of dark green, oddly cut, with the white face and large blue eyes so wide apart in it—there was that about him which made it not difficult to imagine that, if he was something less than a man, he was at the same time something more than a boy. His self-possession was perfect. The manner in which he dominated the entire road, gazing so quietly and fixedly at them—peering it really was—produced an effect of privileged importance that was not calculated according to his mere size at any rate. Aided, perhaps, by the twilight and the background of dark woods, he certainly managed to convey an impression, strangely insistent, of being other than he was—other, at least, than these three saw him.

And, beyond question, each one saw him differently—at first. The picture varied astonishingly. For the elder girl thought it was a "woman or a shadow," and her sister said it looked like an animal on its hind legs, pausing to start in its flight across the road—a hare, for instance, magnified hugely by the dusk— while the man could have sworn, he declared, that at first he saw several figures, a whole line of them, indeed, which had then suddenly telescoped down into the single outline of this diminutive boy.

And the three accounts seem very suggestive of the curiously confusing effect produced upon their sense of sight from the very beginning.

For a time no one said a word, and up the spines of all three ran chills of various degrees. For the place had turned suddenly lonely; no habitation was in sight; dark woods lay close at hand, with mist creeping everywhere over the sombre landscape; and, immediately in front of them, this imp-thing with the glowing eyes and the confident manner, barring their way. It was eerie; though what there could be about a twilight country lane and an inquisitive little boy to make it so, no one of them could understand.

And then, while a stray breeze brought the dead leaves whirling about their feet in a little rustling eddy, the embarrassing silence was broken by the fourth itself, who in a thin, piping voice, like wind blowing through small reeds, ejaculated a sound that all heard differently.

"Surely it was my name that he called," was the thought in the mind of each.

This, however, they discovered afterwards when comparing notes, and discussing the singular affair from every possible point of view; for at the actual moment the man of the party, remembering the character of the friend they were come to meet, and his love of practical joking, thought to see his hand in the behaviour of the youngster, and cried again with laugh:

"But it's some elaborate trick of Harry's! He has sent the boy ahead to meet us. He is not far off himself at this very moment, and this is his messenger boy!"

But was it really a boy! Did it cast a shadow like the rest of them under the gathering stars? Was it unaccompanied truly, or were those merely shapes of mist that rose and melted so mysteriously into one another beside the hedge yonder? And how was it so vividly impressed upon the minds of all that the boy stood there with a definite purpose, a deliberate mission, and sought to spell some message to their brains? For, afterwards, it came out clearly, that it was this conception of the messenger—of someone come to tell something—that had impressed and perplexed the unimaginative three far more than the mere differences of sight and hearing.

"Let's go back," whispered the younger girl. "He frightens me."

It was the one who had most reason to wish for the arrival of the expected friend, and her voice gave utterance to a secret emotion that was beginning to stir in them all—an emotion of chill presentiment and fear. The imp, however, was far too fascinating for this course to recommend itself just then, and the others soon found their voices and began to ply the little fellow with questions. First of all they asked him who he was and where he lived; and without speaking, he pointed in a vague way, waving his hand generally to include sky and fields as though it were impossible more particularly to give his name or describe the place where he dwelt.

"He doesn't know who he is, or where he lives," cried the girl, who wanted the comforting lights of the inn, and the comfortable presence of the one they awaited. "He's a goblin—of course, but a very nice goblin," she added quickly with an odd little forced laugh. The boy had turned his eyes upon her face. They seemed such old, old eyes, she declared afterwards by way of explanation.

"Do you live in the village?" asked the man next.

The boy shook his head with an indescribable gesture of contempt.

"Then where do you live?"

He opened his mouth so that they saw the white line of his teeth, and he began to utter a sound that was not unlike the throaty notes of a big bird. It continued for some seconds, but no words came. He stared at each of them in turn, the stream of sound broken at intervals by tiny explosions from the lips. It almost seemed as though speech were unfamiliar to him, something he could not manage and was struggling with for the first time. Then they discovered that the child had a dreadful stammer, but a stammer unlike anything they had ever heard before. It was fully a minute before he managed to produce the words, yet in the direction where he pointed finally there was nothing to be seen but ploughed fields looming darkly, and a few ragged and ungainly elms standing like broken pillars in the night.

"Over there—beyond," was what he seemed to say.

They began to realise somewhat vividly that it was a late December evening; the night gathered increasingly about them; in the tops of the high elms a faint wind stirred and whispered; the face of the world grew unfamiliar, as though they were plunged in some desolate region where human help availed not. The shadows had come forth in troops and taken possession of the landscape, somehow altering it. For the moment they forgot their immediate purpose of meeting a hungry bicycle-rider and hurrying back to tea at the inn. The passage of time slipped back, as in dreams, to where it was of no account, and they stood there, half fascinated, half frightened by this imp of a creature who seemed to them about to lift a corner of the veil that hangs ever between the illusions of the broken senses and the realities that lie beyond.

But it was the boy himself who broke the spell by suddenly stepping forward and holding out his hands to them. A smile slipped out of his strange eyes and ran all over his face, making it shine.

"Come," he said, without any sign now of a stammer, "come, and I will show you where I live. Your friend is already there waiting."

And the imp mentioned him by name!

The younger girl—she who most looked forward to his coming—gave a perceptible start, and moved quickly backwards towards the hedge. Something clutched at her heart and made her horribly afraid.

But at the mention of their friend's name, the man of the party burst into a cheery laugh.

"There!" he cried, "I told you it was Harry! It's his idea of a Christmas joke. He's gone on to the other inn, the Black Horse, and sent this imp of darkness to waylay us. Now we shall have two teas to negotiate!" He clapped his hands and turned to the girls behind him. "Come on," he said, "let's follow the youngster to the Black Horse and then send him to fetch the others."

Yet the man's words seemed a sham, signifying nothing, or at most merely cheap bravado. They all stood stock still and made no pretence of moving. Their real business was with this boy who hovered there before them between the dusk and the darkness, his hands still outstretched, an air of invitation in his face and manner. It was the boy's message they wanted, yet dreaded to hear, the real message not yet delivered. His eyes, there in the gloom, were so preternaturally steady, so compelling, so stern almost for a child, the younger girl thought. And they sought ever the one face, disregarding the other two. For each girl was positive he looked only into her own eyes, while the man afterwards declared that the boy looked only at him. To each the illusion was perfect.

Thus it seemed an act of inspiration, bringing relief to the uneasy feelings of them all, when the man walked forward towards the imp, and into those outstretched hands—dropped coppers.

Certainly it was a relief to see him pocket them without an instant's hesitation, for this was an eminently human proceeding. But the thin peal of elfin laughter that followed the action was not what they had expected, and the echoes that came from the leafless woods beyond, and prolonged the sound, made them all turn sharply about and try to face in every direction at once. The echoes had seemed so curiously like real voices.

Then the man, by way of protest against the increasing strangeness of it all, resolved to test the spell more vigorously.

"Come," he cried, laughing rather boisterously, "we'll play puss in the corner. You shall be puss, and each time you get into a corner you shall have a halfpenny."

The boy made no audible reply, but danced about lightly in the twilight in the middle of the lane, while the smile flitted over his face like the reflections of an unseen lantern and the others ran wildly from corner to corner, till the imp had finally won six pence. It was easy for him to win. The moment he made for a corner, its occupant fled screaming into the lane. It was impossible, they felt, to contest the points of a merely human game with such a creature of the shadows and the dusk.

Then occurred the strangest thing of all. The game was over and they were girding up their loins to follow the boy to the Black Horse first, and afterwards to their own inn, when, with a quick motion like the rush of a bird, he darted to the younger girl, flung down all the coppers into her hands, before she even guessed what he was about, whispered some words close to her face, uttered a shrill cry of laughter—and was gone!

"Oh, Oh!" she cried out piteously—and this time there was real pain and terror in her voice. "Now I know! Now I know why I was afraid!"

She half fell backwards across a heap of broken stones, and the other two were swiftly at her side with sympathetic questions of alarm. But she was on her feet again in a second. She ran a few paces down the road to the spot where the boy had so mysteriously vanished. None of them had seen exactly how he went, for one second he was there, and the next he was not there. That was all they knew.

The girl paused and held her hand to her side. She peered into the darkness.

"Harry!" she called faintly; and again with anguish in her voice, "Harry! Are you there?"

They were standing in the level space between the two sharp hills. In front of them, after an abrupt turn, the long white road seemed to run steeply into the sky. And it was down this hill that the coming bicyclist must shape his dangerous course.

"There!" she cried again suddenly, running to the side of the road where the hedge ceased, and an open gap led the sight as a single plunge into empty space. "Oh, I knew it, I knew it!"

And when the others joined her, and peered over the hedge they found themselves looking down into the chasm of a disused chalk pit, at the bottom of which in the faint glimmer of the lime and the starlight, lay the smashed bicycle, with the lifeless body of its rider outstretched beside it.

The Story Mr. Popkiss Told

"Talking of railway accidents—"

"But we weren't," interrupted the prig.

"—and of narrow escapes," continued Mr. Popkiss, ignoring the contradiction and looking like an offended parrot with its head on one side, "reminds me of one."

"Which?" inquired the prig smartly, "the railway accident or the narrow escape?" He was a small young man with red eyes and a face like a weasel. He was also a "psychical student."

"Both," said Popkiss, looking at him over the top of his spectacles, and spreading out his coat-tails before the fire, so that he resembled more than ever a parrot, jaunty, yet slightly ruffled, swinging on its perch.

"Let's have the story," said Brown, in a tone of authority.

And the story began at once; for Brown was "the intellect" of the little party of newspaper men telling yarns round the club fire-place that deserted Christmas-week, when their duties held them in London after everyone else had gone.

"It saved my life, so it *was* nearly an accident," continued Mr. Popkiss ambiguously, "and this is how it happened. *Most* odd, it was."

He buttoned his coat tightly, as though conscious that he resembled a bird, and anxious to dissemble the fact. He was a man of fifty, bald, shabby, timid, and kind-hearted—an unsuccessful solicitor.

"It was last year, on the Boxing Day after Christmas," he began in his high-pitched voice, "and I was in a third-class carriage, going down into Surrey for the New Year's week. I was alone, sitting by the window. It was after ten o'clock, and I was drowsy, but *not* asleep. The window streamed with rain. Outside, everything was black and raw and miserable—utterly cheerless. Just after leaving Wimbledon Station another train drew up alongside, and I watched it through the window of my corner-seat, trying to work up an interest, and wondering which would win. I imagined the two trains were racing—as one is apt to do at such a time—and that all the passengers knew it. But for a long time we both ran an even race, neck and neck, and I remember thinking what a fool our engine-driver was not to put on steam and pull ahead.

"Faster and faster we went. It annoyed me that all these stupid passengers in the other train were so close to me, going to other destinations than mine. It seemed so dull and boring for them. You know the kind of foolish thoughts that wander up and down the mind at such times."

"Quite," said the psychical student; "quite!"

"And I was glad the windows were so blurred by rain that they couldn't see into my carriage—when, suddenly, I turned with a start and found that my own window was clear as crystal, and that I could see with the greatest ease into the carriage running close beside me. Something had sponged the windows clean. And in the corner-seat of that other carriage, so close to my elbow that I could have put my hand out and touched him, sat a man, huddled up in overcoats, and rugs, just as I was."

Mr. Popkiss unbuttoned the top button of his coat to allow more freedom for possible gestures. The group of listeners stared with keen attention. The mind of the weasel-faced student was already busily searching for flaws by means of which he might tear the story to pieces the moment it was finished.

"Quite inexplicably," continued Mr. Popkiss, pitching his voice higher in key but lower in tone, "the figure of this man arrested my attention vividly—almost unpleasantly. The face was hidden by his hand, but there was something about him that made me reflect. It seemed to me that I knew who he was. Like myself, he was alone in an empty compartment. The curious idea entered my head that he was watching me through the fingers over his face; and a mysterious uneasiness I could not account for came over me.

"I made a movement forward to look at him through the middle window—and the man made a precisely similar movement. Through the middle windows of both carriages our eyes met, and in a flash I saw who it was—"

"You recognised him?" asked several voices together.

"I recognised him beyond all question; he was *myself!*" continued Mr. Popkiss, unfastening the second button of his coat; "absolutely myself!"

"Another Popkiss!" exclaimed the psychical student. "You mean a reflection, of course?"

"At first I thought it was a reflection, for the man copied every movement I made—every single movement. I won't bore you with details; but everything I did in my carriage that man also did in his carriage. And yet"—Popkiss mopped his forehead and unbuttoned the last button—"there was something about him—something about the peering face with spectacles—about the silent movements and shadowy appearance—that woke a nameless terror in me. I began to perspire all over. And something in me, too, began to tremble. Each time I turned to look, there he stood, his arms placed precisely as mine were placed, his body in the same attitude exactly, and his spectacled eyes staring straight into my own."

His voice sank to a whisper as he said this. Everyone listened breathlessly. "A projection of your own Double," murmured the student, "or a condition of hysteria inducing a vision," but no one paid any attention to him.

"Yes, and this is how it happened," resumed Popkiss, passing a hand over his bald head, as though the world were so strange a place that it would not have surprised him to find unexpected tufts upon that marble surface, "and I never can persuade you how dreadfully queer I felt.

"Then, suddenly, an idea came to me just as the two trains, were slowing down, still running neck and neck. I *opened the window!* The other man did the same. We put our heads out. There was no question of reflection then. I had to cling to the window sides to prevent myself falling, so great was the shock. For, instead of disappearing, as a reflection must have disappeared, the face of this other man suddenly flamed up through the night in most amazing fashion; and, thrusting his head forward, so that we almost touched one another, I heard his whisper fly across to me through the darkness. The words came with a sense of most appalling reality, and it seemed to me that a wind of ice and snow passed over my cheeks.

"'*Leave this train!*' he said, above the rattle of the metals. '*Leave this train!*'

"And the very next second, before I could answer, or do anything at all, the lights in *his* carriage were extinguished, and the train was running beside me in black darkness!

"But was it running beside me? That was the queer part of it. Was it still keeping up a neck-and-neck race with my own? For when I put my head further out to look, and as soon as my eyes got accustomed to the gloom, lo and behold, there was no train there at all! Both in front and behind the lines were clear. There was no train, and no sign of one.... Five minutes later we ran into Woking Junction."

The psychical student longed to say something, but his mind was so confused with such phrases as "double personality," "veridical dreams," "subliminal consciousness," and the like, that before he could squeeze out a word Mr. Popkiss was at it again, finishing his story:

"It would be impossible to describe to you how, and why, the whole thing so impressed me," he explained softly, "that I actually *did* leave the train at Woking Junction, although my destination was several further stations further on.... All I can tell you is that the train itself—my train—ran off the metals before it had gone another mile down the line, and two people were killed outright, and a dozen injured terribly.... I had to sleep at Woking and go on next day when the debris was cleared away...."

He buttoned up his coat again very quickly, and touched the bell for the waiter.

"Queer, wasn't it?" he observed, looking round him with a thirsty sigh.

Involved discussion followed in a torrent, during the course of which the psychical student gave the group the benefit of much labored explanation. A world in which he could not explain everything by the processes of his own acute little mind was intolerable to him. And when the others, led by Brown, made difficulties, he fell back upon the delightful generalisation that "to imagine such things at all was a sure sign of mental degeneration...."

"What do *you* think of it yourself?" he asked at length of the story-teller.

"I?" said Popkiss, deprecatingly; "oh, I don't think anything at all. It saved my life—and that's enough for me!"

He handed a cigarette to the student who "didn't drink," and sat back in his chair to listen to the next tale.

The Face of the Earth

Finkelstein, like many another German, resembled a weak edition of Bismarck. A little way off the appearance was remarkable, closer, of course, one saw the softness of eye and indecision of jaw that destroyed the illusion.

"I want you to fearful be—of nozzing," he said, looking the young man up and down.

"I am afraid of nothing," said Arthur Spinrobin, believing that the secretaryship was already his.

"Goot," said the old professor. "I take you on!"

And thus Arthur Spinrobln, orphan, penniless, the money provided for his Cambridge education just exhausted, began the high adventure of his life by a three months' engagement to Professor Adolf Finkelstein. The only qualification was that he should know German, have some knowledge of surveying, and be "afraid of nothing." Finkelstein, for reasons best known to himself, lived at the time in a little farmhouse of greystone among the folds of the Dorsetshire hills; and thither Spinrobin, small, round, and active, with cheerful face and sanguine heart, betook himself, as agreed, on September 1.

"It may lead to something," he said to himself at the end of the first week, "but it's all jolly queer. I wonder if the old boy is a spy—or merely a lunatic." He remembered that he was expected to be afraid of nothing. Arrest, high treason, and other ominous words occurred to him; but in the end he rejected them all. "He's one of these Teutonic dreamers—transcendentalist and all that—gone a little bit cracky." Only the map-making puzzled him—uneasily.

For the life they led was not quite ordinary. They had a big sitting-room and a bedroom each in the farm house that was glad enough to take in a couple of boarders. The mornings they spent translating various German passages, beginning with authors like Novalis and Schlegel, and ending with more modern writers that Spinrobin had never heard of. While Finkelstein translated into French, Spinrobin did likewise into English—apparently with a view to simultaneous publication in both languages of some big Essay the German professor was at work on. This Essay was to include these passages, but Finkelstein did not take the secretary into his confidence concerning it. There was an air of mystery about the whole thing. And the translated passages always had to do with one subject, viz., that the Earth was the body of a great Being—living, conscious; that it had organs and a physiognomy; that the beauty of nature was merely a revelation of its personality; and that human beings could no more realise this than a fly on an elephant could realise that it walked upon a living body differing from its own merely in size and habits.

"Some faces are too big to be seen as faces," Finkelstein said one morning to him. Then leaning forward through the tobacco smoke above their work-table he suddenly touched Spinrobin's little turn-up nose with his thick finger. "The ten million microbes there dwelling," he said with an earnestness that made the secretary start, "do not know they are on a human face, *was*?" For he talked German and English indiscriminately. The afternoons they walked together upon the hills, Spinrobin in normal shooting costume, and Finkelstein in baggy, grey knickerbockers, elastic side boots with nails, a loose jacket of Austrian Loden cloth, and a Tyrolese hat. A camera was swung round his shoulder, for he took frequent photographs, which he developed himself.

"Look," he said, pointing to the smooth, rounded hill-tops about them, treeless, with sheep and cattle feeding in groups. "The cheeks of a great face I see. I photograph it now, and later show you somezing your own little sight cannot take in. *Ach!* The camera is fine for that. *Wer weisst? Wer weisst?*"

But the chalk pits drew him most, and he was forever taking photographs or making sketches of them, and asking his secretary to draw accurate plans showing the exact relation they bore to one another; and poring over the results on paper, at home till the smoke got too thick to see, and he would put them away with a sigh and discuss plans for the morrow. In particular there were two pits about a mile apart that interested him, with a third some hundreds of feet below them, very deep, with a ragged edge where gorse and furze bushes grew in a fringe along the lips.

"There we have it, I think," he used to say in German, after wandering for hours from one to the other, and studying endless photographs and plans of them at home, "there we have it. Wait und see if I am not right." All of which bewildered the secretary hopelessly until one day, in his chief's absence, he peeped into his bedroom, and saw on the walls his own series of maps, distorted out of all truth or accuracy, with the pits marked in red, and the whole presenting different aspects of a mighty and very dreadful countenance. The two smaller pits were eyes, and the lower deep one with the bushes fringing it like hair, was a mouth, a huge, open, gaping mouth. The sight produced in him an unpleasant sense of alarm and disgust he was at a loss to account for.

"Ach, not here! Do not stumble here!" the German cried one day when Spinrobin slipped near the edge of the bigger pit, and his face was so white that for a moment it seemed almost as if the depths of chalk below had shot up some curious message of reflected light upon his skin. And for some reason he never could explain quite to himself, the secretary always avoided that particular pit afterwards. A certain sense of personality pervaded it; and when the Professor told him the stories (corroborated in some measure, too, by the farmer) about the number of sheep and cattle it devoured yearly, the sense of dread—though he laughed at it—increased. One evening, too, coming home alone, he heard the wind whistling and booming round its white sides, polishing them to smoothness, and the sudden fancy leaped into his brain of a great purring throat. "Absurd!" he laughed, turning with a run in a safer direction; "this old Finkelstein with his crazy anthropomorphism has got into my imagination."

And that very night they translated long passages from Fechner—told with a bold power and originality that made it all unpleasantly real to the ordinarily cheerful, healthy-minded little secretary. "Like your own visionary, ze great Blake," exclaimed Finkelstein. In the middle, curiously excited (and using a vigorous English phrase utterly incongruous to the professional type, and picked up heaven knows where!) "zis Fechner has a great Imagination that bangs straight through into Reality!"

Thus there gradually grew up about the innocent Spinrobin a queer sense that the world was no longer quite the same as he had hitherto seen it. This Fechner, whom the Professor studied, laid a new spell upon him. The water for fish; the air for birds; the ether—well, the ether, too, in turn had its own denizens: worlds! The stars were alive; the planets great spiritual Beings; the earth on which he lived was the physical body of some vast Intelligence that boomed its mighty way through space just as he himself pattered with quick little footsteps across a field. Moreover, Finkelstein elaborated the theory of his fellow countryman with singular conviction.

"Ze worlds are ze true angels," he said, "and not imachination is ze music of the spheres. Ach! I will proof it to everypody when I gif out zis great book I write." Then, puffing his pipe voluminously into his secretary's face, he would become enthusiastic and more confidential. The worlds, he declared, were some kind of Beings superior to men and animals, but alive and conscious in the same sense. He dwelt upon the analogy till water came into his soft eyes, and his gesticulations threatened the crockery as well as Spinrobin's own astonished features. Arms and legs, he said, after all, are only crutches to enable ill-constructed creatures to get about—whereas the worlds have no need for them, being round. Eyes are equally unnecessary, for they find their way through the ether without them infallibly. For lungs—their whole surface is in continual commerce with the winds; and for circulation, the rivers, springs, and rains are unceasing. Also all the worlds are in most delicate touch with one another, keenly sensitive to the last variation; and where they grow cold—they die.

"*Ach! Donnerwetter!* They starve!" he would cry with something between anger and laughter, as though his uncouth imaginations were really true. And Spinrobin, hearing all this from morning till night, and having practical explanations given to him during their walks among the hills, reached a point before long where he became exceedingly uncomfortable. Those maps and tortured photographs haunted his dreams with their suggestions of Races that it is not good for man to look upon....

He kept incessant watch upon Finkelstein. It came to him somehow or other that the work, and the walks, and all the rest of it were a labored pretence. The German dreamer had some very practical, matter-of-fact purpose behind all his imaginative writing and talking. It made him uneasy. Once or twice on the hills he caught Finkelstein looking at him with a singular expression in his eyes—

an expression that made him inclined to run or to cry for help, or do something to draw attention to themselves; and on more than one occasion he was certain he heard something treading softly in the night about the door of his bedroom. And Spinrobin, though not a coward, was decidedly of the timid order. He did not like it! It bewildered his respectable and commonplace soul.

"There," exclaimed Finkelstein, in his native tongue, one November evening, when a first spray of snow had whitened the hills, "there you see it well. The snow helps to bring it out—the great whitened face with glorious features! Ach! Ach! In these desolate places where men have done little to obliterate or disturb, you can see more plainly." He indicated the curious configuration of the hills about them. From the high point on which they stood, Spinrobin's awakened imagination easily permitted him to trace the "great whitened face" the enthusiastic German referred to. The pits marked the two eyes, now closed by the shadows of the dusk; and he saw the large, deep, capacious mouth, gaping wide open beneath its fringe of hair-like trees and bushes. It certainly bore a curious resemblance to a vast Face thrust up from below, the features outlined by the powdered snow.

The man came close to his side, and began to talk very rapidly. The secretary's knowledge of German was good, but the other talked so quickly, using such strange phrases and clipping his words with such guttural gymnastics that he found it difficult to follow.

The only thing he gathered generally was that Finkelstein was indulging his imagination, aided by a grotesque humor, in describing the Death of the Earth. The snow and cold made him forecast the time when the body of the earth would be finally dead; and the cause, he declared—here came in the grotesque humor—was that she could no longer feed her internal fires. Mouths, channels, monstrous funnels to act as feeding pipes should be constructed, and the old earth should be kept alive for ever. Or she might even be fed through smaller holes like these very pits—he pointed to them, catching Spinrobin suddenly by the arm—just as human beings might be fed through the pores of the skin!

Spinrobin jumped away from his side in the middle of the strange outburst. They had approached nearer to the edge of the big pit than he cared about.

"My imachination runs me away!" cried the Professor. "Come let us get home to supper. For it is our duty to feed our own bodies before we feed the earth"; and he laughed aloud as he followed his startled secretary down the stony hill-path back to the farm. During the next few days he made frequent reference, however, to this bizarre notion of feeding the dying earth through holes in her surface—pores in her skin. Spinrobin watched him more carefully than before.

Apparently he was not the only person who watched him, for one afternoon that same week the farmer came abruptly into the secretary's room, and asked for a private word with him. Finkelstein was out. Briefly the man came with a warning. "You seem innocent like," explained he, "but you ain't the first secretary he's had down here, nor the first that's disappeared."

"But I've not disappeared," gasped Spinrobin.

"You may do, though—in the cold weather."

The old man was cryptic and mysterious. He received a big price for his rooms, he explained, but—well, he could not help giving a warning to such a nice young fellow as Spinrobin.

The secretary felt his flesh begin to crawl, and a sudden light dawned upon him. The step of the German already sounded in the hall below, and he turned with a quick question to the friendly farmer. It was guess work, but apparently it hit the bull's-eye.

"The sheep and cattle, then, that disappear—?"

"Oh! But he pays me big prices for them—?"

The approaching steps of Finkelstein sent the farmer about his business, but Spinrobin went into his room and locked the door. He began to understand things better. His first quarter was up that week. He came to an abrupt decision. Finkelstein could get a new secretary! ... and next day when he chose a discreet opportunity to announce his decision with plausible excuses, the Professor merely fixed his watery eyes on his face with the remark in German. "I regret it. You have been a patient and admirable secretary—just the material I want for my great—my great purpose." But the phrase "just the material" was ominous and stuck in Spinrobin's mind. Somehow he had come now to loathe the man, his voice, eyes, and gestures. His speculations no longer interested him as before. They touched secret springs of abhorrence and alarm in the depths of him. The figure with Tyrolese hat, baggy knickerbockers and shapeless legs ending in the ridiculous elastic side boots became cloaked with suggestions of a strange horror he could not in the least explain to himself.

And it was a week later—his last day in fact—when a sound woke him at two in the morning, and he peeped out of his window and saw Finkelstein in the moonlight standing with the Loden cloak about his shoulders and throwing up small stones to attract his attention. The moon was reflected in his big spectacles. He carried a long stick. Grotesquely forbidding he looked.

"Come out," he whispered gutturally, holding up a finger to enjoin silence, "come out and see. It is too wonderful! *Ach*! It is too wonderful!" He was greatly excited it seemed.

"What?" stammered little Spinrobin, half-frightened. It was like a figure in a nightmare he felt, a figure he was compelled to obey, for his unlined young soul was very sensitive to suggestion, and this German undoubtedly exercised unconscious hypnotic influence over him.

"The pits are working!" continued the thick German voice. "Only once in a lifetime you see such a thing, perhaps. Ach, but quick; come, quick. It is the feeding-time. I show you! *Was?* The feeding-time...!"

A crowd of conflicting emotions in the breast of the shivering Spinrobin—curiosity, fear, wonder, and a rash courage of youth that urged him to see this extraordinary adventure to its end—found their resultant expression (to this day he cannot quite explain how!) and brought him in a few minutes to the side of the German outside. They moved rapidly up the hill.

Moonlight lay over the whole tossed landscape of mountain and valley, and a gusty south-west wind from the sea boomed and echoed in the hollows. He heard it swish through the patches of long grass about their feet, and past his ears. The German, wrapped in his cloak, and holding his long stick partly concealed, led the way. His calves, thought Spinrobin, looked just like sausages. At any other time he could have laughed.... Instead, he pattered behind, shivering.

"Hark!" whispered Finkelstein, stopping a moment for breath, after a mile of silent climbing. "Now, you hear it."

And the secretary heard in the distance that booming sound of the wind as it rushed like mighty breathing about the mouth of the big pit. The same intense curiosity that had brought him out on this mad expedition overcame the instinct to turn and run—for his life. Finkelstein, he saw, was making sudden awkward movements under cover of his cloak. They were standing some fifty yards from the edge now. The great opening gaped there in the moonlight down the steep slope in front.

"It is the great cold," the German was crying, half to himself, "the cold that means death! She cries for food! Listen." He was very excited. "*Ach!* The great service you shall perhaps render!"

The wind rose with a wild roar about them, freezingly cold; it shouted horribly in the depths of the capacious opening in the hill-side. It cried with shrill swishing sounds as it rushed through the fringe of bushes that grew along the dizzy edge.

"She cried for you, for you, for you! *Ach!* You are so privileged as that!" called out Finkelstein, the crisis of his mania full upon him, and fairly dancing with excitement. "It is only young food she wants. She refuses me again...!" And a lot more that Spinrobin did not understand.

The whole thing, and the ghastly dementia of this crazy German was very clear to him now! He was an active, nimble-footed little fellow, but somehow or other he stumbled at the first step. The German's arm shot out, and the rope at the end of the long stick whistled dreadfully in the air as it flew towards him, and entangled itself about his legs. It flashed in the moonlight—death in its coils.

Spinrobin yelled and struggled. Finkelstein breathing hard, came up along the shortening rope hand over hand towards him, pulling him nearer and nearer to the edge. They rolled and bumped down the precipitous slope, the German just managing to keep out of reach, and the mingled shouting of the two voices rose in wild clamor through the night.

"But why struggle?" cried the lunatic. "There will be no pain, no pain. And you are worth fifty sheep or cattle...!" The spectacled eyes shone like little lamps of silver.

"You shall come too, you brute!" shrieked Spinrobin, at last catching him by an elastic boot and dragging him down upon the ground with a crash. They rolled a bit. Close to the brink, caught by the fringe of gorse bushes which tore and scratched him (though he only knew it afterwards when he saw the scars), they stopped. The rope was hopelessly entangled about their feet. For a second the struggle ceased. Spinrobin heard a loosened stone drop past them, and land with a distant clatter far below. He made a tremendous effort. But the German wriggled free, and stood over him.

Spinrobln, dizzy and exhausted, closed his eyes. The wind rose with a booming roar, and to his terrified imagination, it seemed like great arms that spread out a net to catch him as he fell.

"You feed her! You feed her! *Ach*; it is fine...!" The wind tore away with his words.

A moment later he would have toppled over to his death, when one of the gorse bushes, to his utter amazement, stood upright, struck the figure of the German a resounding blow in the chest that sent him spinning backwards to the ground, and at the same instant clutched Spinrobin's feet, and dragged him up into comparative safety.

It was the farmer, who had been disturbed by their leaving the house, and had followed them up the hill. But Spinrobin never knew quite how it happened. He fairly spun—mind and body....

How they managed between them to truss the maniac with the rope and stick, and carry him back was not without humor; but the full meaning of the "secretaryship" (for which Spinrobin never received his salary) was only apparent some weeks later when the advertisement caused by the adventure drew out the whole facts.

For Finkelstein, it appeared, with his singular form of homicidal mania, was proved by the joint investigations of the English and German police to have been the author of at least three mysterious "disappearances" of young men who had acted as his secretaries; and his remarkable lunacy that imagined the Earth to be a living Being who required human sustenance to keep her alive (he, Finkelstein, being High Priest of the Ceremony), is now minutely recorded for all who care to read, in the Proceedings of the Psychological Societies of both countries.

The Message of the Clock

Suddenly, in most singular fashion, Smith, the patent agent, became aware of the clock upon his mantelpiece.

His mind was an exact one, dealing soberly with life as he saw it, and the way he saw it was as a series of hard, pellet-like facts, behind which he never divined a possible flaming glory. The artistic temperament touched him not. Religion, beauty, wonder—all that tended to make clients unreasonable or things in life seem other than they are—he loathed. Yet here he was, on the eve of Easter, still postponing his country visit, simply because the poor woman in the flat below—who painted pictures and starved in the process—lay dying. Here he was, lingering on in town almost against his will, scarcely knowing why he did so, held there by something that was not a fact, and despising himself (with a kind of curious amazement) for so doing.

For it was not the blunt fact of the woman's dying that kept him; it was something intangible connected with her dying. This much he realized: it was something queer.

And thus, as he sat pondering the matter between the hour of tea and dinner, he became suddenly aware, in this curious fashion, of the presence of the clock. It was startling.

Now, a clock was merely a piece of mechanism—clumsy mechanism—for had he not filed hundreds of specifications to improve them? His own specimen was square and ugly, with a dirty white face, and holes for two keys. Never before had he noticed how it ticked even, and it had no "strike." Yet now, with abrupt insistence, he became aware in the stillness that its steady little hammering note claimed attention—that it ticked, indeed, almost like a voice. For the first time he realized that it was there—busy and important—fussy! It was a Presence. He was no longer quite alone. So strong, indeed, was the feeling that he turned to look at it, as he might have turned to someone who stood waiting beside him with a message. And this was an extraordinary idea to enter the mind of Smith, the patent agent: a clock, ticking out a communication!

"Quarter to seven," he observed. "And probably wants winding."

This last he added by way of explanation to himself. He moved forward to insert the key—then stopped short. "Can't be that," he murmured. "I wound it only this morning—"

Puffing hard at his pipe, he stood and stared; he listened. By some process of the mind he did not understand—and instinctively opposed—it was borne in upon him that this ticking of the clock led up to something—to a certain moment. It was like a telegraph instrument clicking out a message, a little voice consciously drawing his attention to something—to something that was *about to happen.* Without understanding it quite, Smith experienced the imaginative truth that, if the mind dwells long enough upon an object, that object becomes invested with a personality. The voice of that clock became alive, and held intercourse with him. But why it should have led him to think something was going to happen—and happen at seven o'clock—perplexed him to the point of positive annoyance.

This was a state of mind the patent agent regarded with suspicion and dislike. He deliberately tried to think of something else; yet without success. His thoughts always turned back to the personality of the woman downstairs who lay dying, the artist whom he had seen, though never spoken with, and about whom he had gathered all kinds of intimate details owing to that curious leakage that turns a House of Flats into a huge Whispering Gallery.

Her mode of life, he always felt, in some inexplicable way challenged his own, as though character created an atmosphere that could spread mysteriously through bricks and mortar like an emanation, to affect other minds. Insensibly, often, he had found himself contrasting her life with his: his self-centred, utilitarian, highly moral existence, believing only in "facts"; and hers, the vain fluttering of a soul after Beauty—achieving nothing, yet shedding about her an atmosphere of light, considering all she possessed as belonging to everyone in need of it. He knew, for instance, how she often kept her models when she had no work for them, and even fed them to her own want. The servants carried some rather wonderful stories about—stories that made him feel uncomfortable till he banished them.... So that when he had heard a few days before that she lay dangerously ill—lonely, perhaps dying—he contrasted his jolly Easter in the country with her own dismal prospects, and the instinct stirred in him to stay on a little in town... perhaps to help... perhaps only to *know*... he scarcely understood himself... yet he had stayed....

Again the ticking of the clock interrupted his reverie.

"Ten minutes to seven," he read.

It was very curious; he could not keep his mind from her. On the floor below all was silent. A wind sang mournfully past the walls, carrying a million raindrops that beat their tiny hammers upon the windows. Queer new thoughts attacked his mind, showing him in swift, fugitive vision possibilities of life that a temperament like hers might hold. Perhaps the truth was that this little wave of unwonted sympathy touched into being a new corner of his own consciousness. The figure of the woman, as he had once passed her on the stairs, rose with haunting persistence before him. She had no beauty, strictly speaking, this elderly Irish woman, but her face had that touch of soul that painted it sometimes with a burning glory, and was gone, so that all who saw it experienced a sudden and inexpressible yearning for high things.

And he, Smith, had caught her once or twice with that look. It was very wonderful, very radiant. It had made him pause and ask himself whether, after all, it was she that was wasting time, or himself. Her motto, he had heard, was

"Help others, and pass on"; and she practised it, passing on without reward; she gave herself freely, not counting the cost—time, money, sympathy. Yet, here she was at this moment dying, almost in want, nothing saved, nothing put by, nothing achieved—a failure. Was it worthwhile—this life of unpractical dreaming? He had wondered about it before. He wondered about it now....

Again the voice of the clock drew his attention.

"Five minutes to seven."

It was very haunting, this persistent calling of the clock; he began to feel unaccountably ill at ease and restless. A sensation of eeriness came over him. He wished the hour of seven were past. He drew the curtains closer to shut out the sighing of the wind. More than once he looked over his shoulder, expecting something, he knew not what.... Once he even thought of going downstairs to inquire of the nurse.... Perhaps he might be able to help.

He was still sitting, however, in his armchair opposite the mirror when the sound of the door opening softly behind him drew his attention. The curtain on the rod made it swish audibly. He instantly looked up and saw the figure of the very woman he had been thinking about reflected in the glass before him. In her eyes was that flame seen sometimes in the eyes of the mad, sometimes in those of religious enthusiasts—that lightning of the disturbed soul which seeks to reconcile an inner glory with the common light of the sun. Only, with her now, the soul was not disturbed; the flame was steady and permanent; and an expression of peace and happiness, extraordinarily beautiful, rested upon her features as the mirror gave them back to him.

She was sleep-walking—he realized that, of course—under the stress of fever or delirium. He must act promptly and get her downstairs again, or call for the nurse. Yet he found himself able to do none of these things. He could only stare, with a sense of wonder so exquisite that it was pain—stare at the radiant and beatific expression in the mirror before him.

Amazed, and yet not amazed—conscious, too, of a kind of elevating terror—he then stood bolt upright and tried to turn and face her. Finding this was somehow impossible, he tried to speak. This also failed him. He could not move his lips. The beauty of that look held him spellbound and speechless. He stood motionless, staring at her image in the glass—the image of this dying woman, silent and wonderful behind him—unbelievably glorious!

Then, with extraordinary softness, the whisper of a voice floated to his ear: *"It is more wonderful even than I dreamed. It is—and it was—worthwhile!"*

Smith suddenly realized something new, and his heart gave a horrid jump. He turned sharply round, a terror of the unknown clutching him. The room was absolutely empty.

The ticking of the clock, sounding up till now like a tiny hammer in his brain, had ceased; and he saw that the hands pointed to seven. The mechanism had accountably run down.... It was only on the following day, however, he learned that the human mechanism had also run down at the same moment.

The vision he dismissed easily as a dream, but that running down of the clock puzzled him dreadfully for years....

The Singular Death of Morton

Dusk was melting into darkness as the two men slowly made their way through the dense forest of spruce and fir that clothed the flanks of the mountain. They were weary with the long climb, for neither was in his first youth, and the July day had been a hot one. Their little inn lay further in the valley among the orchards that separated the forest from the vineyards.

Neither of them talked much. The big man led the way, carrying the knapsack, and his companion, older, shorter, evidently the more fatigued of the two, followed with small footsteps. From time to time he stumbled among the loose rocks. An exceptionally observant mind would possibly have divined that his stumbling was not entirely due to fatigue, but to an absorption of spirit that made him careless how he walked.

"All right behind?" the big man would call from time to time, half glancing back.

"Eh? What?" the other would reply, startled out of a reverie.

"Pace too fast?"

"Not a bit. I'm coming." And once he added: "You might hurry on and see to supper, if you feel like it. I shan't be long behind you."

But his big friend did not adopt the suggestion. He kept the same distance between them. He called out the same question at intervals. Once or twice he stopped and looked back too.

In this way they came at length to the skirts of the wood. A deep hush covered all the valley; the limestone ridges they had climbed gleamed down white and ghostly upon them from the fading sky. Midway in its journeys, the evening wind dropped suddenly to watch the beauty of the moonlight—to hold the branches still so that the light might slip between and weave its silver pattern on the moss below.

And, as they stood a moment to take it in, a step sounded behind them on the soft pine-needles, and the older man, still a little in the rear, turned with a start as though he had been suddenly called by name.

"There's that girl—again!" he said, and his voice expressed a curious mingling of pleasure, surprise and—apprehension.

Into a patch of moonlight passed the figure of a young girl, looked at them as though about to stop yet thinking better of it, smiled softly, and moved on out of sight into the surrounding darkness. The moon just caught her eyes and teeth, so that they shone; the rest of her body stood in shadow; the effect was striking—almost as though head and shoulders hung alone in mid air, watching them with this shining smile, then fading away.

"Come on, for heaven's sake," the big man cried. There was impatience in his manner, not unkindness. The other lingered a moment, peering closely into the gloom where the girl had vanished. His friend repeated his injunction, and a moment later the two had emerged upon the high road with the village lights in sight beyond, and the forest left behind them like a vast mantle that held the night within its folds.

For some minutes neither of them spoke; then the big man waited for his friend to draw up alongside.

"About all this valley of the Jura," he said presently, "there seems to me something—rather queer." He shifted the knapsack vigorously on his back. It was a gesture of unconscious protest. "Something uncanny," he added, as he set a good pace.

"But extraordinarily beautiful—"

"It attracts you more than it does me, I think," was the short reply.

"The picturesque superstitions still survive here," observed the older man. "They touch the imagination in spite of oneself."

A pause followed, during which the other tried to increase the pace. The subject evidently made him impatient for some reason.

"Perhaps," he said presently. "Though I think myself it's due to the curious loneliness of the place. I mean, we're in the middle of tourist-Europe here, yet so utterly remote. It's such a neglected little corner of the world. The contradiction bewilders. Then, being so near the frontier, too, with the clock changing an hour a mile from the village, makes one think of time as unreal and imaginary." He laughed. He produced several other reasons as well. His friend admitted their value, and agreed half-heartedly. He still turned occasionally to look back. The mountain ridge where they had climbed was clearly visible in the moonlight.

"Odd," he said, "but I don't see that farmhouse where we got the milk anywhere. It ought to be easily visible from here."

"Hardly—in this light. It was a queer place rather, I thought," he added. He did not deny the curiously suggestive atmosphere of the region, he merely wanted to find satisfactory explanations. "A case in point, I mean. I didn't like it quite—that farmhouse—yet I'm hanged if I know why. It made me feel uncomfortable. That girl appeared so suddenly, although the place seemed deserted. And her silence was so odd. Why in the world couldn't she answer a single question? I'm glad I didn't take the milk. I spat it out. I'd like to know where she got it from, for there was no sign of a cow or a goat to be seen anywhere!"

"I swallowed mine—in spite of the taste," said the other, half smiling at his companion's sudden volubility.

Very abruptly, then, the big man turned and faced his friend. Was it merely an effect of the moonlight, or had his skin really turned pale beneath the sunburn?

"I say, old man," he said, his face grave and serious. "What do you think she was? What made her seem like that, and why the devil do you think she followed us?"

"I think," was the slow reply, "it was *me* she was following."

The words, and particularly the tone of conviction in which they were spoken, clearly were displeasing to the big man, who already regretted having spoken so frankly what was in his mind. With a companion so imaginative, so impressionable, so nervous, it had been foolish and unwise. He led the way home at a pace that made the other arrive five minutes in his rear, panting, limping, and perspiring as if he had been running.

"I'm rather for going on into Switzerland tomorrow, or the next day," he ventured that night in the darkness of their two-bedded room. "I think we've had enough of this place. Eh? What do you think?"

But there was no answer from the bed across the room, for its occupant was sound asleep and snoring.

"Dead tired, I suppose!" he muttered to himself, and then turned over to follow his friend's example. But for a long time sleep refused him. Queer, unwelcome thoughts and feelings kept him awake—of a kind he rarely knew, and thoroughly disliked. It was rubbish, yet it made him uncomfortable, so that his nerves tingled. He tossed about in the bed. "I'm overtired," he persuaded himself, "that's all."

The strange feelings that kept him thus awake were not easy to analyse, perhaps, but their origin was beyond all question: they grouped themselves about the picture of that deserted, tumble-down chalet on the mountain ridge where they had stopped for refreshment a few hours before. It was a farmhouse, dilapidated and dirty, and the name stood in big black letters against a blue background on the wall above the door: "La Chenille." Yet not a living soul was to be seen anywhere about it; the doors were fastened, windows shuttered; chimneys smokeless; dirt, neglect, and decay everywhere in evidence.

Then, suddenly, as they had turned to go, after much vain shouting and knocking at the door, a face appeared for an instant at a window, the shutter of which was half open. His friend saw it first, and called aloud. The face nodded in reply, and presently a young girl came round the corner of the house, apparently by a back door, and stood staring at them both from a little distance.

And from that very instant, so far as he could remember, these queer feelings had entered his heart—fear, distrust, misgiving. The thought of it now, as he lay in bed in the darkness, made his hair rise. There was something about that girl that struck cold into the soul. Yet she was a mere slip of a thing, very pretty, seductive even, with a certain serpent-like fascination about her eyes and movements; and although she only replied to their questions as to refreshment with a smile, uttering no single word, she managed to convey the impression that she was a managing little person who might make herself very disagreeable if she chose. In spite of her undeniable charm there was about her an atmosphere of something sinister. He himself did most of the questioning, but it was his older friend who had the benefit of her smile. Her eyes hardly ever left his face, and once she had slipped quite close to him and touched his arm.

The strange part of it now seemed to him that he could not remember in the least how she was dressed, or what was the colouring of her eyes and hair. It was almost as though he had *felt*, rather than seen, her presence.

The milk—she produced a jug and two wooden bowls after a brief disappearance round the corner of the house—was—well, it tasted so odd that he had been unable to swallow it, and had spat it out. His friend, on the other hand, savage with thirst, had drunk his bowl to the last drop, too quickly to taste it even, and, while he drank, had kept his eyes fixed on those of the girl, who stood close in front of him.

And from that moment his friend had somehow changed. On the way down he said things that were unusual, talking chiefly about the "Chenille," and the girl, and the delicious, delicate flavour of the milk, yet all phrased in such a way that it sounded singular, unfamiliar, unpleasant even. Now that he tried to recall the sentences the actual words evaded him; but the memory of the uneasiness and apprehension they caused him to feel remained. And night ever italicizes such memories!

Then, to cap it all, the girl had followed them. It was wholly foolish and absurd to feel the things he did feel; yet there the feelings were, and what was the good of arguing? That girl frightened him; the change in his friend was in some way or other a danger signal. More than this he could not tell. An explanation might come later, but for the present his chief desire was to get away from the place and to get his friend away, too.

And on this thought sleep overtook him—heavily.

The windows were wide open; outside was a garden with a rather high enclosing wall, and at the far end a gate that was kept locked because it led into private fields and so, by a back way, to the cemetery and the little church. When it was open the guests of the inn made use of it and got lost in the network of fields and vines, for there was no proper route that way to the road or the mountains. They usually ended up prematurely in the cemetery, and got back to the village by passing through the church, which was always open; or by knocking at the kitchen doors of the other houses and explaining their position. Hence the gate was locked now to save trouble.

After several hours of hot, unrefreshing sleep the big man turned in his bed and woke. He tried to stretch, but couldn't; then sat up panting with a sense of suffocation. And by the faint starlight of the summer night, he saw next that his friend was up and moving about the room. Remembering that sometimes he walked in his sleep, he called to him gently:

"Morton, old chap," he said in a low voice, with a touch of authority in it, "go back to bed! You've walked enough for one day!"

And the figure, obeying as sleep-walkers often will, passed across the room and disappeared among the shadows over his bed. The other plunged and burrowed himself into a comfortable position again for sleep, but the heat of the room, the shortness of the bed, and this tiresome interruption of his slumbers made it difficult to lose consciousness. He forced his eyes to keep shut, and his body to cease from fidgeting, but there was something nibbling at his mind like a spirit mouse that never permitted him to cross the frontier into actual oblivion. He slept with one eye open, as the saying is. Odours of hay and flowers and baked ground stole in through the open window; with them, too, came from time to time sounds—little sounds that disturbed him without being ever loud enough to claim definite attention.

Perhaps, after all, he did lose consciousness for a moment—when, suddenly, a thought came with a sharp rush into his mind and galvanized him once more into utter wakefulness. It amazed him that he had not grasped it before. It was this: the figure he had seen was *not the figure of his friend.*

Alarm gripped him at once before he could think or argue, and a cold perspiration broke out all over his body. He fumbled for matches, couldn't find them; then, remembering there was electric light, he scraped the wall with his fingers—and turned on the little white switch. In the sudden glare that filled the room he saw instantly that his friend's bed was no longer occupied. And his mind, then acting instinctively, without process of conscious reasoning, flew like a flash to their walk of the day—to the tumble-down "Chenille," the glass of milk, the odd behaviour of his friend, and—to the girl.

At the same second he noticed that the odour in the room which hitherto he had taken to be the composite odour of fields, flowers and night, was really something else: it was the odour of freshly turned earth. Immediately on the top of this discovery came another. Those slight sounds he had heard outside the window were not ordinary night-sounds, the murmur of wind and insects: they were footsteps moving softly, stealthily down the little paths of crushed granite.

He was dressed in wonderful short order, noticing as he did so that his friend's night-garments lay upon the bed, and that he, too, had therefore dressed; further—that the door had been unlocked and stood half an inch ajar. There was now no question that he had slept again: between the present and the moment when he had seen the figure there had been a considerable interval. A couple of minutes later he had made his way cautiously downstairs and was standing on the garden path in the moonlight. And as he stood there, his mind filled with the stories the proprietor had told a few days before of the superstitions that still lived in the popular imagination and haunted this little, remote pine-clad valley. The thought of that girl sickened him. The odour of newly turned earth remained in his nostrils and made his gorge rise. Utterly and vigorously he rejected the monstrous fictions he had heard, yet for all that, could not prevent their touching his imagination as he stood there in the early hours of the morning, alone with night and silence. The spell was undeniable; only a mind without sensibility could have ignored it.

He searched the little garden from end to end. Empty! Opposite the high gate he stopped, peering through the iron bars, wet with dew to his hands. Far across the intervening fields he fancied something moved. A second later he was sure of it. Something down there to the right beyond the trees was astir. It was in the cemetery.

And this definite discovery sent a shudder of terror and disgust through him from head to foot. He framed the name of his friend with his lips, yet the sound did not come forth. Some deeper instinct warned him to hold it back. Instead, after incredible efforts, he climbed that iron gate and dropped down into the soaking grass upon the other side. Then, taking advantage of all the cover he could find, he ran, swiftly and stealthily, towards the cemetery. On the way, without quite knowing why he did so, he picked up a heavy stick; and a moment later he stood beside the low wall that separated the fields from the church-yard—stood and stared.

There, beside the tombstones, with their hideous metal wreaths and crowns of faded flowers, he made out the figure of his friend; he was stooping, crouched down upon the ground; behind him rose a couple of bushy yew trees, against the dark of which his form was easily visible. He was not alone; in front of him, bending close over him it seemed, was another figure—a slight, shadowy, slim figure.

This time the big man found his voice and called aloud: "Morton, Morton!" he cried. "What, in the name of heaven, are you doing? What's the matter—?"

And the instant his deep voice broke the stillness of the night with its clam-our, the little figure, half hiding his friend, turned about and faced him. He saw a white face with shining eyes and teeth as the form rose; the moonlight painted it with its own strange pallor; it was weird, unreal, horrible; and across the mouth, downwards from the lips to the chin, ran a deep stain of crimson.

The next moment the figure slid with a queer, gliding motion towards the trees, and disappeared among the yews and tombstones in the direction of the church. The heavy stick, hurled whirling after it, fell harmlessly half way, knocking a metal cross from its perch upon an upright grave; and the man who had thrown it raced full speed towards the huddled up figure of his friend, hardly noticing the thin, wailing cry that rose trembling through the night air from the vanished form. Nor did he notice more particularly that several of the graves, newly made, showed signs of recent disturbance, and that the odour of turned earth he had noticed in the room grew stronger. All his attention was concentrated upon the figure at his feet.

"Morton, man, get up! Wake for God's sake! You've been walking in—"

Then the words died upon his lips. The unnatural attitude of his friend's shoulders, and the way the head dropped back to show the neck, struck him like a blow in the face. There was no sign of movement. He lifted the body up and carried it, all limp and unresisting, by ways he never remembered afterwards, back into the inn.

It was all a dreadful nightmare—a nightmare that carried over its ghastly horror into waking life. He knew that the proprietor and his wife moved busily to and fro about the bed, and that in due course the village doctor was upon the scene, and that he was giving a muddled and feverish description of all he knew, telling how his friend was a confirmed sleep-walker and all the rest. But he did not realize the truth until he saw the face of the doctor as he straightened up from the long examination.

"Will you wake him?" he heard himself asking, "or let him sleep it out till morning?" And the doctor's expression, even before the reply came to confirm it, told him the truth. "Ah, monsieur, your friend will not ever wake again, I fear! It is the heart, you see; *hélas*, it is sudden failure of the heart!"

The final scenes in the little tragedy which thus brought his holiday to so abrupt and terrible a close need no description, being in no way essential to this strange story. There were one or two curious details, however, that came to light afterwards. One was, that for some weeks before there had been signs of disturbance among newly made graves in the cemetery, which the authorities had been trying to trace to the nightly wanderings of the village madman—in vain; and another, that the morning after the death a trail of blood had been found across the church floor, as though someone had passed through from the back entrance to the front. A special service was held that very week to cleanse the holy building from the evil of that stain; for the villagers, deep in their superstitions, declared that nothing human had left that trail; nothing could have made those marks but a vampire disturbed at midnight in its awful occupation among the dead.

Apart from such idle rumours, however, the bereaved carries with him to this day certain other remarkable details which cannot be so easily dismissed. For he had a brief conversation with the doctor, it appears that impressed him profoundly. And the doctor, an intelligent man, prosaic as granite into the bargain, had questioned him rather closely as to the recent life and habits of his dead friend. The account of their climb to the "Chenille" he heard with amazement he could not conceal.

"But no such chalet exists," he said. "There is no 'Chenille.' A long time ago, fifty years or more, there was such a place, but it was destroyed by the authorities on account of the evil reputation of the people who lived there. They burnt it. Nothing remains today but a few bits of broken wall and foundation."

"Evil reputation—?"

The doctor shrugged his shoulders. "Travellers, even peasants, disappeared," he said. "An old woman lived there with her daughter, and poisoned milk was supposed to be used. But the neighbourhood accused them of worse than ordinary murder—"

"In what way?"

"Said the girl was a vampire," answered the doctor shortly.

And, after a moment's hesitation, he added, turning his face away as he spoke:

"It was a curious thing, though, that tiny hole in your friend's throat, small as a pin-prick, yet so deep. And the heart—did I tell you?—was almost completely drained of blood."

La Mauvaise Riche

If seeing is believing the story, of course, is justified, and stands foursquare as a fact, for certainly both my cousin and myself saw the thing as clearly as we saw the village church and the wooded mountains beyond, which were its background. There may, however, be other explanations, and my cousin, who is something of a psychologist, availed himself volubly of the occasion to ride his pet hobby. He easily riddled the saying that seeing is believing, while I listened as patiently as possible. Although no psychologist myself, I knew that the phrase was as inadequate as most other generalizations. Indeed, there is no commoner act of magic in daily life than that of sight, by which the mind projects into the air an image, translated objectively from a sensation in the brain caused by light irritating the optic nerve. "The picture on the retina, upside down, anyhow," he kept telling me afterwards, "is not the object itself that throws off the light-rays, is it? You never see the actual object, do you? You're merely playing with an image, eh? It's pure image-ination, don't you see? It's simple magic, the magic that everybody denies."

Yet, somehow, nothing he could offer by way of explanation satisfied me. The question form of his sentences, moreover, irritated. I rather clung to "seeing is believing," and I think in his heart he did the same, for all his cloud of words.

It was evening, and the summer dusk was falling, as we tramped in silence up the hill towards the village where my cousin, with his wife and children, occupy the upper part of an old chalet. We had been climbing Jura cliffs all day; it had been arduous, exciting work, and we both were tired out. Conversation had long since ceased; our legs moved mechanically, and we both devoutly wished we were at home. "Ah, there's the cemetery at last," he sighed, as the landmark near the village came into view. "Thank goodness!" and I was too weary even to make the obvious commentary. The relief of lying down seemed in his mind. With a grunt by way of reply I glanced carelessly at the rough stone wall surrounding the ugly patch cut squarely from the vineyards, and at the formal pines and larches that stood, plume-like, among the peasant graves. "Old mère Corbillard is safe and snug in her last resting-place," he added, as we passed the painted iron gate, "and a good thing too!" There was relief in his tone, but a moment later there was vivid annoyance. "Izzie;" he cried, stopping short, "what are you doing again in there? You know your mother forbade you to go any more. What a naughty, disobedient child you are!" And he called to his fourteen-year-old child to come out. She came at once, but listlessly, and not one whit afraid. He scolded her a little. "I was only putting flowers on the grave," she said. Her face wore a puzzled, scared expression, and the eyes were very bright—she had wonderful brown eyes—but it was not her father's chiding that caused the look.

She took our arms with affectionate possession, as her way was, and we all three laboured up the hill together. No more was said; her father was too tired to find further fault. "Please don't tell mother, Daddy, will you?" she whispered, as we reached the chalet and went in; "I promise faithfully not to go again." He said nothing, but I saw him give her a kiss, and I gave her one myself. The feeling was strong in me that she was frightened and needed protection. I put my arm tightly round her, giving her a good warm hug. The pleading, helpless look she gave me in return I shall not soon forget.

The memory of "old mère Corbillard" no one cared to keep alive—the wealthy peasant who had died a week ago. Known as "la mauvaise riche," because of her miserly habits, she was also credited with stealing her neighbours' cats for the purpose of devouring them—"lapin de montagne," as the natives termed the horrid dish. Her face was sinister—steel-grey eyes, hooked nose, and prominent teeth—and had the village soul been more imaginative or superstitious, she would certainly have been called a witch. As it was, she was merely passed for "méchante" and distinctly "toquée." Held in general disfavour, she was avoided and disliked, and she repaid the hatred well, thanks to her money. She lived in utter solitude, the one companion, oddly enough, to whom admittance was never denied, being—Izzie. "Oddly enough," because, while the old woman was half-imbecile, maliciously imbecile, the child, on her side—to put it kindly—was unusually backward for her age, if not mentally deficient. But Izzie's deficiency was of mild and gentle quality—a sweet child, if ever there was one. And the parents, while barely tolerating the strange acquaintanceship, never knew how frequent the visits were. They always meant to stop the friendship, yet had never done so. Izzie, true solitary, kept to herself too much. She loved the old woman's stories. They hesitated to say the final No. Thus, at first, they let her go to put fresh flowers, which she picked herself, upon the grave, until, feeling that her too constant journeys there were morbid, the ultimatum had gone forth that they must stop. "It's queer that you should care to go so often," said her father. "It's not right," added her mother, the parents exchanging a look that meant they scented some unholy influence at work. "But I promised to do it every day," said Izzie frankly. Then further explanations elicited the unwelcome addition: "She said she would come and fetch me if I didn't"—and the influence of the old woman seemed defined. "Ha, ha!" said mother's eyes to father; "so the old wretch frightened her apparently into the promise," and they congratulated themselves that the mischief had been stopped in time.

The incident was slight enough. The imagination of the backward child, perhaps a little morbidly inclined owing to her love of solitude, had been unduly stimulated. It had been gently, wisely corrected, and the matter was at an end. Yet, somehow, for me, it lingered in my memory, as though something very vital lay at the core of it.

There followed forty-eight hours of soaking rain that kept us all indoors, and after it a day of cloudless sunshine that made everybody happy. We romped and played with the children, basked in the delicious heat, and were generally full of active mischief. Mother, mending stockings and trying to write letters, had a sorry time of it. But joy and forgiveness ruled the day, and one was ashamed to feel vexation at anything with such a sun in the heavens. Only Izzie, I noticed, kept apart; she was listless and indifferent, joining in no games; her thin, pale face, in contrast to the strange brilliance of her eyes, was evidence to me of some force busily at work within. But she kept it fairly well concealed; it seemed natural for her to moon about alone; I think no one else noticed that her behaviour was more marked than usual. With the cunning of the slow-witted she avoided me in particular, guessing that I was ready to make advances. She divined that I understood. Hiding my purpose as well as possible, I kept her closely under observation, and after supper, when she strolled off alone down the road between the vineyards, I called to Daddy to come and have a pipe. We followed her. The moment we caught her up she turned and took her place as usual, an arm to each. How tall she seemed; she almost topped her father. She kept silence, merely walking in step with us, and holding us rather close I thought, as though glad of our presence though she had started off alone. At first Daddy made efforts to draw her into conversation—efforts that failed utterly. For my part, I let her be, content to keep her arm firmly in my own, for there was very strong in me the feeling that I must protect and watch, guarding her from something that she feared yet was unable to resist. We talked across her, I guiding the conversation towards fun, and she was so tall that we had to stoop and lean forward to see each other's faces.

Hot sun had dried the road up, and the evening was still and peaceful. We paced slowly to and fro, turning always at the village fountain, and again at the crest of the hill where the descent went steeply towards the cemetery. And here, at each turning, Izzie lingered a moment and looked down the hill. I felt perceptibly the dragging on my arm. Once, at the fountain, I made to follow the road through the village. "No," said the child, with decision I disliked intensely, "let's go back again," and we obeyed meekly. "Little tyrant," said her unobservant father.

The mountains rose in a wall of purple shadow, their ridges outlined against a fading sky of gold and crimson. Thin columns of peat smoke traced their scaffolding across it faintly, then melted out. From time to time a group of labourers from the vineyards passed us, singing the Dalcroze songs, taking their hats off, and saying "Bon soir, bonne nuit." We knew them all. Izzie watched them go—with almost feverish interest. I got the queer impression she was waiting till the last group had gone home. She certainly was waiting for something; there was a covert expectancy in her manner that stirred my former uneasiness. And this uneasiness grew stronger every minute. I could hardly listen to my cousin's desultory talk. At last I brought things suddenly to a head, for it was more than my nerves could stand. Abruptly I stood still. The other two, linked arm-in-arm, stood with me.

"Daddy," I said sharply, "let's go in," and was going to add peremptorily, "take Izzie with you," when the words died away on my lips and the tongue in my mouth went dry. My blood seemed turned to ice. For a second I stood in rigid paralysis. For the figure between us, she whose arms were linked in ours was not Izzie, but another. A gaunt, lean face peered close into my own through the dusk as I stooped to see my cousin, and the eyes were of cold steel-grey instead of brown. The skin was lined and furrowed, and projecting teeth of an aged woman gleamed faintly below the great hooked nose. It was mère Corbillard who stood between us, hanging her withered hands upon our arms, her sinister face so close that her straggling thin grey hair even touched our shoulders.

The dreadful sight was as vividly defined as the white face of my cousin which I saw at the same instant just beyond; and by his ghastly pallor, and the water in his eyes, I knew that he had seen her too. His lips were parted, his right hand was raised and clenched. I thought he was going to strike, but instead, wrenching himself violently free, he sprang to one side with an expression of horror that was more a cry than actual words. There was a shriek; whose I dare not say; it may have been my own for all my scattered senses can remember. To this day what I recall was the sensation of death upon my arm, and the glare of those steely eyes that peered triumphantly into my own—then a momentary darkness.

All happened in less than a second. The figure had broken loose from between us, and was racing down the road like a flying shadow—towards the cemetery. Yet the figure we watched an instant before starting in frantic pursuit was unmistakable—Izzie.

To my cousin belongs the reward of prompt action and recapture. He simply flew. And he caught the child long before she reached the forbidden gates. Weeping, white and frightened, we half carried her indoors, and explained to her alarmed mother that she had been taken suddenly ill, a *crise de nerfs*, as Daddy, with presence of mind, described it. It was not the first time; Izzie had been too often hysterical to cause undue anxiety. Mother will never know the truth unless she reads this story, which is unlikely, since her mending and darning leave her little leisure for newspapers. My cousin and myself have discussed the thing *ad nauseam*, and, as I have indicated, he explained it in a variety of ways. But neither of us know what Izzie thought or felt. We, of course, dared not ask her, and the child has never volunteered a word. That she was severely frightened only is clear. She never passes the cemetery alone now, and the name of old mère Corbillard has not passed her lips a single time. My cousin's discovery of the horror, however, coincided with my own. Comparing notes proved that. He had been aware of no uneasy sensations previously, as I had been. Telepathy, therefore, was the clue he finally decided on. "It covers more ground than the word 'possession,' and has besides," as he said, "a sort of scientific sound."

SECTION 2: IMAGINATION AWAKES

Amongst Blackwood's early unreprinted stories is "Stodgman's Opportunity," one of his first sales to the *Westminster Gazette* after the success of *John Silence*. In it he compares the imaginative against the unimaginative and shows how an unusual experience will fire the imagination of one but do nothing to another.

Blackwood was becoming fascinated with the idea of what stimulated the mind to move from the mundane towards the fantastic. An early story, "Imagination," collected in *Ten Minute Stories*, but published as early as December 1910, showed how Blackwood stirred out of his own writer's block when he heard the sound of pan pipes which unlocked the spiritual dam within him following his travels in the Caucasus. He explored this idea of both growing self-awareness and the stimulation of the imagination in several stories and I have selected three others here amongst his previously unreprinted material to show the diversity of his approach.

"Who Was She?," published in *The New Witness* in June 1913 is an early draft of what became chapters 3 to 5 in *The Promise of Air*, but here the characters have different names and the central idea stands on its own without the subsequent embellishment of the novel. Blackwood shows how asking a simple question—that of the title—can unlock thoughts within and start an individual on an entirely new life.

"The Night-Wind" was published in *Country Life* for 9 May 1914. This original version, reprinted here, shows that Blackwood developed the story around the characters in his successful novel *A Prisoner in Fairyland*, published a year earlier. In that novel Henry Rogers, known as Uncle Henry to his cousin's children, seeks to recapture the wonders of his childhood and becomes involved in various spiritual adventures with those children in Switzerland. After that book Blackwood began a series of stories for an obvious sequel, starting with "The Story Hour" in *The Morning Post* for 18 November 1913. The key story is "The Night-Wind" where, Uncle Henry shows the children how to befriend and play with the Night Wind. He uses his imagination to stimulate theirs. In converting it into the novel "The Night-Wind," it becomes the chapter called "Imagination Wakes." When he came to weave these stories into what became *The Extra Day* he changed all the names thereby isolating the book from its predecessor, but there is no doubt in this story as to what Blackwood originally planned. In these stories Uncle Henry is another portrayal of Blackwood himself—his middle name was Henry.

"Genius" is a product of the post-war Blackwood, when he had become rather more cynical and he was struggling to regain his pre-war spiritual nourishment.

The story again explores the source of an author's inspiration which is discovered to be something quite different than expected.

All of these stories show various ways in which the creative spirit can be stimulated.

—*Mike Ashley*

Stodgman's Opportunity

Jonathan Stodgman was one of the writing fraternity. He was always talking about "placing" articles, getting "editors to look at my stuff," and all the rest of it. His "stuff" was good, too—of the solid and instructive kind. An article by Jonathan Stodgman was a guarantee of accuracy; and this was essential when its main interest depended upon the picturesque marshalling of facts, dates, measurements and scientific data generally. Proof-readers had no trouble with Stodgman's "stuff."

But Stodgman himself would willingly have sacrificed the goodwill of all the proof-readers in the world for a single pennyworth of a better quality than accuracy, and one of which he was utterly destitute. He had no imagination—not even enough to write a magazine story. And he knew it.

At the moment he was engaged upon a "paper" dealing with the "soils of London." It was an "ordered" article for a technical journal, to run to about three thousand words, and he had just reached a point where definite practical information was necessary. On the stroke of seven o'clock he threw down his pen and went out, remembering that he was to dine at the club with several members of his craft. The sky was aflame with crimson, and exquisitely tinted clouds were reflected in puddles down the darkening street, but he never noticed flaming skies or clouds reflected in puddles. Purchasing a ticket for threepence—he lived some way out—he dived underground into one of the many pipes that burrow in a mysterious network below London, and was hurried away to his destination without delay.

In the train his mind dwelt exclusively upon clays, sands, loams, and gravel; he also reflected upon drainage, subsidence caused by moisture, and the porous qualities of sand. But being weary and overworked, his thoughts merely turned in a vicious circle. Stupid and heavy, Stodgman felt.

"I must see those builders tomorrow," he reflected, "and get the actual facts about the area and depth—especially the depth—of the London clay." He sighed and lit a cigarette. Then he noticed the compartment was not "smoking," and he dropped the cigarette and ground his heel on it. His thoughts about the London clay continued dully.

The train roared and rattled meanwhile, and the stations flew by so fast that Stodgman suddenly realised with a jerk that he would forget to get out unless he kept his thoughts from wandering. He took the ticket out of his pocket and read it.

"But where in the world did I get *this*?" he exclaimed with surprise, examining the bit of pasteboard carefully. It was crimson and the edges were fringed with neat little spots of shining gold like stars. "And what the dickens does it mean?"

His surprise increased suddenly very much indeed. But it was more than surprise. Something in it touched oddly upon the borders of alarm, and he became aware of a curious sensation of faintness, with an unpleasant sinking of the heart.

"That's queer," he thought, meaning partly the alarm and partly the card. On it, in wee white letters, he read the words, "*Pass one.*"

He instantly fumbled through his pockets for the right ticket, but could not find it. His gloves turned thick and all his fingers were thumbs. He had a dim recollection that the booking-clerk had smiled curiously at him when he bought it. He searched furiously and got hot in the process. That tube ticket was nowhere to be found, and his hands stuck in his pockets as though they were full of clay. The train, meanwhile, began to slow down.

"The devil!" he exclaimed. "What's the matter with me?"

A strange sense of panic got hold of his mind. He felt like a fat woman with a dozen parcels climbing about in a bus. He began to breathe in a quick, flustered sort of way, and the breathing came a trifle hard.

Impulses, of course, were foreign to Stodgman's nature; but on this occasion he had one—a very strong one. He realised that he wanted to get out at once. He was in the wrong train. More—there was something uncommonly queer about the train itself!

It stopped with a lurch and a swagger, and Stodgman went to the door with the hop-skip-and-jump peculiar to tube travellers. The sooner he was out of it the better. A dreadful oppression came over him.

At the platform with the sliding doors, however, the conductor stopped him with a menacing face. The man's face was positively dark.

"Can't get out now," he muttered. "You're too late. Everybody's out long ago—everybody but you and me. You've missed yer chance!"

Something in the voice, face and manner of the conductor made him feel extraordinarily bewildered and afraid. He turned to look, and saw to his amazement that the whole compartment was empty. Already the carriage swayed from side to side as the train moved on again and got into its stride. Something in the queer way it moved, too, touched his sense of terror—like a thing of life, it moved—a living creature—an animal in a hurry!

A cold thing stirred in his heart, rising by jumps to his throat, making it difficult to get his words out. It was exactly like a nightmare. He remembered afterwards he had wished that it *was* only a nightmare.

"Let me out, you idiot!" he tried to shout angrily; "I've paid for my ticket." But his voice sounded weak and faint, hardly audible above the roar of the tunnel.

"Tickets ain't nothin'," the conductor roared. "You orter have a pass, not a ticket, to get out of *this* train."

"I have got a pass, you — — — !" Stodgman shrieked, now genuinely terrified.

"Too late now, any'ow," the man shouted above the din. "Too late now. We're fairly caught—both of us."

The train was rushing onwards, whistling as it went. Stodgman suddenly got the horrible impression that it was running on legs instead of on wheels—a hundred short iron legs—legs that raced along the sleepers; that it was some gigantic antediluvian beast come to life again after sleeping for centuries in the soil. The whistling and shrieking were just the sounds such a monster would make; they were not the noises of a train at all. He could feel it panting, leaping, struggling in its speed. And he was *inside* it!

"But what does it all mean? Where are we going to?" he cried in real anguish. "Tell me at once, you———." And in his heart he was most dreadfully afraid— afraid of the answer the man would make. He felt he already knew what it would be.

There came a sudden, complete hush when the carriages seemed to stop swaying and run on velvet and rubber. The roar ceased, the shrieking and whistling died away. The conductor left his post between the swinging doors and crept forward into the car. He put his lips to Stodgman's ear, with his hand up to help the sound.

"Shall I tell yer what it is?" he whispered in a way that made his hearer's flesh crawl. "I'll tell yer, then," he added, as Stodgman stared speechless in his eyes, finding no words.

The conductor drew himself up and caught a swinging strap over his head. His face was like death.

"We're lost!" he hissed, "lost in the clay; the London clay's got us at last! We're done for, we are!"

Stodgman sprang to his feet, a sudden raging fury taking the place of his terror. His hands seized the wretched conductor by the throat. He had just the time to realise that the throat was iron when a voice behind him brought him to his senses with a violent start.

"—road Station! —road Station!" it called, and Stodgman leaped to his feet and had exactly three seconds to dash out through the door before the train moved on again. It was the gradual stopping of the carriages that had produced the silence of his dream. He staggered out upon the platform, still thinking of gravels, loams and clay, but chiefly amazed by the vividness of his four-minute nightmare.

"One's head invariably falls forward when one sleeps in a train," he reflected as he rose in a lift to the surface of the world. "I really must think up an article on that—'Curious Postures of the Head in Sleep,' or something of the kind, perhaps."

After dinner, in the smoking-room, Stodgman regaled his companions with an account of his dream. More or less bored, the majority barely listened to the end, so anxious was each to cap the dream with one of his own. Only one of them, the teller noticed, was silent; and *he* listened with rather a flushed face and attentive manner. Before they broke up for the night this fellow, whose name was O'Flynn, came up to Stodgman and asked a question or two on his own account.

"The Pass with crimson, with a fringe of stars?" he asked; "and the train had turned alive with legs and wings that might have whipped you clean up into the sky? That's a capital idea, you know, for the beginning of a yarn."

"Capital," said Stodgman, politely.

"Going to use it for anything?" asked O'Flynn.

"My dream? Oh dear, no. There's no copy in a dream nowadays. By the bye, talking of copy, do you know any reliable builders or contracts who can tell me…&c…&c…?"

It was a couple of months later, while engaged upon an article called "Great Bridges of the World," that Stodgman came across a gorgeously imaginative fantasy, charmingly illustrated, in *The Premier Magazine*, called "The Night Journey." It was all about the adventures of a man who found himself in a queer tram, and whose ticket turned out to be a pass to a most bewitching place outside London, where the writer took his reader and entertained him with much charm and power of imagination.

"Good yarn, by Jove, that!" Stodgman exclaimed after reading it through to the end. "How those fellows do invent, to be sure! I only wish I could do it myself, but such ideas never come to me."

Then he glanced at the signature of the author. "Michael O'Flynn," he read; "let me see, now. I met a fellow of that name somewhere not so very long ago. I wonder where it was."

Then he dismissed the subject and switched back his mind on to the "Great Bridges of the World."

Who Was She?

There were times in the life of Arthur Minns when he didn't know whether he was standing on his head or his feet. "Everything looks different suddenly," as he expressed it. He saw things upside down, or inside out, or backwards forwards. And the condition first betrayed itself one afternoon when he returned unexpectedly from work—he was traveller to a publishing house—and found his wife talking over the tea-cups with a caller. He burst into the room before he knew that any one was there, and did not know how to escape without appearing rude. He sat down and fingered a cup of tea. They were talking of many things, the sins of their neighbours in Maida Vale, chiefly, and after the pause and interruption caused by his unwelcome entrance, the caller, searching for a suitable subject, asked:

"You've heard about Captain Fox, I suppose?"

Mrs. Minns opened her eyes as though to read the other's thoughts. Evidently she had not heard.

"What's the latest about *him?*" she enquired cautiously.

"He's going to marry her," was the reply. "I know it for a fact. But don't say anything about it *yet*, because I heard it from Lady Spears, who...." She dragged a good deal of Burke into the complicated explanation, making it as impressive as she could. Captain Fox was a gay young spark, no better than he should be, who paid rather frequent visits upon the young widow of the ground-floor flat, who should have been better than she was. The widow made her living by literature—phrase used by the other occupants of the building but not by the neighbourhood—and "the Captain" was well connected, very. Hence the malicious interest in their doings. To find that honest courtship explained the friendship was something of a disappointment. Mrs. Marks, the caller, being chiefly responsible for the darker interpretation, wished to be the first to announce the innocent one, to claim authorship, indeed.

"Who'd ever have guessed *that?*" exclaimed Mrs. Minns, off her guard a moment. "You always told me—"

The face of her caller betrayed a passing flush.

"One always hoped," she began primly, when the other interrupted her with a firm, clear question. It was this question that first started the odd condition enjoyed subsequently by Minns, and referred to in the opening sentence. Mrs. Minns asked it, and Mrs. Minns was a good, clean, honest soul, while Arthur Minns was even simpler—a hard-working, gentle, saving and generous little man who knew the selling value of an author as well as he knew the title of every book his firm had published in the past twenty years. Just at this moment his wholesome little mind was wondering sweetly whether Captain and Mrs. Fox would be happy in their married life. *He* had been uncommonly happy himself; he longed for others to be the same. His natural thought ran spontaneously upon the chances of the new couple—on lines domestic, financial, love-in-a-cottage, children and the rest. Yet vaguely only: there was nothing he could have *said*.

"Who *was* she, I wonder. Do you know?" came the amazing question.

And, hearing it, Arthur felt his world turn upside down a moment. He realised, that is, that his excellent, dear little wife saw it upside down. Which came to the same thing. For his wife was a good, true woman, no modern complexity in her. Her present gossip was merely tact—adopting her caller's mood from sheer politeness. And for his wife to ask such a question was as if he had asked it himself. He felt ashamed. His world turned inside out. He rose abruptly, finding the energy to invent a true-escaping sentence:

"You ask who she *was*," he said, not with intentional rudeness, yet firmly, "when what you ought to ask should be—"

Both ladies stared at him with surprise, waiting for him to finish. He was picking up the cup his sudden gesture had overturned.

"Who and what she *is*," concluded Mr. Minns, with the astonishment of positive rebuke in his tone. "What *does*—what *can* it matter who she was? It's what she *is* that's of importance. The Captain's got to live with *that*. 'Who she was' is like thinking backwards and seeing things upside down." And then the escaping-sentence: "If you'll excuse me, Mrs. Marks, I have to go upstairs to see a book,"—he hesitated, stammered, and ended in confusion—"about a book." And off he went, making a formal little bow at the door. He went into the dining-room down the passage, vaguely aware that he had not behaved very nicely. "But, of course, I'm not a gentleman exactly," he said to himself; "what's called a gentleman, that is. Father was a chemist at Guildford."

He stood still a moment, then dropped into a chair beside the table with the red and black check cloth. His mind was working on all by itself, as it were.

"What I said was true, anyhow. People always ask, 'Who was she?' What the devil does that matter? It's what you *are* that counts. Father was a chemist, but I—I—"

He got up and walked over to the clock, because the clock stood on the mantelpiece, with a mirror behind it. He wanted to see his own face. He stared at himself a moment without speaking, thinking, or feeling anything. He put his tie straight and picked a bit of cotton from his shoulder.

"I am Arthur Minns, not a gentleman quite, not of much account anywhere perhaps, but a true workman, earning £250 a year, knowing all about the outside, but nothing about the inside of books; thirty-seven years old, with a boy at the Grammar School, and a girl of sixteen in the house, and married to—to—" He paused, turned from the mirror, and sat down. Who *was* she, now? It cost him an effort to remember—"To Mary Lumley, daughter of a corn-chandler in Norfolk, who might die any moment and leave us enough to live on," he went on, in a more comfortable position, passing his hand over his forehead; "and my life is insured, and I've put a bit by, and Alfred's to be a solicitor's clerk, and everything's going smoothly except that taxes—"

The sound of an opening door disturbed him. He felt all confused in his mind. He heard Mrs. Marks saying loudly, "And please say good-bye for me to your usband," it was suspiciously like a dropped h—as though intending he should hear and understand she bore him no ill-will for his bad manners, and, as the steps went downstairs, the two questions came back upon him like pistol-shots:

"Who *was* she? Who *am* I?"

He realised he had been wandering from the point.

"I'm a centre of life, independent and unafraid," thought flashed an answer. "I'm what I make myself, what I think myself. I'm *not* seeing things upside down; I'm beginning to think for myself, and that's what it is. No one, nor nothing, nor anything anywhere in the world," he went on, mixed in speech, but clear in mind, "can prevent me from being anything I feel myself, will myself, say I am. I've never read nor thought nor bothered my head about things before. By heavens! I'll begin! I *have* begun—"

"What's the matter, Artie? Have you got a headache, or is it the books bothering you, dear?" His wife had stolen in upon him.

She put her hand upon his forehead, and he got up from his chair and faced her.

"I've made a discovery," he said, with exhilaration in his manner, "a great discovery." He looked triumphantly at her. "I am."

"*What* are you?" she asked, thinking he was joking, and his sentence left unfinished on purpose.

"I *am*," he repeated with emphasis. "I have discovered that I am, that I exist. Your question to that woman made me suddenly see it."

His wife looked flustered, but said nothing. Arthur continued:

"As yet, I don't know exactly what I am, but I mean to find out. Up till now I've been automatic, just doing things because other people do em. But I've discovered that's not necessary. I'm going to do things in future because I want to. But first I must find out *why* I am what I am. Then the explanation'll come—of everything. Do you see what I mean? It's a case of 'Enquire within upon everything.'"

"Do you mean you're going to start in the writing or publishing line, Artie?" It had always been her secret ambition.

"That may come later," he told her, "when I've something to say. For it's big, you know, it's really big, this discovery of mine. Most people never find it out at all. She"—indicating with his thumb the direction Mrs. Marks had taken—"hasn't, for instance. She simply isn't aware that she exists. She isn't."

"Isn't what, dear?"

"She is *not*, I mean, because she doesn't know she is," he said loudly.

"Oh, that way. I see." Mrs. Minns looked a wee bit frightened.

"There are strange, big things about these days, I know," she said after a pause, thinking of the books with queer titles his employers published. "You have been reading too much, dear, thinking and—"

"Mary," he interrupted, in a tone that convinced her his head was momentarily turned, "that's the whole trouble. I've never thought in my life."

"But why should you, dear?" she soothed him, wondering if fits began this way, or if people who lost their memory and wandered off had symptoms like this first. "You always do your work splendidly. Don't think, is what I say. It always leads to trouble—"

"Hardly ever—till this moment," he was saying in the grave, emphatic way that so alarmed her. "Not even when I asked you to marry me, when Alfred was born, or Joan, or when we took this flat, or anything."

"You've made a great success of your life without it anyhow, Artie, dear. And no woman could ask more than that. D'you feel unwell? Joan can fetch Dr. Monson in a moment."

"I feel better and bigger and stronger," he replied, "than ever in my life before. I have never been really alive till this moment. I *am*—and for the first time I know it. I'm experiencing." He stopped short, as Joan went down the passage, pausing a moment to look in, then tactfully going on her way again. "Mary," he said, as their heads turned back from the door together, "do you know what 'experiencing' is? D'you realise what the word means?"

She sat down, resting her arms upon the table. She looked quietly into his eyes, as one who is about to speak out of greater knowledge.

"Artie dear, I *have* had experiences—experiences of my very own, you know."

"Yes, yes, I know, you good old soul. I know, I know. But what I mean is— do you get the meaning, the real meaning of the word?"

She sighed audibly. "Not *your* meaning, perhaps," she meant. But she did not say it. She was a precious woman, words few in her.

"It means," he said, delighted with her exquisite silence, "it means—er—" He thought hard a moment. "Experience," he went on, "is that 'something' which changes potatoes into nourishment, and so into emotion. That's it. Until you eat potatoes, you don't exist. Until you have experiences, you don't exist. When you have experiences and know that you have them, you—*persist*."

She gasped aloud. She took his hand—very quietly, hoping he would mistake it for a caress, while surreptitiously she felt his pulse.

"Artie, dear," she said, softly as in their courtship days—she loved him very dearly—"such ideas don't come into your head from nowhere. Has someone been talking to you? Have you been reading these books?"

For his pulse was very quiet.

"Have you been reading the firm's books, dear?"

She asked it gently, forgivingly, as a mother might ask her boy. "Have you been tasting father's whisky?" The books were meant to sell to booksellers, to the public, to people who needed that particular kind of excitement. Her husband was to be trusted. He was not supposed to know what they contained. His *line* of trade was chiefly medical, psychological, religious, philosophical. Fiction was another "line"—for the apprentice. Arthur was an "expert" traveller. He was expected to talk about his wares, but not as one who read them. Merely their selling value was his strong point.

By the expression of his face she knew the answer.

He leaned back in his chair, just as he did sometimes when he asked what there was for dinner—the same real interest in his eyes—and he answered very calmly:

"My dear, I have. *Cogito ergo sum*. For the first time I understood, in theory, that I existed. My reading taught me that. But I never knew it in practice until just now, when I heard you ask that question about the future Mrs. Fox: 'Who *was* she?' And then I knew also that you—"

"You what?" enquired Mrs. Minns, bridling.

"Were unaware that you existed," he replied point blank.

"Aren't you a little beside yourself, Arthur—sort of excited, or something?" she asked, proud of her tact and self-control. "What else could I have said? How could I have put it different?"

"Mary," he answered gently, "you should have said, 'What *is* she?' For that would have meant you thought for yourself. It would have meant that you knew you *were*, and that you knew she *was*."

"Original," said Mrs. Minns slowly, catching her husband's meaning.

"True," he answered, "just as when, years ago, you were looking at the prehistoric things in the Crystal Palace grounds, and the band was playing a waltz, and the sun was lovely, and you said, 'Yes.' Do you remember?"

Some how or other she had got upon his knee, and their faces were close together. She understood his meaning—in a way. She looked into his glorious eyes. He *was* the exceptional man she had always believed him to be. Something big, caught from his proximity, stirred strangely in her. She said, at random, something bigger than she knew:

"Then you mean, that until a person thinks for himself upon the common little everyday things of life, he's not really alive—independent, true, *real*, as it were? Is it that, Artie darling?"

He smiled indulgently. He kissed her paternally. He realised what a long way he had travelled.

"That's part of it," he replied, kissing her. "To ask who she *was*, is to accept the judgment of the common mass. To ask what she *is* means that you think for yourself—and want the truth. If a man asked me who *you* were—I'd—" Mr. Minns made a violent movement that half shook her from his knee.

"What dear?" she murmured adoringly.

"—knock him down," said Mr. Minns with grandeur.

Then Joan came in noisily, singing down the corridor as she came. But, before she could ask whether it was to be cold lamb or curry for supper, her father was on his feet.

"I'm going to take you both out to-night," he said. "We'll dine at a restaurant in the West End."

And they did.

II.

Now Joan was no ordinary girl; some called her backward, some considered her deficient, but the majority described her as a natural idiot. Tall, slim and dark, with plenty of hair and the eyes of a wild animal, she was out of the common in an unattractive sort of way. Tom, her brother, with the mind of a solicitor's clerk, looked down upon her; her mother, fond, conventional, socially ambitious, despaired of her; her father alone held the opinion, "There's something in that girl. She's always herself. But town-life over-weights and hides her; and in the end will suffocate. It'll snuff her out. She's meant for country." He was aware of something unusually real in her. They were great friends. "I want more air," she said once. "In a field or garden I'd grow enormous like a bean plant. In these streets I'm just a stone squashed down by crowds. I'm in a hole and can't breathe. I prefer a fewity." Even her words were her own like this. "I'd like room to dance in. Life is a dance. I'd learn it in a field. I'd be a bird girl."

It was her father's secret ambition too: a cottage, a garden with things that grew silently into beauty, flowers, vegetables, plants; sweet laughing winds; the rush of living rain at midnight; water to drink from a deep, cool spring instead of from metal pipes; a large, inviting horizon in which a man might lose himself; and above all—birds, birds, birds. Both he and Joan loved birds.

"After a month in real private country—loose country, talking, dancing, running country—" She paused.

"Liquid, fluid, as it were," he put in, delighted.

"Yes, deep and clear as a river, when it avoids cities," she went on, "in country like that, do you know what'd happen to me, father, after a few months of waiting?"

"I know, but I can't quite say," he answered. "Tell me, child, for I'd love to hear your own description."

"I'd fly," was her answer. "Everything in me would fly about like a bird, picking up things, and all over the place at once without a plan—a fixed, heavy plan like a street or square in London here—and yet getting on all the time—getting further."

"And how would you learn, dear?"

"Birds," she laughed. "There's bird-teaching, I'm sure." She flitted across to another chair as she said it. She came closer to her father, who was listening with

both ears, watching, drinking in something he didn't understand yet knew was
true—somewhere.

"You're rather like one, d'you know," he smiled. "Like a bird, I mean."

She was perched on his knee before he knew it. Her small voice twittered on
into his ear. Something about her sparkled, flashed and vanished, and it reminded him of sunshine on swift-fluttering wings through the speckled shade
of an orchard. She darted, whirred, and came to rest. He stroked her.

"Father, you know everything before I say it," she went on, her face shining
with happiness that made her almost beautiful. "If I could only live like a bird,
I could *live*. Here it's all a big, dirty cage." She flitted to the window, pointing
to roofs and walls and chimney-pots, black with grime. The same instant she
was back again upon his knees. "To live like a bird is to be alive, I'm sure, I'm
sure. I know it. It's all routing here."

Whether she meant rotten, routine, or living in a rut, he did not ask. He felt
her meaning. He stroked her.

"There's a nest in a garden waiting for us somewhere," he said, living the
dream with her in his heart. "And it's got an orchard, high deep grass, wild flowers, hills in the distance, with a tremendous sky where the winds go tearing
about like the rush of an enormous bird, and real country people who drop in
of an evening and say real things. All alive, I mean, and always moving. They
say the country's stagnation. It isn't. It's a perfect rush—"

"Like a bird, of course," she put in, chirruping with pleasure. "Oh, father,
think hard about that place, and we'll attract it nearer and nearer, till in the end
we drop into it and grow like—"

"Beans," he laughed.

"Birds," she rippled, and hopped from his knee across the room, and was
down the passage and out of sight before he could draw another breath.

There was something alert as lightning in the girl. She woke a similar thing
in him, too. It had nothing to do with brain as intellect, or with reason, or with
knowledge in the ordinary sense the world gives to these words. But it had to
do, he dimly felt, with another bigger thing. What that bigger thing might be
perplexed him. He was aware that it drove hugely past, alertness in such a massive thing conveying the impression of magnificent power. There was un-
speakable grandeur in it somewhere, glory, dignity, beauty; yet this subtle
alertness too, and this swift, protean sparkle. It was towering as a night of stars,
alluring as a peeping wildflower, but prodigious also as though all the oceans
flowed suddenly between narrow banks in a flood of clearest water, very rapid,
terrifyingly deep. For a robe it wore the lustrous colouring of untold age. His
imagery, when he tried to visualise it, grew mixed. He called it Experience. But
sometimes he told himself he knew its Christian name—its familiar, little, intimate nickname—and that was Wisdom.

And so he was rather glad that Joan, like himself, was but half educated; that
she was backward, and that he knew, relatively, only the outsides of books. For

facts, he vaguely felt, might come between them and this august yet precious thing they knew together. Birds could teach it, but Ornithology hid it.

Lately, however, as his wife divined, he *had* been dipping in between the covers of the goods he travelled in. Caught by the bait of several drugging titles, he had nibbled—in the train, in waiting-rooms, in the "parlours" of commercial hotels where he put up for the night. He had found names and descriptions of various things, but they were the names and descriptions given by others to their own sensations. The ordered classification merely developed snapshots. He recognised photographs of dead things that *he* had always known alive. The names made stationary what for him had danced with incessant movement. Only he did not realise this until he saw the photographs. The alleged accuracy of a photograph was a shouting insolent falsehood, pretending that what was alive was dead, that what rushed was stationary. Dogs and savages cannot recognise the photographs of their masters. The resemblance has to be taught. Everything flows, his shilling *Heraclitus* told him. He had always known it. Joan lived it. Birds taught it. To classify is to photograph—a prevarication. To publish a snapshot of a jumping horse was to teach what is not true. To boast about it is to glory shamelessly in ignorance. The sole value of names, of classification, of photographing lay in stopping life for an instant so that its flow might be realised—as a momentary stage in an incessant process. And he looked at a group of acquaintances his wife had "Kodaked" ten days ago, and realised with delight how they all had rushed away, torn on ahead, lived, since she had told that lie in black and white about them.

Joan, catching him in the act of destroying it, had said, "I know why you're doing that, father."

"Why?" he asked, half ashamed and half surprised.

"Because you don't want to stop them," was her answer, "and because it wasn't fair of mother to catch them in the act like that."

And, as he stared at her curious peeping face, she came quickly up to him, saying passionately, imploringly:

"Oh, *do* let's get into the country soon, and live along with it, and grow and know things. I feel so stuck still here, and always caught-in-the-act like that photo. It's so dead. The streets are all nailed down on to the ground. In the country they run about—"

He interrupted her on purpose:

"But in a city life is supposed to be much richer than in the country," he said. "You know that?"

"It goes round and round like a circle, though; it doesn't go *on*. I'm living other people's lives here. I want to live my own. Everybody here lives the same thing over and over again till they get so hot they get ill. I want to be cool and naked like a fern. Here I'm being photographed all day long. Oh, father, I'm so tired of it. Do let's go soon and live hoppily like the birds."

"You mean happily?" he asked, laughing with her.

"It's the same thing," she laughed back, "it's like wings or running water—
    Flow, fly, flow,
    Wherever I am, I *go*;
    Live on the run,
    Like a bird—it's fun,
    Flow, fly, flow!"

... and was dancing to and fro over the carpet, when the door opened and in came her brother Tom.

He looked surprised, ashamed, then vexed. It was Saturday afternoon. He had been six months now in the office.

"I've brought Mr. Halliday with me," he said, "to have tea. We've just been to a matinée at the Coliseum. Joan, this is Mr. Halliday, our junior clerk. My sister, Harold."

Joan instantly looked gauche and ugly. She shook hands with a speckled youth, whose shy want of manners did not prevent his eyeing her all over. He sat down beside his friend, talking of the singing, dancing, juggling and so on that they had witnessed. All the time he talked *at* something else in her. But she hid it away as cleverly as a bird hides its nest. The callow youth, without realising it, was hunting for a nest. In the country he might have found it. He would have been sun-burned, for one thing, instead of speckled. The wind, the rain, the starlight would have guided him. His natural instinct would have flowed out in a dance of spontaneous running movement. Here, however, it seemed rigid, ugly, diseased. He was living the life of others.

"You were dancing just as we came in," observed Mr. Halliday. "Does that line of things attract you? You are going on the stage, perhaps?"

Joan looked past him out of the window, and saw the swallows flashing about the sky.

"I *can* dance," she replied, "quite wonderfully, but not on a stage."

"But you'd be a great success, I think, from what I saw," opined the callow junior clerk. And somehow he said it falsely, unpleasantly.

She didn't flush, she didn't stammer, at first she didn't answer even. She watched the swallows a moment, as though she had not heard him.

"You stare, you don't watch and enjoy," she said suddenly, turning upon him. "And an audience like that...!" She stopped, got up from her chair, put her head out of the open window and spat into the street. When she turned back, she saw that her mother had come into the room and was leading the others into the dining-room for tea. Her father's face wore a singular expression—it seemed, of exultation. Tom, black as a thunder-cloud, waited for her.

"You're nothing but a little barbarian," he said angrily. The life of others he led had been sorely wounded. "I can never bring Mr. Halliday here again. You're simply not a lady."

"I'm a bird," she laughed in his face. "And you men can never understand that, because no man has a bird in him, but only a creepy, crawly animal. We go on two legs, you on four."

"I'm ashamed of you, Joan. You're nothing but a savage." He snapped at her. He could have struck her. His face was flushed, but his neck thin, scraggy, white. "In the City we—" he began with a clown's dignity.

"Live like rats in a drain," she interrupted quickly, perched a moment on her toes in front of his face. "You don't breathe or dance. Tom," she added with a gesture of her arms like flapping wings, "if you were alive, you'd be—a mole. But you're not. You're a lot of other people. You're a herd—always enclosed and always feeding."

She danced down the corridor and into her room, locked the door, slipped out of some tight clothing, and began to sing her bird-song of incessant movement:

Flow! Fly! Flow!
Wherever I *am* I *go*;
I live on the run
Like the birds—it's fun!
Flow, fly, flow....

She sang it to a tiny, uneven, twittering melody that was made up of half notes. It went on and on, repeating itself without end. It seemed to have no real end at all.

III.

"Oh, she's all in the air," people said. And it was truer than they knew. She had an affinity with all that flew. This bird-idea was in her heart and blood. Whatever flew, whatever rose above the ground, whatever passed swiftly, suddenly, from place to place, without deliberation, without calculation, without weighing risk and profit—this appealed to her. Yet there must be steadiness in it somewhere too, and it must get somewhere. A swallow or a butterfly she approved, but not a bat. The latter, for all its darting swiftness, was a sham; it was an earth-crawler really, frightened into ridiculous movement by finding itself aloft like a blown leaf; like a flying fish, it was wrong and out of place. But the former were perfect. They were ideal. They were almost spirits.

And when her father said he was glad she was half educated, he only meant glad that she had left school and teachers before her butterfly mind had become a rigid, accurate, mechanical thing. She might play with books as he himself did, fluttering over the covers, smelling their perfume, glancing at sentences and chapter headings, at indices even, but she must not build nests in them. A book, like a photograph, was an evillish thing that nailed a flowing thing into a fixed pattern. In the author's mind an idea was true, but when he had put it down in black and white he had put down only a snapshot of it: the idea was already far away; when printed it was merely the pattern of its coffin that the reader saw.

"Not poetry-books," Joan qualified this, "because poetry runs clean off the page. It's alive and wingy. It sings my bird-song—

Flow, fly, flow,
Wherever I *am*—I *go!*"

She had this unerring instinct for the bird in everything, the quality that
flashes, darts, is gone before it can be killed by capture. A bird is everywhere
and nowhere. It's all over the place at once. Look at it, and it's no longer there;
listen to it, and it's gone. Touch it, and you catch a sunbeam that warms the hand
but loses half its beauty. Catch it—and it's dead. But no one ever caught a swallow or a skylark naturally on the wing. Even the eye, the mind, the following
thought grows dizzy in the effort.

For the cow in the field she had no song. "Wherever I am, I stay," was without a tune of its own. A cow couldn't leave the ground. She wanted something
with incessant movement that could touch the earth, yet leave it at will. Wings
and water could. Birds and rain both flew. Half the time a river (the only real
water for her) flowed over the earth without stopping on it, and half the time
it was a cloud in the sky, yet never lived there. "Flow, fly, flow; wherever I *am*,
I *go*,"—this was the little song of life and change and movement that came out
of her curious heart and mind. "Live on the run, like a bird, *that's* fun!"

She applied her principle unconsciously to people, too. Few men had the bird
in them except her father. Mother was a badger, half the time out of sight below the earth. She felt respect, but no genuine love, for mother.

"A whale or a badger, I really don't know which," she said. "That's Mother."

"Joan, I cannot allow you to speak in that way of your parent and my wife."
The sentence was unreal. He chose it deliberately, as it seemed, from some book
or other. It was sparklingly true, what she said, only it could not be said. "You
were born out of mother, and so must think her holy."

"I only meant that she is not birdy," was the answer, "and that she likes fat,
salt water, or sticky earth. I mean that I never see her on the surface much, and
never for an instant *above* it. A fish is all right, but not a half-and-half thing."

"She built your nest for you. She taught you how to fly. Remember that." He
lit his pipe to hide the laughter that would bubble up.

"But she never flew with me, father—as you do," Joan replied triumphantly.
"Besides, you know, I *like* whales and badgers. I only say they're not birds."

She paused, stared hard at him a moment, and then, with anxiety in her tone,
she added: "And you said that as if someone had taught it you, Father. Some
one's put bird-lime near you—some book, I suspect."

"Grammar's all right enough in its way," he told her hurriedly (meaning that
there were correct and incorrect ways of saying a thing), and so the little matter was nicely settled up, and they flew on to other things as their way invariably was. But, after that, whenever mother was in the room, they thought of
something under ground or under water that emerged for a brief moment to
stare at them and wonder (heavens!)—how they lived. *They* wondered how (on
earth!) she lived. They were in different worlds.

For a long time now Arthur Minns, "travelling" in tabloid knowledge, had been absorbing what is called the Spirit of the Age. On the paper wrappers of his books—chiefly Knowledge Primers—were printed neat and striking epitomes of the contents. Written by expert minds, these epitomes were admirable brief statements. There was no room for argument. They merely gave the entire book in a few short sentences that hit the mind—and stayed in it. They left the impression that the problem was proved, though actually it was merely stated. Hundreds of those statements he had read, until they flowed like a single sentence through his consciousness, each *résumé* a word, as it were, in the phrase describing the knowledge—or at least the tendencies—of the day. Minns was thus a concise phrase-book, who taught the grammar of the twentieth century. For his Firm, alert and enterprising, had the gift of scenting a given tendency before it was understood by the mass—while still "in the air," that is—yet while the mass still wanted to know about it; then of choosing the writer who could crystallise it in simple language that made the man in the street feel at home and up to date. The What's-in-the-Air-To-day Publishing Co. was well named; it had the bird quality. These Picturesque Knowledge Primers sold like wildfire. They purveyed knowledge in tabloid form and advertised the hungry public into nourishment. The latest thing in politics or in diseases, in painting or in flying, in feminism or call-of-the-wild, in music, scouting, cubism, futurism, feeding, dancing, clothing, ancient philosophy redressed, or modern pulpit pretending to be neo—everything that thrills the public to-day, from pageantry and Dalcroze to higher thought and psychics, they touched with clever condensing accuracy of aim, and grew fat upon the proceeds. The stream of little books flowed forth, written by birds, distributed in flocks, scattered broadcast like seed in a wind, each picked up eagerly and discarded for the next—winged knowledge in sparrow doses. The Managing Director, Fox Martin (*né* Max Levi), was a genius in his way, sure as a hawk, clairvoyant as a raven. His *Bergson* sold as successfully as his *Exercises for the Bedroom*—because he chose the writer. He hovered, swooped, struck—and the primer was caught and issued in its thousands. His advertising was consummate, for it convinced the ordinary man he ought to know that particular thing-in-the-air-today, just as he ought to wear a high collar with his evening clothes or a slit in his coat behind with flannels. He aimed at the men as the machine-made novel aims at the women.

Minns, *the* traveller *facile princeps*, for this kind of goods, knew, therefore, everything that was "in-the-air-to-day," without knowing in the least why it was to be believed, or what the arguments were. And yet he knew that he was right. He knew things as a bird does, gathering them on every wind, and shaping his inner life swiftly, unburdened by reasoning calculation built on facts. Thus, useless in debate, his mind was packed with knowledge. He was a walking Index.

And the feeling in him that everything flowed and nothing was stationary was strong. He dealt in shooting ideas, not in dead, photographic detail. He flashed from one subject to another; flowed through all categories, ancient and modern; skimmed the cream off modern tendencies, and swept above the knowledge of the day with a bird's-eye view, unburdened by fact or argument.

Of late, moreover, he had enjoyed these curious upside-down and inside-out experiences, because he had filled himself to the saturation point, and become, as it were, stationary. He could hold no more without—a change. He stopped. He took a snapshot photograph of himself, realised that he existed as a separate, vital entity, and thenceforward watched himself expectantly to see what the change was going to be, for he knew he would not stay still. Hitherto he had been mechanical, whereas now he was an engine capable of self-direction—an engine stoked to the brim. When the air is at the saturation point, the tiniest additional percentage of moisture causes rain to fall. It's the final straw that makes the camel sit down and consider the next step. So with Arthur Minns. He was ready to discharge.

And it was this chance remark of his under-ground wife asking who the widow *was* that took the photograph, and made him say, "I am." All he had read was included in the affirmation. The epitomes had become part of his consciousness. Like the weary camel, like the moisture tired of balancing in the air, he wanted to sit down now and consider. His daughter's longing for the country was his too. And it was she who now brought out all this.

At dinner that night in a West End restaurant near Piccadilly Circus he broached the subject and listened patiently to his wife's objections.

"What's the good, even if we had the means, Artie? Burying ourselves like that."

Joan hopped, as it were. She recognised her mother's instinctive dread that she would go under ground or under water and never come up again.

"None of the nice people, the county families, would call. There'd only be the vicar and the local doctor, or p'r'aps a gentleman-farmer or two. We know much better class in town, and there's always chances of getting to know better still. Besides, who'd there be for Joan? The girl wouldn't have a look-in, simply. And the winters are so sloppy in a country cottage. Think of the Sundays. And the chickens and pigs I really couldn't ever abide, and howling winds at night, and owls in the eaves, and rats in the attics. You see, we'd have no standing at all."

"But just a week-end cottage, Mother," Joan put in, "just a place of flowers and orchards and a little stream to flit down to overnight, so to say—*that* now you'd like, wouldn't you?"

"Oh, that's different," she said more brightly, "only that's not what father means. He means a place to live in altogether. The week-end idea is right enough. That's what everybody does who can afford to. Lady Spears has a bungalow on the Thames. But that means more money than we shall ever see, and even for that you want to keep a motor or a horse and dog-cart, or a little steam launch to get about in. Then the handy places are very expensive, and we couldn't go very far because of Tom. Tom could come down and bring his friends if it was near enough."

"Grandfather might give us a little nest cheap," suggested Joan. She didn't "see" Tom in the cottage.

But mother turned up her nose as she sipped her glass of Asti Spumante that accompanied the west-end dinner by way of champagne. She didn't approve of Essex.

"Nobody lives there," she said. "There's no society. Your grandfather only stays there because his father did before him and there's the business to keep going. If we ever did such a thing as to move to the country, it'd have to be the Surrey pinewoods or the Thames."

She looked across the table questioningly at her husband. The music played ragtime. The waiters bustled. There was movement and excitement in the air about them. Arthur looked quite distinguished in his evening dress, and she felt proud and distinguished herself. She only wished he were a publisher. Still, no one need feel ashamed of being interested in the book line. Literature was not a trade.

"Some place, yes, where the country's really alive," he agreed. "I don't want to vegetate any more than you do, dear, I can assure you."

"Nor I, mother," laughed Joan. "I simply want to fly about all the time."

"Johanna," was the reply, half reproachfully, "you always talk as if we kept you in a cage at home. The more you fly the better we like it; I only say choose places worth flying to—"

Her husband interrupted abruptly.

"It was nothing but a little dream of my own, really," he said lightly. "A castle in the air, an airy adventure, a flash of country in the brain." He laughed and called the waiter.

"Black, white, or Turkish?" he asked his wife. "And what liqueur, dear?"

"Turkish and Grand Marnier," was the prompt reply, and she would have said *"fine champagne"* only felt uncertain how *fine* should be pronounced. They sipped their coffee and talked of other things. It was no good, this speculative talk, it was too much in the air. The key of mother's mind was always: Who *was* she? She lived underground, using the worn old narrow routes. Joan and her father made their own pathways in the trackless medium of the air. During the remainder of the evening they kept to the earth beside mother.

That night in the pokey flat, after the girl had gone to bed, Mrs. Minns observed to her husband:

"Do you know, Artie, I think a little change *would* do her a lot of good. She's getting restless here, and seems to take to nobody. Why not take her with you sometimes on your literary trips?"

This was her name for his journeys to provincial booksellers when soliciting orders for his employer's wares, or when occasionally he was sent to interview one of the Primer writers upon some detail of length, material, or date of completion.

"If we could afford it," he replied.

"Father might help," she said, showing that she had considered the matter already. "It would be good for her—educational, I mean."

Her husband agreed, and they fell asleep on that agreement.

A few days later a reply was received from Mrs. Minns's father, the corn-chandler in Essex, enclosing a cheque for £20 "as a starter." The parents were delighted. Joan preened her wings and began at once her short flying journeys about the country with her father. He avoided the Commercial Traveller Hotels and took her to little Inns, where they were very cosy together. They went from Northumberland to Cornwall, and from Norfolk to the edge of Wales. She acquired a bird's-eye knowledge of the map of England. These short trips gave her somehow the general "feel" of the various counties, each with its different "note," in much the same way as the Primers gave her father his surface impression of England's mental condition. She noticed and remembered the living arteries which are rivers, he the streams of thought and theory which are tendencies. The two maps were shown and explained, and each was wonderfully alert in understanding the other's meaning. The girl drank in her father's knowledge, while he in his turn "felt" the country as a dancing sheet beneath them, flowing, liquid, alive. A new language grew into existence between them, a kind of shorthand, almost a symbol language. They realised it first when talking of their journeys at the dinner-table, and Mrs. Minns looked puzzled. Her face betrayed an odd anxiety; she asked perplexed questions, looking up at them as a badger might look up at wheeling pigeons from the opening of its hole. Mentally she turned tail and dived out of sight below ground, where, with her feet on solid earth, her back and sides touching material that did not yield, she felt more at home, the darkness comforting and safe.

Joan and her husband flew too near the sun. It dazzled her. They could have talked for hours without her catching the drift, only they were far too fond of her to do so. They resented going underground with her, but they came down and settled on earth, folded their wings, used words instead of unintelligible chirrupings, and chatted with her through the opening of the hole.

One afternoon, then, in Chester, they received a telegram from her that, for a moment, stopped the flow of things, though immediately afterwards the rush went on with greater impetus than ever.

"Father passed away return at once funeral to-morrow Epping."

And the family found itself with a solid little income of its own, free to fly and settle where it would. The London nest became impossible.

The Night-Wind

There were certain things that Uncle Henry, as a writer of "historical novels," had to explain, or else admit himself a disgraceful failure. For he sometimes read fancy bits aloud to the children, using the latter as a standard. These fancy bits were generally scenes of action: Escape; a Duke landing by night and dressed as a woman to avoid discovery; a dark man stealing "'storical" documents from a tapestried chamber in a frightful castle where bats and cobwebs shared the draughty corridors. These and the like he read aloud, judging their success by the reception accorded to them. "Thank you very much, Uncle," meant failure; the imagination was left untouched. But questions were an indication of success; the scene was alive and real; the audience wanted more details. For he knew that it was the "child" in his readers that enjoyed such scenes, and if Jinny and Jimbo felt no interest, neither would Mr. and Mrs. William Smith of Peckham. To squeeze a question out of Maria, the youngest, however, raised hopes of at least a Second Edition!

The night scenes, of course, were always windy: sometimes they were stormy. Either the wind rose at an unexpected and unwelcome moment, or else it dropped just when the cover of its roar was needed by the villain; at other times it merely misbehaved itself generally, as night-winds do. But as a rule it wailed, moaned, whistled, cried, sang, sighed, sobbed or—soughed. Keyholes and chimneys were its favourite places, and sometimes the rafters knew it too. Thus to the children, it became a known, expected thing with tastes and habits of its own. They looked for "Mr. Night-Wind," and recognised it when it came. "A night-wind story, please," was a classical form of attack between tea and bedtime. It had a personality, and led a mysterious existence. It had qualities, privileges, prerogatives. It acquired a definite *locus standi* in the mythology of the country house. Owing to its various means of vocal expression—singing, moaning, and the rest—a face belonged to it with lips and mouth; teeth too, since it whistled. It ran about the world, and so had feet; it flew, so wings pertained to it; it blew, and that meant cheeks of sorts. It was a large, swift, shadowy being whose ways were not the ordinary ways of daylight. It struck blows. It had gigantic hands. Moreover, it came out only after dark—an ominous and suspicious characteristic rather.

"Why isn't there a day-wind too?" inquired Jinny thoughtfully.

"There is, but it's *quite* a different thing," Uncle Henry explained calmly. "You might as well ask why midday and midnight aren't the same because they both come at twelve o'clock. They're simply different things, you see."

"Of course," Jimbo helped him unexpectedly; "and a man can't be a woman, can it?"

Mr. Night-Wind's nature, accordingly, remained a mystery rather, and its sex, in spite of the deceptive "Mr.," was also undetermined. Whether it saw with eyes, or just felt its way about like a blind thing, wandering, was another secret matter undetermined. Each child visualised it differently. Its hiding-place in the daytime was equally unknown. Owls, bats, and burglars guessed its habits best, and that it came out of a hole in the sky was, perhaps, the only detail all unanimously agreed upon. It was a pathetic being rather.

This Night-Wind used to come crying round the bedroom windows sometimes, and the children liked it, although they did not understand all its melancholy beauty. They heard the different voices in it, although they did not catch the meaning of the words it sang. They heard its footsteps too. Its way of moving awed them. Moreover, it was forever trying to get in.

"It's wings," said Jinny, "big, dark wings, very soft and feathery."

"It's a woman with sad, black eyes," thought Jimbo, "that's how I like it."

"It's someone," declared Maria, who was asleep before it came, so rarely heard it at all. And they turned to Uncle Henry who knew all that sort of thing, or at any rate could describe it. He found the words. They lay hidden in his thick back hair apparently—there was none on the top!—for he always scratched his head a good deal when they asked him questions about such difficult matters. "What is it *really*—the Mr. Night-Wind?" they asked gravely; "and why does it sound so *very* different from the wind in the morning or the afternoon?"

"There *is* a difference," he replied carefully, realising it for the first time now that they asked. "It's a quick, dark, rushing thing, and it moves like—like anything."

"We know *that*," they told him contemptuously, yet with considerable patience.

"And it has long hair," he added hurriedly, looking into Jimbo's staring eyes. "That's what makes it swish. The swishing, rushing, hushing sound it makes—that's its hair against the walls and tiles, you see."

"It *is* a woman, then?" said Jimbo proudly.

All looked up, wondering. An extraordinary thing was in the air. A mystery that had puzzled them for ages was about to be explained. They drew closer round the sofa, and Maria blundered against the table, knocking some books off with a resounding noise.

"Hush, hush!" said Uncle Henry, holding up a finger and glancing over his shoulder into the darkened room. "It may be coming now.... Listen!"

"Yes, but it is a woman, isn't it?" insisted Jimbo, in a hurried whisper. He had to justify himself before his sisters. Uncle Henry must see to that first.

The big man opened his eyes very wide. He shuddered. "It's a—Thing," was the answer, given in a whisper that increased the excitement of anticipation. "It certainly is a—Thing! Now hush! It's coming!"

They listened then intently. And a sound *was* heard. Out of the starry summer night it came, quite softly, and from very far away—upon discovery bent, upon adventure. Reconnoitering, as from some deep ambush in the shrubberies where the blackbirds hid and whistled, it flew down against the house, stared in at the nursery windows, fluttered up and down the glass with a marvellous, sweet humming—and was gone again.

"Listen!" the man's voice whispered; "it will come back presently. It saw us. It's awfully shy—"

"Why is it awfully shy?" asked Jinny in an undertone.

"Because people make it mean so much more than it means to mean," he replied darkly. "It never gets a chance to be just itself and play its own lonely game—"

"We've called it things, too," objected Maria.

"But we haven't written books about it and put it into poetry," Uncle Henry corrected her with an audacity that silenced them. "We play our game; it plays its."

"It plays its," repeated Jimbo, amused by the sound of the words.

"And that's why it's shy," the man held them to the main point, "and dislikes showing itself—"

"But why is its game lonely?" someone asked, and there was a general feeling that Uncle Henry had been caught this time without an answer. For what explanation could there possibly be of that? Their faces were half triumphant, half disappointed already.

He smiled quietly. He knew everything—everything in the world. "It's unhappy as well as shy," he sighed, "because nothing will play with it. Everything is asleep at night. It comes out just when other things are going in. Trees answer it, but they answer in their sleep. Birds, tucked away in nests and hiding-places, don't even answer at all. The butterflies are gone, the insects lost. Leaves and twigs don't care about being blown when there's no one there to see them. They hide too. If there are clouds, they're dark and sulky, keeping their jolly sides towards the stars and moon. Nothing will play with Mr. Night-Wind. So it either plays with the tiles on the roof and the telegraph wires—dead things that make a lot of noise, but never leave their places for a proper game—or else just—plays with itself. Since the beginning of the world the Night-Wind has been shy and lonely and unhappy."

It was unanswerable. They understood. Their sense of pity was greatly touched, their love as well.

"Do pigs really see the wind, as Daddy says?" inquired Maria abruptly, feeling the conversation beyond her. She merely obeyed the laws of her practical, matter-of-fact nature. But no one answered her; no one even heard the question. Another sound absorbed their interest and attention. There was a low, faint tapping on the window-pane. A hush, like church, fell over everybody.

And Uncle Henry stood up to his full height suddenly, and opened his arms wide. He drew a long, deep breath.

"Come in," he said splendidly.

The tapping, however, grew fainter and fainter, till it finally ceased. Everybody waited expectantly, but it was not repeated. Nothing happened. Nobody came in. The tapper had retreated.

"It was a twig," whispered Jinny, after a pause. "The Virgin Creeper—"

"But it was the wind that shook it," exclaimed Uncle Henry, still standing and waiting as though he expected something. "The Night-Wind—"

A roaring sound over the roof drowned his words; it rose and fell like laughter, then like crying. It dropped closer, rushed headlong past the window, rattled and shook the sash, then dived away into the darkness. Its violence startled them. A deep lull followed instantly, and the little tapping of the twig was heard again. Odd! Just when the Night-Wind seemed furthest off it was all the time quite near. It had not really gone at all; it was hiding against the outside walls. It was watching them, trying to get in. The tapping continued for half a minute or more—a series of hurried, gentle little knocks as from a child's smallest finger-tip.

"It wants to come in. It's trying," whispered someone.

"It's awfully shy."

"It's lonely and frightfully unhappy."

"It likes us and wants to play."

There was another pause and silence. No one knew quite what to do.

"There's too much light. Let's put the lamp out," said a genius, using the voice of Jinny.

As though by way of answer there followed instantly a sudden burst of wind. The torrent of it drove against the house; it boomed down the chimney, puffing an odour of soot into the room; it shook the door into the passage; it lifted an edge of carpet, flapping it. It shouted, whistled, sang, using a dozen different voices all at once. The roar fell into syllables. It was amazing. A great throat uttered words. They could scarcely believe their ears. The wind was shouting with a joyful, boisterous shout: "Open the window! *I'll* put out the light!"

All heard the wonderful thing. Yet it seemed quite natural in a way. Uncle Henry, still standing and waiting as though he knew not exactly what was going to happen, moved forward at once and boldly opened the window's lower sash. In swept the mighty visitor, the stranger from the air. The lamp gave one quick flicker and went out. Deep stillness followed. There was a silence like the moon. The shy Night-Wind had come into the room.

Ah, there was awe and wonder then! The silence was so unexpected. The whole wind, not merely part of it, was in. It had come so gently, softly, delicately too! In the darkness the outline of the window-frame was visible; Uncle Henry's big figure blocked against the stars. Jinny's head could be seen in silhouette against the other window, but Jimbo and Maria, being smaller, were merged in the pool of shadow below the level of the sill. A large, spread thing passed flutteringly up and down the room a moment, then came the rest. It settled over everything at once. A rustle was audible as of trailing, floating hair.

"It's hiding in the corners and behind the furniture," whispered Uncle Henry; "keep quiet. If you frighten it—whew!"—he whistled softly—"it'll be off above the tree-tops in a second!"

A low soft whistle answered to his own; somewhere in the room it sounded; there was no mistaking it, though the exact direction was difficult to tell, for while Jimbo said it was through the keyhole, Jinny declared positively that it came from the door of the big, broken cupboard opposite. Maria stated flatly, "Chimney."

"Hush! It's talking." It was Uncle Henry's voice breathing very low. "It likes us. It feels we're friendly."

A murmur as of leaves was audible, or as of a pine bough sighing in a breeze. Yet there were words as well—actual spoken words:

"Don't look for me, please," they heard. "I do not want to be seen. But you may touch me. I like that." The children spread their hands out in the darkness, groping, searching, feeling. "Ah, your touch!" the sighing voice continued. "It's like my softest lawn. Your hair feels as my grass feels on the hill-tops, and the skin of your cheeks is smooth and cool as the water-surface of my lily ponds at midnight. I know you"—it raised its tones to singing. "You are children. I kiss you all!"

"I feel you," Jinny said in her clear, quiet voice. "But you're cold."

"Not really," was the answer that seemed all over the room at once. "That's only the touch of space. I've come from very high up to-night. There's been a change. The lower wind was called away suddenly to the sea, and I dropped down with hardly a moment's warning to take its place. The sun has been very tiresome all day—overheating the currents."

"Uncle, *you* ask it everything," whispered Jimbo, "simply everything!"

"Say how we love it, please," sighed Jinny. "I feel it closing both my eyes."

"It's over all my face," put in Maria, drawing her breath in loudly.

"But my hair's lifting!" Jinny exclaimed. "Oh, it's lovely, lovely!"

Uncle Henry straightened himself up in the darkness. They could hear him breathing with the effort. "Please tell us what you do," he said. "We all can feel you touching us. Play with us as you play with trees and clouds and sleeping flowers along the hedgerows."

A singing, whistling sound passed softly round the room; there was a whirr and flutter as when a flight of bees or birds goes down the sky, and a voice, a plaintive yet happy voice, like the plover who cry to each other on the moors, was audible:

"I run about the world at night,
Yet cannot see;
My hair has grown so thick these millions years,
It covers me.
So, like a big, blind thing

I run about,
And know all things by touching them.
I touch them with my wings;
I know each one of you
By touching you;
I touch your *hearts!*"

"I feel you!" cried Jinny. "I feel you touching me!"

"And I, and I!" the others cried. "It's simply wonderful!"

An enormous sigh of happiness went through that darkened room.

"Then play with me!" they heard. "Oh, children, play with me!"

The wild, high sweetness in the windy voice was irresistible. The children rose with one accord. It was too dark to see, but they flew about the room without a fault or slip. There was no stumbling; they seemed guided, lifted, swept. The sound of happy, laughing voices filled the air. They caught the Wind, and let it go again; they chased it round the table and the sofa; they held it in their arms until it panted with delight, half smothered into silence, then marvellously escaping from them on the elastic, flying feet that tread on forests, clouds, and mountain tops. It rushed and darted, drove them, struck them lightly, pushed them suddenly from behind, then met their faces with a puff and shout of glee. It caught their feet; it blew their eyelids down. Just when they cried, "It's caught! I've got it in my hands!" it shot laughing up against the ceiling, boomed down the chimney, or whistled shrilly as it escaped beneath the crack of the door into the passage. The keyhole was its easiest escape. It grew boisterous, singing with delight, yet was never for a moment rough. It cushioned all its blows with feathers.

"Where are you now? I felt your hair all over me. You've gone again!" It was Jinny's voice as she tore across the floor.

"You're whacking me on the head!" cried Jimbo. "Quick, quick! I've got you in my hands!" He flew headlong over the sofa where Maria sat clutching the bolster to prevent being blown on to the carpet.

They felt its soft, gigantic hands all over them; its silky coils of hair entangled every movement; they heard its wings, its rushing, sighing voice, its velvet feet. The room was in a whirr and uproar.

"Uncle! Can't *you* help? You're the biggest!"

"But it's blown me inside out," he answered, in a curiously muffled voice. "My fingers are blown off. It's taken all my breath away."

The pictures rattled on the wall; loose bits of paper fluttered everywhere; the curtains flapped out horizontally into the air.

"Catch it! Hold it! Stop it!" cried the breathless voices.

"Join hands," he gasped. "We'll try." And, holding hands, they raced across the floor. They managed to encircle something with their spread arms and legs. Into the corner by the door they forced a great, loose, flowing thing against the wall. Wedged tight together like a fence, they stooped. They pounced upon it.

"We've caught it!" shouted Jimbo. "We've got you!"

There was a laughing whistle in the keyhole just behind them. It was gone. The window shook. They heard the wild, high laughter. It was out of the room. The next minute it passed shouting above the cedar tops and up into the open sky. And their own laughter went out to follow it across the night.

The room became suddenly very still again. Someone had closed the window. The twig no longer tapped. The game was over. Uncle Henry collected them, an exhausted crew, upon the sofa by his side.

"It was very wonderful," he whispered. "We've done what no one has ever done before. We've played with the Night-Wind, and the Night-Wind's played with us. It feels happier now. It will always be our friend."

"It was awfully strong," said Jimbo, in a tone of awe. "It fairly banged me."

"And awfully gentle though," Jinny sighed. "It kissed me hundreds of times."

"I felt it stroking me all down the back," announced Maria.

"It's only a child, really," Uncle Henry added, half to himself, "a great wild child that plays with itself in space—"

He went on murmuring for several minutes, but the children hardly heard the words he used. They had their own sensations. For the wind had touched their hearts and made them think. They heard it singing now above the cedars as they had never heard it sing before. It was alive and lovely, it meant a new thing to them. For they had their little aching sorrows too; it had taken them all away: they had their little passionate yearnings and desires; it had prophesied fulfilment. The dreamy melancholy of childhood, the long, long days, the haunted nights, the everlasting afternoons—all these were in its wild, great, windy voice, the sighing, the mystery, the laughter too. The joy of strange fulfilment woke in their wind-kissed hearts. The Night-Wind was their friend; they had played with it. Now everything could come true.

And next day Maria, lost to the Authorities for over an hour, was at length discovered by the forbidden pigsties in a fearful state of mess, but very pleased and happy about something. She was watching the pigs with eyes brimful of questioning wonder and excitement. She was listening intently too. She wanted to find out for certain whether pigs really—really and truly—saw—anything unusual!

Genius

To know greatness at close quarters, to be intimate with its processes and habits, is not given to many. A hedge surrounds the genius; the majority know of him by his works and by report. To speak with Hildritch, genius of the first order, to hear him addressed familiarly as Billy, to be beside him in his play and breathe his atmosphere when the fire of inspiration was upon him were privileges accorded to few indeed. Yet they were vouchsafed to Tomkyns by some generous twist of fate, to Tomkyns whose one gift in life was an unshakeable faith in his fellow-kind, who saw the best in everybody and, even when faced with undeniable evil, turned his eyes away to find the good.

Owing to circumstances over which he had no control, Tomkyns found himself swept into the familiar circle of the great man's life. He looked over the hedge. "Come and spend a week with us; my wife and I shall be delighted to have you," said Hildritch. And Tomkyns, feeling himself privileged beyond his deserts, thus found himself inside the hedge. He talked with Billy Hildritch face to face, observed the processes and habits of his genius, observed the fire of inspiration light up and die alternately, and breathed his hero's atmosphere.

"I've known only one great man in my life," he would say, then turn his eyes away. The privilege he had tasted still affected him profoundly. He was a modest, pleasant little man, round of face and body, owner of a comfortable car and a comfortable income, of which latter he gave away more than half to needy beggars whom most called parasites. He played tennis, he played with the children, he sang songs in his throaty tenor to the accompaniment of Mrs. Hildritch, he enjoyed his country visit absurdly. But his main preoccupation was with the great man himself whose writings, indeed, it was that had brought the sweetness into his life, or, rather, brought into fuller blossom perhaps the kindly devotion that already was in his character. Filled with admiration, worship, faith, with a touch of reverence, too, that was close to awe, he watched observantly the habits and processes of genius.

The privilege was not treated lightly; to know a great man, a mind that had deservedly won this adjective, to be side by side with such a personality in the close quarters of his intimate family life, and to note the way he worked—all this had a human and psychological value that constituted it a real experience for Tomkyns. The dictum that no man is a hero to his valet proved wrong. Intimacy pieces affectation and shows up pose, but it can only emphasise true greatness. Hildritch had neither pose or affectation; his work proved his power, the fineness of his character increased rather than diminished at close quarters. A great artist, a great man. Big, simple, modest, his genius conveyed that touch of wonder which is the hall-mark of all uncommon men.

There was mystery, of course, too, as Tomkyns speedily discovered. How should there not be, indeed, with the processes of genius. Whence came the afflatus, the mood, the inspiration, with that suddenness which ever attends the wayward manifestation of these divine gifts? How, then, did he shape and clothe these splendid visions with that simple yet convincing interpretation which delighted the army of his readers? Oh, to have sat at the little desk inside his mind and watched the marvellous process in its detail!

Tomkyns, like everyone else, even like Mrs. Hildritch herself, had to supply these inaccessible items as best he could. It rather disappointed him, frankly, that Mrs. Hildritch had grown too familiar with the problem to feel the respectful wonder that he himself felt. "Oh, Bill's a real artist, you see," she explained with inexplicable lightness. "All artists get ideas automatically. As to dramatising them, as Billy does, why, they simply can't help it."

It was the commercial side that seemed to interest her most—sales, reviews, advertisement. There were the children to educate, of course. It evidently pleased her, too, when another great writer, a rival possibly, received a public set-back. "Poor Freddy!"—she knew him by his first name, of course— "There's a dreadful notice of his new book in the *Times* this morning." But her eyes sparkled. Her husband's sales, and her husband's health seemed, however, her chief preoccupations. "If you get a good advance on this novel," she mentioned, "we might buy that car and do a tour in Wales. It would set you up, dear." She would urge him then to finish the book soon, "get on with it," being the term made use of.

And this distressed the admiring Tomkyns not a little. No genius, he reflected, as though he had invented the idea, ever ought to marry. He admired and watched in silence after this; he kept his questions to himself, at any rate. His unique experience must not be tarnished. Hildritch had no peculiarities, he noticed with pleasure, unless his habits of seeking the woods and the lonelier parts of the wild garden can be considered peculiar. Like many another, he found his inspiration with Nature. In the middle of playing with the children, immediately after a game of tennis or, suddenly, at the end of a conversation, his fine great head would jerk upwards, he would sniff the air, as it were—and off he would go. His wife would note his going, but would not interfere, beyond perhaps calling after him some caution about the risk of a chill, or a question as to when he would be back. "Oh, I'll be all right, dear," was his answer.

No one ever offered to accompany him. Tomkyns would have given his soul to go, had he dared. Hildritch would return in due course, his eyes alight, his mind charged with ideas, his conversation brilliant. If he did not retire to his room to work, the evening would then be wonderful, the talk at dinner with grand flights of imagination, lively discussions afterwards, the little country cottage aflame and alight with the fires of genius at full blast.

Mrs. Hildritch, on these occasions, contributed little, so that Tomkyns again felt disappointed in her. She sat silent, even preoccupied, adding hardly more than, "Yes, dear.... No, dear," to the talk. To Tomkyns fell the role of feeding the great mind with such comments, questions, and observations as his common-place intelligence could suggest. And it was here that Hildritch showed so plainly his power, his modesty, his creative imagination, for whatever Tomkyns said—it was often foolish and ordinary enough—the other took up and passed through the alembic of his great fiery mind. There was no sneer, no depreciation, no contradiction. Hildritch caught at the least remark, seized it, played with it, re-made it, showed it aglow with life and beauty.

These evenings were very wonderful. Tomkyns was glad when he saw his hero slip away into the woods. This communing with Nature produced such exquisite results. In the mornings Hildritch was never visible. He breakfasted upstairs and worked in solitude. No rule was more strictly kept than that which forbade his being disturbed on any pretext at all. He appeared first at lunch, a little exhausted sometimes, but the fires alight still in his eyes, his occasional absent-mindedness very natural. The respect and admiration in Tomkyns became genuine hero-worship.

Thus it was that one day the force of his devouring curiosity made him bold; the wonder in him as to *how* Hildritch found beauty and inspiration in the solitude of those woods consumed him. His effort was common-place, but passionate admiration prompted it: "The trees," he ventured, as they rested a moment after their evening game of tennis, "that bit of wild garden—they mean much to you?" He almost added, "Sir." "You find *everything* there—don't you?"

He felt he was intruding unwarrantably, that his question was impertinent, was even sacrilege. The reply of the great man enchanted him by its simplicity: "They lead everywhere," he said, with a delightful smile, "to heaven—or to hell." Then, as he buttoned his coat and prepared to go, Mrs. Hildritch, in a dreadful anti-climax, shouted something from the drawing-room window, and little Gladys came running up, holding letters in her hand. "Mummy says, will you post these for her, please."

Tomkyns felt the shock of it, but Hildritch showed admirable self-control. He smiled patiently, took the letters, nodded to his friend, and was gone into the lonely woods his soul desired. Tomkyns, deeply chagrined, with contemptuous pity in his heart towards Mrs. Hildritch, but an increase in wonder towards the patient husband, allowed a suitable interval to pass—then went after him.

The trees closed round him; there was a hush, a twilight, a peace. A bird sang here and there, a jay flew swiftly overhead, a rabbit scuttled. Striving hard to find what his hero found—inspiration, beauty, wonder—he found nothing but a rather oppressive silence, damp dead leaves of yesteryear underfoot, a melancholy gloom, and a desire to escape into the fading sunlight. A conviction that Hildritch was a superior being increased in him. He meditated deeply, following his wondering thoughts. Then, finding a tiny path, he followed that.

The twilight deepened into dusk, the sun went down, the first stars appeared. He had now left the oppressive wood and was on the common-land. He went idly on. A bicycle, with its lamps lit, passed him, and a short distance ahead lay a group of huddled houses, lights shining in their windows.

He paused presently in front of one of these, reflecting vaguely that it must be time to turn homewards, and as he reflected he raised his eyes and saw the lighted window facing him. The blind was down, a pale yellow blind, and on it was a shadow silhouetted sharply. It was the shadow of a man. The shadow was holding a glass. It lifted the glass to the lips and drained it. Then it stretched out an arm and another arm appeared and took the empty glass. The head belonging to the first arm nodded. He saw a hand go up and wipe the mouth.

Tomkyns recognised the shadow—and turned his eyes away.

SECTION 3: NATURE INSPIRES

This section looks at ways in which Blackwood's own imagination was inspired. Writing in his autobiography *Episodes Before Thirty* in 1923 Blackwood said that "By far the strongest influence in my life . . . was Nature; it betrayed itself early, growing in intensity with every year. Bringing comfort, companionship, inspiration, joy, the spell of Nature has remained dominant, a truly magical spell." It was a spell he shared with his father, for although Blackwood, Sr., had an evangelical religious conviction which he tried to inculcate in his children, he also enjoyed going for long walks with young Algernon and inspired in the youth the sheer pleasure of the living Earth.

So when sent to Canada in 1890, aged just twenty-one, with the purpose of making a living as a farmer, and failing miserably at every job he turned his hand to, Blackwood found solace in Nature. He had become a theosophist, following the teachings of Madame Blavatsky, and joined the Toronto branch of the Society, contributing to their magazine *Lucifer*. One of his earliest published essays, "Thoughts on Nature" appeared in *Lucifer* in December 1890.

After ten suffocating years in Canada and New York, Blackwood returned home to England in 1899. Surrounded by family and, for a while, holding down a job sufficient to finance some of his travels, Blackwood started to write about his experiences for various British magazines such as *Macmillan's* and *Blackwood's*. Amongst these were several relating to his experiences in Canada from which I have selected "'Mid the Haunts of the Moose." This essay relates to an expedition that Blackwood undertook in October 1898 in the lake territory near Deux-Rivières in Quebec. It was this expedition that inspired several of Blackwood's stories, including the murder tale "Skeleton Lake" and his classic, "The Wendigo."

In June 1900 Blackwood and his friend Wilfrid Wilson decided to canoe the full length of the River Danube. In the event they did not complete the entire journey but did enough for the experience to be imprinted firmly in Blackwood's mind, and it resulted in probably his best known story, "The Willows." The expedition is recorded in detail in "Down the Danube in a Canadian Canoe."

That expedition and others almost imprinted upon Blackwood's mind the significance of location or, as he calls it in the title of a later essay, "The Psychology of Places." This and "The Glamour of Strangers" show how Blackwood was becoming attuned to both the places he visited and the people he met there. Both of these would inspire thoughts and ideas and lead to stories. So would his ruminating on the flora and fauna, especially birds, as shown in "On Wings." The idea of flight represented total freedom and escape to Blackwood and it fea-

tures strongly in many of his works. It is through flight that Jimbo escapes his
psychological prison in *Jimbo*. It is through spiritual flight that a New Age
dawns on the world in *The Promise of Air*. And flight, akin to dance, gives rise
to the atmospheric conclusion to his story "The Wings of Horus." This tri-
umvirate of essays show how Blackwood harmonised with his surroundings and
how these inspired some of his most imaginative works.

The final three essays in this section reveal his impressions of the other key
landscapes of his life—the Jura, on the border of Switzerland and France,
where Blackwood spent many winters skiing and writing, and where many of
his stories are set; the Caucasus, where Blackwood traveled in 1910 and which
inspired *The Centaur*; and Egypt. Blackwood first travelled to Egypt in January 1912 and, as the essay here shows, it overwhelmed him. Amongst the stories inspired by the visit are "Sand" and "A Descent Into Egypt," both of which
consider the immensity of Egypt in size and time—features explored here in detail.

These essays show just how much Blackwood's writings related to his love for
and affinity with his surroundings and how the wildness and beauty of these
remote places can liberate and inspire the imagination.

—Mike Ashley

Thoughts on Nature

There are moments in the sweet stillness of early morning, when strange and novel thoughts flow in upon the soul and when the harmonies of nature produce symphonies of music so sweet and wild, and withal so exquisite, that the spirit of the privileged beholder is stirred to its most mysterious depths and thrills with new and inexpressible emotions. The magic of evening is eminently soothing; it lulls the spirit, tired out with the trials and worries of a long day; its influence partakes of the nature of a narcotic, which, for the time, supplies a balm that smooths over the pains and big realities of the active life battle. It sleeps on the soul of the weary one, as moonlight sleeps on the surface of a calm lake, wakening only the lightest and most pleasurable ripples of reflection; but it can never "trouble the waters," nor call into action those energies that lie in the deeps, as the wind-storms do, racing over the ocean waters; neither can it awaken those highest energies—"noble longings for the strife"—the nobler will-potencies, which, in a lofty mind, cannot fail to be evoked by the wondrous freshness, vigour, novelty, and almost unearthly loveliness of an early morning scene.

As the darkness of the night slowly merges into the first streaks of the sunrise lights, the beholding spirit seems to leave its own plane of consciousness and to enter that of the surrounding nature-life, to commune, indeed, with the potencies which, above and behind all natural phenomena, render them beautiful, mysterious or weird. Then, too, we seem to be in perfect sympathy with the "unknown" (not the "unknowable") which gives to all such beautiful scenes their wonderful life and high spirituality. Then it is that the spirit understands intuitively the expressive voices of the trees, and is more susceptible to the sweet cadences of the song of the stream as it rushes along over the pebbles; playfully springing up to kiss the leaves of some low-hanging bough or to carry from them some message born of night's lightest breeze and purest dew to old father ocean, away in the far distance, under the glare of the noon-day sun—to that grand old ocean whose murmur, too, at such a time has a deeper significance than usual and to the spirit rightly attuned will, in smothered roars along the lone shore, disclose something of "what is unknown." It is at this hour of early morning that one may seem to hear faint echoes of the weird whisperings in which the forms of nature converse during the great silences of the night.

High up among the wild mountains such a scene to a sensitive spirit will be one of awe, power and indescribable grandeur. As, one by one, the dark giants rearing up into the unmeasured depths of the sky first catch a glimmer of the returning light and, as the winds, that all the long night through have slept on the cold solitudes of inaccessible ice-fields, begin again to breathe along the still, shadowed slopes, where myriads of pines point, like long fingers, heaven-ward, imparting to all they touch an indescribable sense of aloofness and strong beauty, of "power apart and inaccessible" which belongs not to the softer char-acteristics of the great midday heats—as these morning airs stir the wild grasses and pass from one rocky monster across intervening valleys in deepest slum-ber to others more distant still, a new sense thrills through us and we partici-pate, as far as may be, in the life throbs of the great nature spirits by whom we are surrounded; we are raised aloft to their cool heights of repose, and almost gain an entrance into that spiritual and far more beautiful world of which our own is but an imperfect reflection—an image, distorted and to pass away.

By the greater power that lies around us on such an occasion we are enabled, perhaps some of us for the first time, to comprehend the exquisite beauty that lies in the combined poetry and music of the wind among the pine boughs and the majestic power freed by the cataract, the crashing of rock-falls or the thun-ders of the snow slides.

> "These are the voices of the mountains;
> Thus they open their snow lips
> And speak to one another
> In the primæval language lost to man."

But another poet gifted with far deeper insight into the real essence and na-ture of things on beholding some such scene of wildness, exclaims:—

> "Spirit of Nature I here!
> In this interminable wilderness
> Of worlds, at whose immensity
> Even soaring fancy staggers,
> Here is thy fitting temple.
> Yet not the lightest leaf
> That quivers to the passing breeze
> Is less instinct with thee:
> Yet not the meanest worm
> That lurks in graves and fattens on the dead,
> Less shares thy eternal breath."

The poet who gave birth to the above lines had a passing glimpse of a great truth, one that can only be appreciated and therefore thoroughly enjoyed by the Theosophist.

Again the same sweet singer says:—

> "Spirit of Nature! No!
> The pure diffusion of thy essence throbs

Alike in every human heart.

• • •

Thine the Tribunal which surpasseth
The *show* of human Justice,
As God surpasses man.
Soul of those mighty spheres
Whose changeless paths through heaven's deep silence lie;
Soul of that smallest being,
The dwelling of whose life
Is one faint April sun-gleam."

He elsewhere says that

"Every heart contains perfection's germ,"

But the whole truth in all its grandeur with the marvellous evolution of life from its source through all forms back again to the beginning had not dawned on his mind.

So again, we find that this poet, who writes so beautifully about one, like himself, creating "forms more real than living man," never really perceived that "form is illusive, and that the reality is a principle which is independent of form."

Nevertheless he has glimpses of highest truth; as for instance, when he expresses the inexorable justice of the Karma which every man is slowly and surely weaving for himself and his future, even as he has in the past brought about his present condition and circumstances.

"And all-sufficing nature can chastise
Those who transgress her law, she only knows
How justly to proportion to the fault
The punishment it merits."

He never fully realised, though, the full meaning of the word he was so fond of using and which represented what he justly worshipped without ever comprehending that he was worshipping in reality, not the highest, but only the shadow of the highest—NATURE. He saw through a glass darkly, and only in part did he grasp the great Truth that, as the author of "Magic, White and Black" puts it—"Nature has the same organisation as man, although not the same external form."

'Mid the Haunts of the Moose

Deux Rivières is a stopping-place—it can hardly be called a station—on the Canadian Pacific Railway before you come to Port Arthur and Winnipeg, and the few wooden shanties of which it consists stand on the border-line between Quebec and Ontario. It stands, moreover, on the edge of that vast wilderness that stretches unbroken to James Bay, the southern loop of Hudson's Bay itself. Just below this little "lumber village" runs the Ottawa river, icy cold, swift, and narrow. It has not here attained the width and power that many miles farther on render it of paramount importance to the lumber trade; and, last year in October, when our little party went up into this wilderness to hunt moose, we found that the Ottawa river here formed the dividing-line between danger and safety. In Ontario *l'orignal* (moose) was still protected by Government, and had been for three years; but in Quebec, across the river, any one who could get within range of a moose after October 1 was allowed to shoot it. The moose seemed to know where they were well off, for Ontario was reported "thunderin' full of 'em," whereas Quebec was comparatively deserted.

"It's easy huntin'," an indiscreet fellow in Deux Rivières observed to us as we made ready to start; "you can shoot yer moose on one side of the river and bring ower his horns and pelt on the other. The game-warden ain't agoin' to hunt for that carcass, you bet. And even if he do, he ain't agoin' to find it before the wolves and meat hawks and ants have had their go at it." The licence for each gun is £5; and the fine for shooting out of season is exceedingly heavy. It is divided between the warden and the man who reports the discovery.

No camera can ever reproduce the still beauty of that morning scene when we left the train at 5 a.m. and made ready to leave the little outpost of civilisation. The cool autumn air, fragrant with a hundred scents from the surrounding woods, was still hazy with the smoke of forest-fires that had been smouldering all the summer. Through this gauze-like veil the maples and birches, already turned to gold and crimson beneath the touch of early frosts, shone with a strange luminous beauty that for miles in every direction lit up the ocean of trees with flaming patches of glory. And all was still and silent. There was no wind astir, and the air only trembled very faintly to the musical roar of the waterfalls and tumbling rapids of the Ottawa below. A few human figures moved here and there among the little wooden shanties.

The river swept swiftly round a sharp bend, and rushed on to a dangerous fall two hundred yards farther down. Along either bank there was a vigorous back-water. To cross this water with our packs, tents, &c., we embarked in a clumsy lumber barge propelled by immense oars. The first backwater carried us a considerable distance up-stream, the men heading the boat straight across all the time, and rowing as hard as they could. Then we suddenly entered the main current, and were swiftly borne down the centre of the stream, the boat turning round like a huge top all the way. The banks seemed to fly past. The roar of the fall, and the horrible edge where the river dropped abruptly out of sight, seemed to us unpleasantly close, when the prow of the boat caught the other back-water and our direction was instantly reversed. With a shudder and a splash the unwieldy boat spun round and shot up-stream again, finally landing us in safety at a spot exactly opposite our original point of embarkation. During this brief but exciting journey the French-Canadian oarsmen regaled us with pleasant stories of boats swept over the falls and lives lost in the spring when the river was high and the strength of the two backwaters was easily miscalculated by a few seconds.

Then, for two days and two nights we travelled by canoe and "portages" inland to the lake of Cogawanna, whose lonely beaches were said to be haunted by "the biggest moose yer ever seen." The scenery these two days was in a sense monotonous. Miles upon miles of undulating forest and low hills—no open spaces, except black patches of desolation, where fires had consumed the underbrush, and licked the branches off the giant trees till they had died. The second growth on the scene of a fire is never the same as the trees that were destroyed, but usually silver birch or scrub-oak and maple. Everywhere we passed these lighter greens among the sombre shades of the hemlocks, cedars, and pines. Lakes of all sizes and shapes came suddenly into view, blue as the Mediterranean, or green and black as the ocean itself. The constant repetition produced the sense of monotony; but the real charm of it all lay in the utter loneliness and remoteness from the scenes of men's labours. Wild-duck of all descriptions we saw; cranes, huge fish-hawks, divers, laughing loons, eagles, tracks of otter, mink, bear, deer, and occasionally of wolves along the shores— and moose-tracks, where the great beasts had blundered through the dense scrub to find a drinking-place. But no men, not even Indians; no farms, no shanties. We had the great woods to ourselves. Chipmunks, chattering on the crests of lofty pines, dropped cones upon us as we glided silently by, close to shore. Loons dived in front of us, and popped up again, many hundreds of yards away, with fish in their beaks. More than once, as we turned a sharp corner, a startled buck looked up and stared in amazement at us before it turned and crashed away into the forest, "whistling" as it went. There were no mosquitoes. The cold nights had mercifully destroyed them. No singing-birds, nor any of brighter plumage than the rich blue of the blue jay and the light greys of the meat-hawks or carrion-birds. No wild-flowers, or hardly any. The merciless winter does not encourage their growth. Better still, no flies, no snakes, no poisonous insects of any kind. There is a decided note of grimness in these northern woods of Canada,—almost as if the shadow of the cruel winter hung somewhere in the air, even in summer, and held up a warning finger: "This is sacred to the life of the forest. You may venture here in the warm months, but never let yourselves be caught here when the frost comes, and the snow on the wings of the north wind."

Meanwhile, we had reached the old haunts of the lumber companies. On all sides we saw their traces. In days gone by there had been lumber-camps at remote points. In the deep snows the men cut the trees and "skid" them over the slippery surface to the edge of the nearest water. The logs are piled up 20 feet high on the shores, and when the ice melts they are tumbled down into the water, and in huge "booms," acres in extent, are floated for weeks down streams and across lakes till they reach the Ottawa river and eventually the great sawmills. In the spring these booms choke up many a good fishing-stream. Perhaps the first big fellow gets caught by a projection on the bank. Instantly the others pile up on his back, till in a few hours a towering heap of logs dams the river and forms a "jam." To break a jam is to lead a forlorn hope, and it is not uncommon in these solitudes to come across a plain wooden cross, close to some tumbling stream, with the inscription roughly hewn with a knife, "Jean Garnier," or "Jim Smith, killed by jam"—with the date. And these lonely graves beneath the "murmuring pines and the hemlocks" have their poetry and their lesson of duty nobly done without hope of reward.

The apology for this digression is that the lumber companies proved of great value to us. In order to skid the logs they have to cut roads, so that the horses may have a tolerably clear path. These roads are on the surface of the snow, lying perhaps four feet deep, and in the springs are only recognisable as faint vistas in the forest. They always lead to water. Following these woodland vistas, canoeing down winding lakes shut in by lofty cliffs and dotted with picturesque islands, we covered the fifty miles that lay between us and our destination. About sunset on the second day our "birch-barks" grated in a sandy bay of Cogawanna's northern shore, and we pitched a permanent camp on a promontory covered with silver birches and maples.

Water-fowl of various descriptions scattered with whirring wings as we landed, and more than one porcupine ambled leisurely away into the woods when we began to chop the tent-poles and get the stones for the fireplace. When the sun finally disappeared, the shadows of the night fell over a camp as cosy as any hunter could desire, and perhaps a little more comfortable, because one of the party happened to be a young lady. The stillness was almost unearthly when the moon rose over the lake, silvering untold distances, and throwing impenetrable shadows under the trees. I sat over the little fire at the mouth of my tent long after the others were asleep. It seemed unnatural that the whole country should be so silent when the woods were full of life—moving life too. Everything alive in the forest moves at night and rests by day. The woods travel in the darkness. At that very moment, as I sat in the cold moonlight looking out upon immense stretches of forest, there was not a hundred yards anywhere in which some living creature was not moving. Yet there was no sound—not the breaking of a twig or the crackling of a dry leaf beneath the lightest paw. Nothing but silence, and moonlight, and the stars, and distance. As I imagined the moose prowling and feeding not very far from us, they almost seemed to me a survival of the antediluvian monsters, a species all by themselves, having no part or portion with the degenerate animals of modern days.

With the earliest morning came the sound of fish jumping in the lake and the chipmunks scampering through the trees overhead. But the excitement began at breakfast (trout and buckwheat cakes), when one of the men announced the discovery of fresh deer-tracks not half a mile behind our tents. Deer are not plentiful in these regions. The wolves keep their ranks thin. No wolf can catch a deer in the woods; but in the winter, ferocious with long fasts, they chase them on to the ice, and soon get their teeth into their tender flanks. They double more easily than deer on the slippery surface, and, being lighter, do not sink so deep in the soft patches of snow. The barking of a few wolves in pursuit of a deer sounds like the fighting and snarling of a lot of angry dogs. It must be an unpleasant sound to have at your heels at any time, and the poor deer makes the most frantic efforts, but only slips from side to side, growing momentarily weaker, till it is at length overhauled and torn to pieces. The discovery of deer so close to us was only exciting because it meant we should not lack fresh meat; but moose was the magic word in our camp, and the first thing to do was to find out where the moose were in relation to ourselves. These creatures, it may be said, move generally in groups of four or five, or less. Several groups of this size travel in the same direction, and cover practically the same country at the same time. In this sense they may be described as moving in widely scattered herds. They get over vast distances, moving with great rapidity, and the enormous territory at their disposal of course makes difficult hunting. You must have iron muscles and be tireless. A fresh moose-track—that is, one with no water or cobwebs in it—may be followed fifty miles, the creature always keeping half-a-dozen miles ahead of the hunter. If, meanwhile, it chooses to take to the water, the tracks of course are lost, and so much time has been wasted, that's all! The utmost caution has to be observed. Their ears are sharper than those of a deer. If a twig snaps beneath your mocassin, or your coat brushes noisily against a low branch of some maple-tree, they will put another mile to their credit before you have gone a hundred yards.

It is upon their unrivalled powers of scent, however, that they chiefly depend for their safety. Nature, or evolution, has endowed them with a proboscis of rare proportion, and their title of "Hebrew of the Woods" is thoroughly deserved. In the wide nostrils gaping at the end of that expansive muzzle, the least scent, the faintest odour, is faithfully registered, and the owners are off at top speed in less than a second. With their heads lowered, and in spite of the bull's spreading horns, they charge through the woods at full tilt, crashing through the densest underbrush as if it were standing hay, and smashing young tree-stems as if they were the stalks of sunflowers. Everywhere, in these northern woods, can be seen the traces of their passage—trunks with the bark scraped off, broken saplings, tufts of hair caught on pointed branches, and on the ground the imprint of their hoofs and tremendous stride.

Accustomed to the dim twilight of the great woods, the eyeballs of these creatures are oblique, as with deer, and do not seem to be specially sensitive. They never turn their heads at shadows. Provided the wind is right, you can approach a moose to within a few feet, if you go straight in front of him, and he will never see you. If he does raise his head, it will mean that his ears have warned him of your approach. If you can fool his ears and his nose, you can put salt on his tail, say the hunters. But wind and rain are the best aids. Noisy weather is good hunting weather. The roar of the branches, the rattle of the rain, and the constant dripping from the trees upon the leaves on the ground, combine to drown the inevitable sounds of your approach. Then there is good chance of success. The front legs of the moose are longer than the hind ones. To drink (if the bank be steep) he has to kneel; to crop the sweet shoots of the wild rice they must assume the humble attitude of prayer. Their food consists chiefly of the ground hemlock, whose low bushes cover the ground in the neighbourhood of big hemlock-trees, and can be easily got at in winter by scraping away the surface snow; but they are also fond of the topmost leaves of the young maples, which their great height enables them to pull down with ease. On all sides, where moose have been travelling in the autumn, the maple saplings can be seen bent double to the ground. When the earth is too hard to hold a track, the experienced hunter can follow the path of a moose for miles, by observing where he has cropped the hemlock and the sweet maple leaves on both sides as he sauntered slowly along, enjoying his vegetarian meal.

In the great heats of July and August these animals suffer terribly from the sun, owing to the thickness of a hairy skin that also keeps them warm when the thermometer is 40° below zero. In these months they commonly wade into the lakes and stand up to their necks in the cool water, where the Indians, to their shame, slaughter them without mercy. They offer a large target, as may be imagined, and, though strong swimmers, cannot get away from the bullet in time. These same Indians affirm that the bear is the shyest animal of the woods. Bruin certainly is a very wary beast; but the moose, in my humble opinion, comes in an uncommonly close second. On all sides you can see the rotten logs the bears have torn open in their search for ants and honey, and the deep trail leading up to, and away from, them; but the bear itself is probably miles away, covering the ground in that rolling, tumbling gait of his that carries him along at incredible speed. It is no uncommon sight to surprise a bear among the low fruit-bushes, no matter what way the wind is. When berries are thick you may stumble frequently enough upon them in the midst of the blue-berries, with both front paws round a particularly rich clump, and gluttonously devouring the ripe purple fruit. Yet who ever came upon a moose in the middle of his dinner, unless wind and weather and everything else were against him?

The first two days we spent reconnoitring. It was necessary to find out in what special portion of their great park the moose were enjoying the splendid "fall" weather. In three parties of two each, with compasses and canoes, we separated, after a very early breakfast, and spent the day following the freshest trails we could come across. At night we met again round the blazing logs of the open camp-fire, and compared notes. All of us had come across very recent trails of deer, bear, beaver, otter, fox, skunk, even wolves—but the moose-tracks were all old. There was nothing worth following, nothing fresher than a week. They had moved.

"They're travellin' fast, and we've got to shunt along purty fast to get up with 'em."

"Unless they're movin' in a circle, which they often do—darn 'em!"

Then followed the usual consultation of maps, which we laid over a flat stone beside the fire, and studied intently while the owls hooted in the woods behind us, and more than one pair of glowing eyes watched our proceedings from a safe distance.

Ten miles to the north of us Garden Lake stretched its lonely bays and arms over an immense surface, dotted with wooded islands, on one of which the Indians had built their annual crop of birch-bark canoes. I found the thin strips of cedar, and the root they use for strings, still lying among the long grass. Garden River, the exit of this lake, was trampled and pounded for hundreds of yards along the banks, but the owners of the monstrous hoofs had gone. Blue Lake, to the west of us, with its cold blue waters; Sand Lake, with its yellow stretches of shore; Green Lake, with its deep green waves and precipitous cliffs, Roscoe Lake, Round Pond, Lindsay Lake, and a dozen more besides, all bore traces of the giants' thirst along their quiet shores. Maple leaves had been cropped and ground hemlock devoured; tree stems scraped; projecting twigs left with a tuft of coarse hair streaming in the wind, and the ground manured in patches. But the moose themselves, shy mammoths, were hiding somewhere out of our way, and the second day's search brought us to the trails of their sentries, that were by no means too old for hope. The hoarse croaking of the ravens, always a sign of their neighbourhood, was heard at intervals; and the carrion-birds, that follow them in the air, feeding temporarily on a parasite of their thick hair, and hoping eventually for a whole carcass, were seen flitting about in all directions. This reconnoitring is pleasant work. The air is dry and cool, wonderfully invigorating, and laden with the hundred scents of a primeval forest that stretches unbroken to the icy shores of James Bay. You tread all the time on a carpet of deep moss or crimson and golden leaves. On all sides the partridges are "drumming," or flying quietly into the lower branches of the trees, where half-a-dozen will stand and let you shoot them one by one. Squirrels dart everywhere, chattering and squeaking, with tails erect, and a rare nest of nuts hidden somewhere for the coming winter. The quiet bays of the lakes shelter wild-fowl of all descriptions, and the springs fill your flasks with the best brand of champagne you have ever tasted.

So we peeled the crackling bark from the silver birch-trees and fashioned call-ing-horns, and prepared in other ways for night-watches and vigorous hunt-ing measures generally. The cry of the cow moose is admirably imitated by means of this rude horn. While an amateur exaggerates it into something be-tween a fog-horn and a cornet, the practised hunter produces the long deep "moo" that carries an incredible distance, and rarely fails to bring the bull, if within hearing length, crashing headlong down to his death.

The third day my guide and I loaded our pack with a few provisions, and with tent and canoe started for a series of little ponds beyond the northern shores of Garden Lake. We journeyed all day down "lumber roads" that were simply vis-tas of glowing colour. I was always in front, with a 50-lb. pack strapped across the shoulders and a loaded rifle, while behind me the man, with the canoe over his head like a gigantic pantomime hat, followed awkwardly. Frequent rests were necessary; but who could wish to go fast in such woods on a fine day in Octo-ber, with the blue sky overhead, and the slanting sunlight putting the match to autumn bonfires on every side. We moved as quietly as possible in mocassins.

"Hunt *all* the time; you never kin guess when your chance 'll come."

Once the man stopped suddenly and sniffed the air like a dog. He made a sign to me, and I helped the canoe off his shoulders. He went a few feet ahead of me and pointed to the ground. I looked and saw a heap of gorgeous leaves left by an eddy of wind. It was indeed a patch of beauty; but I thought it strange for this rough woodsman to take so much trouble to show it to me.

"Beautiful, indeed," I whispered.

"Ain't it, though?" he whispered back. "It's a young cow. Guess she ain't been away long either!"

It was not the poetry of autumn that had moved him, but the smell of a moose, and the deep imprint of her body where she had recently rested upon the leaves. I saw it plainly enough when his finger outlined it for me. He kept sniff-ing the air as he gazed.

"There's a moose within...." He hesitated. I gasped. "A couple of miles, maybe," he concluded.

He showed me the faint hoof-marks on the thick carpet of leaves where it en-tered the wood.

"That thar cow was lyin' thar not ten minutes ago. But the wind's wrong, and I guess she smelt us pretty strong."

Speaking for himself, I have no doubt she did!

We followed the trail some distance into the woods. The underbrush was very thick, and we had to scramble on all-fours. The cow had doubled a good deal on her tracks. We presently came to a spot where she had evidently waited a mo-ment.

"She stopped to listen here," he explained, sitting down on a huge fallen tree and gazing sadly at the hoof-marks. "When one of them animals is startled it runs 200 yards, maybe, into the woods, and then stops to listen. This is whar that cow stopped to listen, or I'm a — Injin.

"She didn't stop long," I ventured.

He looked at me without speaking, and then motioned me to follow. For half a mile through the woods we followed the tracks. Soon they began to get longer and wider apart.

"She was scared here. She's runnin'."

The tracks got wider and wider apart, till finally they reached a big tree lying on the ground, with its branches sticking out like the spokes of a wheel in the air. There they seemed to come to a full stop. But the woodsman soon found their continuation—on the other side of the tree.

"That's whar she jumped—see!" he explained. And, measuring it as accurately as we could, it came to 18 feet. A very fair jump, I thought, for a cow moose. To clear the branches she must have crossed the tree at an elevation of nearly 4 feet.

It was just sunset when we reached the shores of Garden Lake and saw the expanse of still water, with dark patches in all directions showing the islands. There was no wind, and not a cloud in the sky; so we launched our canoe in silence, and for the next two hours paddled across the deserted waters, skirting points and islands, and occasionally long reefs of black rocks. Like Hiawatha, we

"Sailed into the fiery sunset,
Sailed into the purple vapours,
Sailed into the dusk of evening,"—

and before we were half-way across this arm of Garden Lake the moon rose over the ridge of forest and silvered a picture of fairy-like enchantment such as I have never seen equalled. It was peace beyond all telling, and the only sound was the water splashing musically against the sides of the frail canoe and the monotonous dripping of the paddles. It didn't matter where we landed to camp. All was ours—islands, points, bays, and mainland. No one could interfere. The loneliness was real.

By the light of the moon, then high in the heavens, we pitched our tent upon the farther shore on the edge of the mighty woods, and after devouring the two partridges shot *en route*, and drinking a quart each of black tea, we crawled into the narrow tent and were soon fast asleep—I in a sleeping-bag with a red woollen nightcap on my head, and my companion in his clothes with his ordinary slouch-hat drawn down over his eyes.

The day following was clear and still. In the afternoon we portaged into a narrow little pond, unhonoured by a name, that lay several miles in the forest, and at a much higher level than the main lake.

"It ain't fur from the ridge, and if they're travellin' in this country they're bound to come within callin' distance." He never deigned to use the word moose. It was always "they" or "them beasts," "cow," "bull," or "calf."

It was late in the afternoon, and very little wind was stirring. Stealthily we lowered the canoe from our shoulders and pushed it into the lake, and then with the utmost care got in ourselves and paddled cautiously down the near shore. The canoe moved on the quiet water like a spirit, silently, almost without ripple, as if it knew what was expected of it. I sat in the bows, the rifle across my knees, and the man propelled us with a slight movement of his wrist, never taking the paddle out of the water. In such still weather the dripping of the drops carries dangerous distances, and the sun shining on its wet blade flashes signals that can be seen literally for miles. Neither of us spoke a word, and, in spite of occasional spasms of "canoe cramp" that shot up my legs and back, I sat motionless. The least movement, and a birch-bark canoe crackles like a pop-gun. The opposite shore, about a quarter of a mile across, lay in front of the sun, and therefore in shadow. The sun was fast nearing the edge of the ridge above. Nothing seemed more likely than that a moose should come down to drink, and nothing less likely than that it should distinguish us from one of the many logs that line the shore beside us. It could never make us out across 400 yards of water. The lake was perhaps two miles long. About half-way down the man stopped paddling, and, with very slow even movements, raised the horn to his lips and blew a long sad "moo," that echoed numberless times before it finally died away in the sea of silent woods round us. Twice he did this, with due intervals and there was no answer; but just as the third "moo" was losing itself in the distance, a new sound rose after the echoes. We paused and listened intently. It was the breaking of branches a long way off.... The guide's keen brown eyes flashed a message to me as I turned my head towards him.

"There he comes... but a long way off."

A tremor ran through me, and I strained my ears so much to listen that I heard the blood singing under the skin. The sound of breaking branches continued to reach us at intervals, each time a little closer than before. Some great animal was moving through the long stretch of forest on the opposite shores. He seemed to be at a spot halfway between the lake and the ridge. It was getting dusk, and drinking-time was close at hand. Every now and then came a louder report, as some young tree was snapped off short, and then followed a period of silence again. The shadows were settling down over the trees. Already the sun was below the ridge, and probably within a short hour of the horizon itself.

"He's feedin'," whispered the man; "he ain't travellin' fast."

"Is he coming this way?"

"Guess so, if we don't scare him any. The wind's right." A puff of air came against our faces at that very moment as if to verify his words. It came from across the water. For another half-hour we waited in cramps and silence. The beast never deigned to answer our cry, nor to hasten his step, yet he was certainly coming nearer and nearer. It was just about drinking-time; but the poor brute did not bargain for a piece of lead in his cup.

"It may be a b'ar," whispered the man.

Scarcely were the words out of his mouth when a roar that made the air shake issued from the shadows directly opposite.

"There he is," whispered the man excitedly, pointing.

It was some seconds before I could distinguish anything at all save the dense growth of bushes that lined the shore. My rifle was raised and ready, but I could see nothing to aim at. Then suddenly the bushes parted and I saw a form, dim and immense, rise up out of the very ground it seemed. The width of the horns was lost in the shadows; but there was no mistaking those broad shoulders and that big brown bulk. Instantly the canoe shot round, and began to move swiftly towards him across the lake. I pointed ready to fire, and the light bark trembled beneath us like a thing of life as we moved steadily forwards. There was a touch of buck-fever; but the steel-tipped bullet sped true, and the monster fell with a crash to its knees.

"Steady—now another one," said the man behind me, urging on the canoe as fast as he could.

A second shot, and the moose rolled sideways into the lake and lay motionless. Next day the other men went over to skin it, and the horns and pelt were just about all they could manage. The horns measured 52 inches across, and there were 28 points.

The night we watched for moose I shall never forget. Sleeping for several hours in the afternoon, we took an early supper, and just as the shadows were falling started out for our adventure. The lake had to be crossed and a mile "portaged"; then a second lake came, and after it a second portage. It was nine o'clock when we cautiously slipped the canoe into the still waters of a secluded pond far from camp. A frosty night without wind seemed in our favour. A host of stars in a sky as clear as winter was the only light we dared use. Wrapping ourselves up in blankets, we crawled in the canoe to a suitable spot twenty yards from shore, and there prepared to wait till the dawn. No tobacco was permissible. No fire could, of course, be made, nor anything cooked. A nip of whisky about two a.m. was all that warmed.

How still the night was. Our breathing seemed the only sound. The pond was barely three-quarters of a mile long, and very narrow. It seemed, so far as we could judge, to be in the direct route the moose had been taking of late. Surely some one of them would deign to drink of its sweet waters at sunrise. Everything alive in the woods travels at night. Everything is awake and moving. Yet, how silently. The shores of the lake rose up into the sky by gentle slopes, and from the shadows of the remoter shore came occasionally the splash of an otter or the wet patter of a mink running along over the stones. Once or twice we distinctly heard a deer drinking; but the noises of our heavier game were not yet audible. Men hunt moose often for days and days in this country without getting even a "smell of one." A New York man, who for years has sought his favourite game in these regions, told me that one season he spent seven weeks here—"hard huntin', you bet, it was, too!"—without seeing a single animal. As I sat cold and shivering in the cramped canoe, passed some of the time working out mathematically the chances that a moose would, or would not, come our way. Millions of square acres, thousands of lakes to drink at, miles of forest—and, then how many moose? My companion interrupted my calculations by pointing to the other shore. Had he heard something, and could so huge a beast move so stealthily? No! It was not a moose. The moon was rising, that was all; and we should soon have to change our position and shift into the shadow. A single motion of the paddle accomplished this, and we glided under the lee of the other shore, with no sound but the rustle of the man's coat-sleeve and the drip-drip of the paddle, as he drew it shining and wet in the moonlight from the water.

As the moon rose over the hill, the shadows deepened along the shores, though retreating a little, and the air seemed to grow colder. A flood of silver light shone on the flat surface of that sea of trees opposite; but behind us we could see nothing at all. It was too dark to distinguish even one tree-trunk from another. Now and then a wave of cooler, richer air seemed to breathe out upon us from the deep recesses at our backs, bringing scents of moss and bark and pine-needles and all that is sweet and good in the heart of the woods. Distant sounds, too, faint and muffled, reached our ears, and kept the blood tingling. I was too excited to feel sleepy. Every minute I thought the hum of indistinct murmurs would grow louder and differentiate itself into the tread of hoofs, the breaking of boughs, the crashing of saplings. Every instant I thought those immense shadows, that foregathered and waxed and waned on the farther shore, would suddenly step forth into the moonlight and assume the shape of a great animal with spreading horns. But the hours passed, and the moon crossed over to the other side, and the stars began to fade. Already the eastern sky was beginning to.... Hark! What was that? A sound like the cracking of distant branches trembled on the air and died away. Presently it was repeated, again, and again. Something was coming at last. It is needless to say what our emotions were, after the long cold night, when we distinctly heard the animals—for there were several—breaking through the underbrush at the far end of the lake and coming out to drink.

A confused mass, a big moving shadow, was all we saw. It was too far away, and the light was too uncertain. Crack, crack, went the rifles, and when the echoes had subsided, we heard the whole hillside crashing to a mighty tread as the moose thundered away at full speed.... And that was our last chance. Soon the sun was up, and after visiting the drinking-place and inspecting the deep hoof-marks, we dragged wearily home the twelve miles to hot coffee and fried trout.

It was a pleasant camp we had there beneath the slender silver birches on the point of a sandy little promontory. On one side was the sandy bay sacred to the men, and in a little cove on the other side the solitary lady-hunter of the party was supposed to disport herself matutinally in the cold waters. As a matter of fact, it was generally believed that she preferred a basin of hot water in the tent; and towards the end of our stay, when it grew really cold, her husband was brought round without difficulty to her view of the situation. The point of the promontory was kept for the guides, though it must be recorded to their honour that they made no ablutionary use of it, and that the deep pools seemed to them better fitted for cleaning the fish and partridges in. From our tent-doors we looked straight down seven miles of blue Cogawanna water. Soon the surface would be a solid sheet of ice, over two feet thick, and covered with snow; but then it was dancing and alive, full of fish, and warm enough even in October to make an occasional swim enjoyable. Cogawanna was a Chippewa Indian who died about 1860, and was buried on a little pine-clad island at the far end of the lake, and in the centre of his favourite fishing-grounds. A grave marks the spot. At its head stands a rude wooden slab in which some one (I never could ascertain who) annually cuts a little deeper the wooden cross. The island just appears in the centre of my tent, and fills its narrow opening as I lie in bed. Cogawanna's grave, too, has its mystery and pathos.

Our guides were thorough woodsmen, hunters by instinct as well as experience, and skilled in all branches of woodcraft. They could build a canoe, carve a yoke for the shoulders to carry it on, or fashion a "dug-out" boat from a log with equal facility. They never get lost as long as they are provided with a compass; and a small axe hanging from the belt, which also holds a hunting-knife, is their chief tool and weapon. They profess contempt for the French-Canadian guides as well as for the Indians. The former are lazy and too often dishonest. Moreover, they have indifferent lasting powers. The Indians, on the other hand, as guides, are untrustworthy in another sense. They are paid by the day, and the longer the trip lasts the more money they make. The consequence is, they keep their hunting-party a safe distance from the game as long as possible. It is always the next day or the day after that they promise to discover it. In this way the inexperienced hunter who relies upon their tender mercies often goes home with a poor bag—just enough to keep up the Indian's reputation (and therefore income) as a game-finder—when he might have had twice the sport. The Indians then report as quickly as possible to the nearest station of the Hudson's Bay Company where the game are lying, and receive orders to go out again and bring back the hides and furs, for which they of course are paid commissions. As guides they generally are paid, with the French Canucks, six shillings a-day. Our men, who came from the Adirondack Mountains (New York State), received twice as much; and they enjoyed the hunting as much as we did!

They are rarely willing, however, to go on an expedition into the woods without plenty of whisky. Our chief guide, as soon as we got into camp, made a "cache" of the bottles somewhere in the dense brush behind the tents, and thus controlled the quantity consumed. The other fellows never knew where it was.

When more was wanted he would only get it at night. Taking a lantern, he would pretend to search among the trees for ten minutes or more, and though the others watched him carefully from a distance, they never could tell when or where he picked it up. Yet he always returned with a bottle.

There was a spawning-bed just opposite our camp, and the speckled and salmon trout fairly swarmed over it. The water was shallow and covered a nice sandy bottom. At night, when the moon was on the water, it was a sight worth observing to see the hundreds of scaly backs sliding and slithering over one another just beneath the surface. A sudden spurt in the canoe often brought the fish knocking and tumbling against its thin sides. The paddles struck them at every stroke.

There were wolves in the neighbourhood, and the lady of the party, an unerring shot and enthusiastic hunter, held these creatures in special abhorrence. She hated to hear them bark. Several nights running some animal had been heard sniffing and snuffing round their tent. The ground was too bare and hard to leave any tracks, and the opinion was divided between a wolf, a bear, and a porcupine. "It seems to be a largish animal," she said.

Just as I was dozing off one night, after a hard day's hunting, I heard voices in the tent next to me.

"There's that thing again," in the lady's voice. "You must get up and see what it is."

"Oh! It's nothing but a silly porcupine," growled the husband. It was a cold night, and those camp-beds are warm and cosy, besides being hard to remake.

"But it's trying to get in."

"That's no reason why I should get out, though." However, the lady thought it was, so after a few more growls he got out of bed, and peeped through the opening of the tent. The moon shone brightly, but only served to make the shadows beneath the trees the darker.

"Take the gun."

"I've got it. Give me the lantern. I hope the beast won't go for my legs, whatever it is."

"Put on your top-boots, then."

A sound of laughter came from the guides' tent beyond. Evidently they were listening as attentively as I was. There were manifold sounds of preparation, and in due course the brave husband, in pyjamas, top-boots, red woollen nightcap, and pea-jacket, issued forth into the cold night. The lantern swung over his arm, and the loaded rifle was pointed. His footsteps were soon lost in the silence, and I lay and listened in my sleeping-bag, praying devoutly that he would not aim hastily and send a bullet whizzing through my canvas or my skin. Suddenly there was a shout, "I see it" and the next instant the rifle cracked. "It's a skunk!" he cried with a roar of laughter. And that's all it was. But the guides thought a good deal of that skunk. The wind was blowing in their direction, and the whole benefit of the penetrating and offensive odour of that otherwise harmless little animal was wafted into their tent. They got up and burned the body—but you cannot burn the stink of a skunk. The language of the guides at intervals during the night was fully as picturesque as the other surroundings of our camp.

Down the Danube in a Canadian Canoe

I.

It was a brilliant day in early June when we launched our canoe on the waters of the Danube, not one hundred yards from its source in the Black Forest, and commenced our journey of four and twenty hundred miles to the Black Sea. Two weeks before we had sent her from London to Donaueschingen by freight, and when the railway-company telegraphed the word arrived we posted after her with tent, kit-bags, blankets, cameras, and cooking-apparatus.

Donaueschingen is an old-fashioned little town on the southern end of the Schwarzwald plateau, and the railway that runs through it brings it apparently no nearer to the world. It breathes a spirit of remoteness and tranquillity born of the forests that encircle it, and that fill the air with pleasant odours and gentle murmurings.

There, lying snugly on a shelf in the goods-shed, we found our slender craft, paddles and boat-hook tied securely to the thwarts,—and without a crack! "No duty to pay," said the courteous official, after examining an enormous book, "and only seventeen marks for freight-charges the whole way from Oxford." She was sixteen feet long (with a beam of thirty-four inches), and had the slim graceful lines and deep curved ribs of the true Rice Lake (Ontario) build. Two or three inches would float her, and yet she could ride safely at top speed over the waves of a rapid that would have capsized a boat twice her size. Splendid little craft, she bore us faithfully and well, almost like a thing of life and intelligence, round many a ticklish corner and under more than one dangerous bridge, though this article will only outline some of our adventures in her over the first thousand miles as far as Budapest.

From the yard of the Schuetzen Inn, where she lay all night, we carried her on our shoulders below the picturesque stone bridge and launched her in a pool where the roach and dace fairly made the water dance. You could toss a stone over the river here without an effort, and when we had said farewell to the kindly villagers and steered out into mid-stream, there was so little water that the stroke of the paddle laid bare the shining pebbles upon the bottom and grated along the bed.

"Happy journey!" cried the townsfolk standing on the bank in blue trousers and waving their straw hats. "And quick return," added the hotel-keeper, who had overcharged us abominably in every possible item. We bore him little malice, however, for there were no inns or hotel-bills ahead of us; and uncommonly light-hearted were we as the canoe felt the stream move beneath her and slipped away at a good speed down the modest little river that must drop twenty-two hundred feet before it pours its immense volume through three arms into the Black Sea.

At first our progress was slow. Patches of white weeds everywhere choked the river and often brought us to a complete standstill, and in less than ten minutes we were aground in a shallow. We had to tuck up our trousers and wade. This was a frequent occurrence during the day and we soon realised that the hundred and twenty-five miles to Ulm, before the tributaries commence to pour in their icy floods from the Alps, would be slow and difficult. But what of that? It was glorious summer weather; the mountain airs were intoxicating, and the scenery charming beyond words. Nowhere that day was the river more than forty yards across, or over three feet deep. The white weeds lay over the surface like thick cream, but the canoe glided smoothly over them, swishing as she passed. Her slim nose opened a pathway that her stern left gently hissing with bubbles as the leaves rose again to the surface; and behind us there was ever a little milk-white track in which the blossoms swam and danced in the sunshine as the current raced merrily along the new channel thus made for it.

Winding in and out among broad fields and acres of reeds we dropped gently down across the great plateau of the Black Forest mountains. The day was hot and clear, and overhead a few white clouds sailed with us, as it were for company's sake, down the blue reaches of the sky. Usually we coasted along the banks, the reeds touching the sides of the canoe and the wind playing over hosts of nodding flowers and fields level to our eyes with standing hay, while, in the distance, the mountain-slopes, speckled with blue shadows, were ever opening into new vistas and valleys. Here the peaceful Danube still dreams, lying in her beauty-sleep as it were, and with no hint of the racing torrent that comes later with full waking. Pretty villages appeared along the banks at intervals. Pforen was the first, snugly gathered into the nook of the hills; a church, a few red-roofed houses, a wooden bridge, and a castle with a fine stork staring down at us from her nest in the ruined tower. The peasants were away in the fields and we drifted lazily by without so much as a greeting. Neidingen was the second, where a huge crucifix presided over the centre of the quaint bridge, and where we landed to buy butter, potatoes, and onions. Gutmadingen was the third; and here a miller and his men helped our portage over the weir while his wife stood in the hot sunshine and asked questions.

"Where are you going to?"

"The Black Sea." She had never heard of it, and evidently thought we were making fun of her. "Ulm, then," Ah! Ulm she knew. "But it's an enormous distance! And is the tent for rain?" she asked.

"No; for sleeping in at night."

"*Ach, was!*" she exclaimed. "Well, I wouldn't sleep a night in that tent, or go a yard in that boat, for anything you could give me."

The miller was more appreciative. He gave us a delicious drink,—a sort of mead, which was most refreshing and which, he assured us, would not affect the head in the least—and told us there were twenty-four more weirs before we reached Ulm, the beginning of navigation. But none the less he, too, had his questions to ask.

"I thought all the Englishmen had gone to the war. The papers here say that England is quite empty."

The temptation was too great to resist. "No," we said gravely, "only the big ones went to the war. [We were both over six feet.] England is still full of men of the smaller sizes like ourselves." The expression on his face lightened our work considerably for the next mile.

Soon after the river left the plateau behind it and took a sudden leap into the Donauthal. We shot round a corner about six o'clock and came upon a little willow-island in midstream. Here we landed and pitched our tent on the long grass, made a fire, peeled the onions, fried our strips of beef with the potatoes, and made excellent tea. On all sides the pines crept down close into the narrowing valley. In the evening sunlight, with long shadows slanting across the hills, we smoked our pipes after our meal. There were no flies and the air was cool and sweet. Presently the moon rose over the ridge of forest behind us and the lights of Immendingen, twinkling through the shadows, were just visible a mile below us. The night was cool and the river hurried almost silently past our tent door. When at length we went to bed, on cork mattresses with india-rubber sheets under us and thick Austrian blankets over us, everything was sopping with dew.

The bells of Immendingen coming down the valley were the first sounds we heard as we went to bathe at seven o'clock next morning in the cold sparkling water; and later, when we scrambled over the great Immendingen weir no villagers came to look on and say *"Engländer, Engländer,"* for it was Sunday morning and they were all at mass.

The valley grew narrower and limestone cliffs shone white through the sombre forests. It was very lonely between the villages. The river, now sixty yards wide, swept in great semi-circular reaches under the very shadow of the hills; storks stood about fishing in the shallows; wild swans flew majestically in front of us,—we came across several nests with eggs—and duck were plentiful everywhere. Once, in an open space on the hills, we saw a fine red fox motionless in his observation of some duck,—and ourselves. Presently he trotted away into the cover of the woods and the ducks quacked their thanks to us. Then suddenly, above Möhringen, just when we were congratulating ourselves that wading was over for good, the river dwindled away into a thin trickling line of water that showed the shape of every single pebble in its bed. We went aground continually. Half the Danube had escaped through fissures in the ground. It comes out again, on the other side of the mountains, as the river Ach, and flows into the Lake of Constance. The river was now less in volume than when we started, clear as crystal, dancing in the sunshine, weaving like a silver thread through the valley, and making delightful music over the stones. Yet most of our journey that day was wading. Trousers were always tucked up to the knees, and we had to be ready to jump out at a moment's notice. Before the numberless little rapids the question was: "Is there enough water to float us? Can we squeeze between those rocks? Is that wave a hidden stone, or merely the current?" The steersman stood up to get a better view of the channel and avoid the sun's glare on the water, and in this way we raced down many a bit of leaping, hissing water; and, incidentally, had many a sudden shock before the end, tumbling out headlong, banging against stones, and shipping water all the time. The canoe got sadly scratched, and we decided at length to risk no more of these baby-rapids. A torn canoe in the Black Forest, miles from a railway, spelt helplessness. Thereafter we waded the rapids. It was a hot and laborious process,—the feet icy cold, the head burning hot, and the back always bent double. Weirs, too, became frequent, and unloading and reloading was soon reduced to a science. In the afternoon the villagers poured out to stare and look on. They rarely offered to help, but stood round as close as possible while we unloaded, examining articles, and asking questions all the time. They had no information to give. Few of them knew anything of the river ten miles below their particular village, and none had ever been to Ulm. Now and then there was a sceptical *"Dass ist unmöglich* (that's impossible)," when we mentioned Ulm as our goal. *"Ach je!* They're mad, — in *that* boat!"

From Donaueschingen to Ulm there is a weir in every five miles, and our progress was slow. Whenever the river grew deep we learned to know that a dam was near; and below a dam there was scarcely enough water to float an egg-shell. But there was no occasion to hurry; everything was done in leisurely fashion in this great garden of Würtemburg, and most of the villages were sound asleep. At Möhhringen, indeed, we got the impression that the village had slept for at least a hundred years and that our bustling arrival had suddenly awakened it. It lay in a clearing of the forest, in a charming mossy bed that no doubt made sleep a delightful necessity. The miller invited us to the inn, where we found a score of peasants in their peaked hats and black suits of broadcloth sitting each in front of a foaming tankard; but they drank so slowly that a hundred years did not seem too long to finish a tankard. There was very little conversation, and they stared unconscionably, bowing gravely when we ordered their stone mugs to be refilled and regarding us all the time with steady, expressionless interest. In due time, however, they digested us, and then the stream of inevitable questions burst forth.

"You bivouac? You go to the sea? *If* you ever get to Ulm! You have come the whole way from London in *that* shell!"

We gulped down the excellent cold beer and hurried away. The river dwindled to a width of a dozen yards and wading was incessant. We lightened the canoe as much as possible, but, our kit having been already reduced to what seemed only strictly necessary, there was little enough to throw away,—a tin plate, a tin cup, a fork, a spoon, a knife, and a red cushion. These we piled up in a little mound upon the bank with a branch stuck in the ground to draw attention. I wonder who is now using those costly articles.

Another series of picturesque villages glided past us: Tuttlingen, famous (as the dirty water proclaimed) for its tanneries, and where a couple of hundred folk in their Sunday clothes watched our every movement as we climbed round two high and difficult weirs; Nendringen, where a kind and silent miller gave us of his cool mead; Mülheim straggling half-way up the hills with its red-brown roofs and church and castle all mingled together in most picturesque confusion, as if it had slipped down from the summit and never got straight again; and Friedigen, where we laid in fresh supplies, and found two Germans who had spent years in California, and whose nasal voices sounded strangely out of place among their guttural neighbours. "Camp anywheres you please," they said, "and no one'll objec' to your fires so long as you put 'em out."

I forget how many more villages ending in *ingen* we passed; but now that the heat of the day, and the labour and toil of wading are forgotten, they come before me again with their still, peaceful loveliness like a string of quaint jewels strung along the silver thread of the river.

Soon the water increased and the canoe sped onwards among the little waves and rapids like a winged thing. The mountains became higher, the valley narrower. Limestone cliffs, scooped and furrowed by the eddies of a far larger Danube thousands of years before, rose gleaming out of the pine-woods about their base. We plunged in among the Swabian Alps, and the river tumbled very fast and noisily along a rock-strewn bed. It darted across from side to side, almost as though the cliffs were tossing it across in play to each other. One moment we were in blazing sunlight, the next in deep shadow under the cliffs. There was no room for houses, and no need for bridges; boats we never saw; big, grey fish-hawks, circling buzzards, storks by the score had this part of the river all to themselves.

Suddenly we turned a sharp corner and shot at full speed into an immense cauldron. It was a perfect circle, half a mile in diameter, bound in by the limestone cliffs. The more ancient river had doubtless filled it with a terrifying whirlpool, for the rocks were strangely scooped and eaten into curves hundreds of feet above us. But now its bottom was a clean flat field, where the little stream, with its audacious song, whipped along at the very foot of the cliffs on one side of the circle.

It was a lonely secluded spot, the very place for a camp. Though only five o'-clock on a June afternoon the cliffs kept out the sunshine. We sank the canoe, to soak up cracks and ease strained ribs, and soon had our tent up, and a fire burning. Then we climbed the cliffs. It was a puzzle to see how the river got in or got out. As we climbed we came across deep recesses and funnel-shaped holes, caves with spiral openings in the roof, and pillars shaped like an hourglass. Across the gulf the ruined castle of Kallenberg stood on a point of rock that was apparently inaccessible, and when the evening star shone over its broken battlements, it might well have been a ghostly light held aloft by the shades of the robber-barons who once lived in it. When we went to bed at ten o'clock the full moon shone upon the white cliffs with a dazzling brilliance that seemed to turn them into ice, while the deep shadows over the river made the scene strangely impressive. Only the tumbling of the water and the chirping of the crickets broke the silence. In the night we woke and thought we heard people moving round the tent, but, on going out to see, the canoe was still safe, and the white moonshine revealed no figures. It was doubtless the river talking in its sleep, or the wind wandering lost among the bushes.

At five o'clock next morning I looked out of the tent and found our cauldron full of seething mist through which the sunshine was just beginning to force a way. An hour later the tent was too hot for comfort.

All day we followed the gorge, with many a ruined castle of impregnable position looking down upon us from the cliffs. The valley widened about noon, and fields ablaze with poppies lay in the sun, while tall yellow flags fringed the widening river. In another great circle, similar in formation to that of Kallenberg, but five times as large, we found the monastery of Beuron with its eighty monks and fifty lay-brothers. We bathed and put on our celluloid collars (full dress in an outfit where weight is of supreme importance) and went up to the gates. A bearded monk, acting as door-keeper, thrust a smiling face through the wicket in answer to our summons and informed us with genuine courtesy that the monastery was not open to visitors at this time of year.

"There are many visitors in summer, I regret," he explained.

"Visitors! How do they get here?"

"By road; they come from long distances, driving and walking."

"But we may never be here again; we are on our way to the Black Sea."

"Ah, then you will see far more wonderful things than this in your journey." He remained firm; so, by way of consolation we went to the Gasthaus Zur Zonne and enjoyed a meal,—the first for a week that we had not cooked ourselves.

It was a quiet, out-of-the-world spot. Monks were everywhere working in the fields, ploughing and haymaking; and it was here I first saw sheep following a shepherd. A curious covered bridge, lined with crucifixes, crossed the river, and we took an interesting photograph of a monk in a black straw hat and gown going over it with a cloud of dust in the blazing sunshine followed by fifty sheep. There was contentment on all faces, but the place must be dreadfully lonely and desolate in winter. We bought immense loaves in the monks' bakery, and matches, cigars, sugar, and meat in a *devotionshandlung* (store for religious articles)!

Sigmaringen, with its old rock-perched castle and its hundred turrets gleaming in the sun, was reached just in time to find shelter from a thunderstorm that seemed to come out of a clear sky. There was a hurricane of wind, and the rain filled the quaint old streets with dashing spray. In an hour it cleared away, and we pushed on again; but the river had meanwhile risen nearly a foot. The muddy water rushed by with turbulent eddies, and the bridges were crowded with people to see us pass. They stood in silent dark rows without gesture or remark, and stared.

Suddenly the storm broke again with redoubled fury. Up went their umbrellas, and we heard their guttural laughter. In a few minutes we were soaked, and no doubt cut a sorry figure as we launched the canoe at the foot of the big weir and vanished into the gathering darkness. We swirled between the pillars of another bridge in sheets of rain and the outlook for a dry camp and a fire was decidedly poor. It was after nine o'clock when we landed in despair under a clump of trees on the left bank, and found to our delight that they concealed a solitary wedge of limestone cliff, and that in this cliff there was an arch, and under that arch a quantity of dry wood. A fire was soon blazing in the strip under the arch,—some three feet wide—and the tent stood beneath the dripping trees. Our waterproof sheets and cork mattresses kept us dry, though all night the rain poured down, while outside we could hear the swollen river rushing past with a seething roar.

Next day the rapids began in earnest. Rapids are to canoeers what fences are to fox-hunters. The first wave curls over in front of the canoe, there is a hiss and a bump, a slap of wet spray in the face, and then the canoe leaps under you and rushes headlong. At Riedlingen, while carrying the canoe across a slippery weir, we fell, boat and all, into the deep hole below the fall, luckily with no worse result than a wetting, for our kit was safely piled upon the bank. At Dietfurt we went into an apparently deserted village to buy milk, but the moment we entered the street it became alive. From every door poured men and women gaping, and the moment they spied the little yellow canoe upon the shore they rushed down in a flock shouting *"E' schiff! E' schiff!"* But, if they ran fast, we ran faster, and were off before the terrible onslaught of questions had even begun. The milk was a mere detail.

At Gutenstein, where we camped in a hay-field, the mowers woke us at dawn, peering into the mouth of the tent. But they made no objections and merely said *"Gruss Gott"* and *"Gute Reise;"* and for an hour afterwards I heard their scythes musically in my dreams as they cut a pathway for us to the river.

At Obermarchsthal we left the mountains behind us, and with them, too, the memory of a pathetic figure. As we landed to go up to the little inn for eggs, an old man, leaning on a stick, hobbled down to meet us. His white hair escaped in disorder from beneath a peaked blue hat, and he wore a suit of a curious checked pattern that seemed wholly out of keeping with the dress of the country. At first, when he spoke, I could not understand him, and asked him in German to repeat his remarks.

"He's talking English," said my companion. "Can't you hear?" And English it was. He invited us up to the inn and told us his story over a mug of beer.

"This is my native village. I was born and raised here, and sixty years ago I ran away from Germany to escape military service. I went to the United States and settled finally in Alabama. I had a shop in Mobile, down South in a nigger town, and as soon as I was ready I wrote to the girl I left here to come out to me. She came and we were married. I've had two wives since out there. Now they're all buried in a little churchyard outside Mobile. And this is the first time I've been back in sixty years," he went on after a gulp of beer. "The village ain't changed one single bit. I feel as though I'd been sleepin' and sorter dreamin' all the while.... The shop's sold and I'm takin' a last look round at the ole place. There's only one or two that remembers me, but I was born and raised here, and this is where I had my first love, and the place is full of memories, just chock full. No, I ain't a goin' to live here. I'm goin' back to the States nex' month, so as I can die there and lie beside the others in the cemetery at Mobile."

The country became flatter and the mountains were soon a blue line on the horizon behind us. At Opfingen we crossed our last weir, and among the clouds in front of us saw the spire of Ulm cathedral, the tallest in the world. A fierce current swept us past banks fringed with myrtle bushes, poppies, and yellow flags. Poplars rose in lines over the country, bending their heads in the wind, and we camped at eight o'clock in a wood about a mile above the town. While dinner was cooking a dog rushed barking up to us followed by three men with guns. They were evidently German Jäger. Two of them were dressed like pattern plates out of a tailor's guide to sportsmen,—in spotless gaiters, pointed hats with feathers (like stage Tyrolese), guns with the latest slings, and silver whistles slung on coloured cord round their necks. They examined the canoe first, and then came up and examined us. One of them, who was probably the proprietor of the land, a surly gruff fellow, had evidently made up his mind that we were poachers. And I must admit that at first sight there was ground for suspicion, for no poacher could possibly have found fault with our appearance.

"What are you doing here?" he asked.

"Preparing to camp for the night," we told him.

"When are you going on?"

"We intend to go into Ulm in the morning."

"Where do you come from; are you Englishmen?"

"Yes; we come from London."

"*Ach was!*" (they all say *Ach was* when they want to be witheringly scornful). "In *that* egg-shell?"

"Certainly."

"And where are you going to?"

"Odessa."

They exchanged glances. "Evidently madmen, and not poachers," said the face of the man with the biggest silver whistle plainer than any words could have spoken it. "Do you know these are private preserves?" was the next question.

"No." My friend, a keen sportsman, sheltered himself scowling behind his alleged ignorance of German, (somehow he always knew our conversation afterwards to a word); but the penny whistle and the immaculate costume of the hunters in a scrubby wood where not even a rabbit lived, excited him to explosions of laughter which he concealed by frequent journeys to the tent.

"What's in that tent?"

"Beds." The *chasseurs* and the keeper went to examine, while the dog sniffed about everywhere. Our beds were not then untied, and the sportsman untied them; but they found only blankets and cork mattresses.

"You have no guns, or dogs, or fishing rods?" We shook our heads sulkily. "And you are only travelling peacefully for pleasure?"

"We are trying to," we said meekly.

"Then you may sleep here if you go on again to-morrow; but don't go into the woods after game." Then the men moved off. Doubtless they were right to ask questions, yet we were so obviously travellers. "Still, our weather-worn appearance and unshaved faces probably made us look more than a little doubtful," quoth my friend, who himself wore a slouch hat that did not add to the candour of his expression.

In the middle of dinner the men suddenly returned from another angle of the wood and examined everything afresh. We offered them some tea in a tin cup which they declined; and at last after watching us at our meal in silence for ten minutes they moved off, evidently still suspicious. Thereafter we always knew them as the *chasseurs*. They were not the only pests, however. Mosquitoes appeared later,—our first—and that night we slept behind the mosquito-netting we had so carefully fitted to the mouth of the tent when we first erected it weeks before in the garden of a London square. During the night someone prowled about the tent. We heard twigs snapping and the footsteps among the bushes; but neither of us troubled ourselves to get up. If they took the canoe, they'd be drowned; and our other only valuables (a celluloid collar apiece, a clean suit for the big towns, and a map,) were safely inside the tent.

In the morning we shaved and washed carefully, and put on our full dress for the benefit of Ulm. We intended to paddle down quietly and stop at the Rowing Club wharf of which we had read; according to the map it was a mile, and the current easy and pleasant. We wished our entrance to be sober and in good taste.

The best-laid plans, however, will sometimes go amiss when you're canoeing on the Danube. We were half way when we heard a roar like a train rushing over a hollow bridge. It grew louder every minute. In front of us the water danced and leaped, and before we knew what had happened we were plunging about among foaming waves and flying past the banks at something more than ten miles an hour.

"It's the Iller," cried my friend as the paddle was nearly wrested from his grasp. "It's marked on the map just about here."

It was the Iller. It had come in at an acute angle after running almost parallel with us for a little distance. It tumbled in at headlong speed, with an icy, tur-

bulent flood of muddy water, and it gave the sedate Danube an impetus that it
did not lose for another hundred miles below Ulm. For a space the two rivers
declined to mingle. The noisy, dirty Iller, fresh from the Alps, kept to the right
bank, going twice as fast as its more dignified companion on the left. A distinct
line (as though drawn by a rope) divided them, in colour, speed, and height,—
the Iller remaining for a long time at least half an inch above the level of the
Danube. At length they mingled more freely and swept us down upon Ulm in
a torrent of rough, racing water. Our leisurely dignified entrance into Ulm was,
like the suspicions of the *chasseurs*, a structure built on insufficient knowledge,
a mere dream. Ulm lies on a curve of the river. Big bridges with nasty thick pillars (and whirlpools, therefore, behind them) stand at both entrance and exit.
How we raced under the first bridge I shall never forget. We were half way
through the town, with the wet spray still on our cheeks, before the sound of
the gurgling eddies below the bridge had ceased behind us. Where, oh, where
was the friendly wharf of that Danube Rowing Club? The second bridge rose
before us. There were crested waves under its arches. Already Ulm was almost
a thing of the past; yet we had hoped to spend at least a week exploring its beauties.

"There it is," cried my friend in the bows, "on the left bank! That old
board,—see it? That's the wharf."

We managed to turn in mid current and point the canoe up-stream. Then, by
paddling as hard as we could, we dropped down past the wharf at a pace that
just enabled us to grasp the rings in the boards and come to a standstill. You'll
never forget Ulm if you arrive there, as we did, in a canoe, when the Iller is in
flood.

II.

We spent a week in the quaint old town of Ulm, but our adventures there have
properly no part in our journey down the river. Only, in passing, I must mention the courtesy of the Danube Rowing Club. Fritz Miller (who rowed at Hen-
ley in 1900 for the Diamond Sculls) is the leading spirit in a list of members who
showed us all possible kindness. They housed and mended our canoe, varnished
it afresh, and gave us better maps. The secret charms of picturesque Ulm unknown to the tourist were shown to us; and in the evenings we used to meet for
music and supper in a quaint little club-room that hangs half of its Roman ma-
sonry over the rushing river.

Here the navigation of the Danube (such as it is) is said to begin. The fierce
current allows no boats or steamers, but immense barges (called *Ulmer
schachtel*) laden with merchandise, are floated down the current to the Bavarian towns below. On arrival they are sold for lumber, the return journey being
impossible.

The Rowing Club takes out eights and fours. Rowing with all their might they move two miles an hour against the current; and it may well be imagined that, with this training, they are well nigh the first rowing club in Germany.

There was a great deal of rain while we were in Ulm and we started again on a rapidly rising river, full of floating rubbish, and rushing at a pace that made it a pleasure merely to stand and watch it from the bank. The Bavarian bank (Ulm is on the frontier line of Bavaria and Würtemburg) displayed black signboards with the kilometers marked in white. We timed our speed by one of Benson's chronometers and found it to be over twelve miles an hour. It was like travelling over a smooth road behind fast horses. My note-book gives an average day, the day, for instance, we left Ulm.

June 19th. The members of the Rowing Club came down in force to see us off at eleven o'clock. Flags were flying in our honour and we heard the men shouting *glückliche Reise* as we shot the middle arch of the bridge on the waves of a rather nasty rapid. The bridge was lined with people, but we only faintly heard their cries for the thunder of the waves. This exceedingly rapid water makes awkward currents as it swirls round the pillars of the big bridges. Behind the arches are always whirlpools, which twist you sideways and toss you from them with ridiculous ease. A wrong turn of the steering paddle and the canoe would be sucked in instead of thrown out, and then—! At a little distance below the bridge the eddies of the whirlpool from adjacent pillars meet in a series of crested waves. The only safe channel lies exactly in the middle. The canoe rises, slaps down again, all its length a-quiver; the first wave breaks under the bows and some of the water comes in, but before enough is shipped to be dangerous the frail craft rises again with a leap to the next wave. Then the race begins. The least wrong twist to left or right and the waves break sideways into the canoe and down she goes. It takes so little water to sink a laden canoe.

To-day, for the first time, we heard the famous song of the Danube,—famous at least to us who had read of it in so many different accounts. It is a hissing, seething sound which rises everywhere from the river. You think steam must be escaping somewhere, or soda-water fizzing out from an immense syphon among the woods on the banks. It is said to be the friction of the pebbles along the bed of the river, caused by the terrific speed of so great a body of water. Under the canoe it made a peculiar buzzing sound accompanied by a distinct vibration of the thin bass-wood on which we knelt.

We swept through Bavaria much faster than we wished, but it was impossible to go slowly. The river communicated something of its hurry to ourselves, and in my mind the journey now presents itself something in the form of a se-ries of brilliant cineomatographs. Delightful were our lunches at the quaint inns of remote villages—black bread, sausage, and such beer!—Lauingen, a town of the sixteenth century, where the spokesman of the crowd said, "I suppose you're both single;" Donauwörth, in a paradise of wild flowers, where the Lech tears in on the right with leaping waves; Neuberg, with a dangerous stone bridge and the worst rapids we had yet encountered. Then a long stretch where the swamps ceased and the woods began to change. Instead of endless willows we had pine, oak, sycamore, birch, and poplar. The river was a mile wide with out-lets into lagoons, like Norfolk Broads, that ran parallel with us for miles and were probably empty mud flats at low water. Fishing-nets were hanging up to dry along the shore, and hay lay sunning itself on the narrow strips of the banks. We passed Ingolstadt, a military post, and then the river dipped down before us into blue hills and we came to Vohburg,—destroyed by the Swiss in 1641, and now, apparently, nothing but a collection of quaint chimneys and storks' nests—and, soon after it, Eining, near Abusina, a Roman frontier station established fifteen years before our era. Trajan's wall crossed the river near here and extended north as far as Wiesbaden.

Then the river narrowed between precipitous limestone cliffs and we entered the gorge of Kehlheim. At its very mouth, between impregnable rocks, lay the monastery of Weltenburg, the oldest in Bavaria. The river sweeping round a bend into the rocky jaws made landing difficult; but we accomplished it, and entered the old courtyard through an iron gate with graceful stone pillars. There were everywhere signs of neglect and decay. The monks' quarters formed one side of the square and the church another; a third side was a wall of rock; the fourth was the river. It was secluded, peaceful beyond description, ab-solutely out of the world. The air was cool, the shadows deep. Fruit-trees grew in the court-yard, and monks (there were only thirteen in all) in black gowns were piling up wood for the winter. A priest was intoning vespers in the church, which boasted a beautiful organ, marble altars, and elaborate carving of the usual gilded sort. The sunshine filled the painted air. Outside over the neglected walls crept vines, and at the far end of the courtyard a wild rose-tree, covered with sweet-smelling blossoms, grew at the foot of crumbling stone steps that led under shady trees to a chapel perched on the cliffs. We toiled up in the heat and were rewarded by a glorious view; from above the monastery was shut in like a nest between river and cliffs.

Later in the day we were driven by a violent thunderstorm to the first land-ing-place we could find. It was a few miles below Weltenburg in the very heart of the gorge. With surprising good fortune we found a cave leading deep into the mountain, and in less than ten minutes we were dry and snug before a fire burning cheerfully for dinner. It was a strange camp,—the storm howling outside and the firelight dancing down behind us into the interior of the cave, which was unnecessarily full of bats.

At Ratisbon, the Castra Regina of the Romans, we were solemnly warned not to attempt to pass under the bridge. "The whirlpools are savage," they told us. "Of the seven arches of this six-hundred-year-old bridge, all but one are forbidden by the police." Leaving the canoe half a mile above we landed and walked down the shore to examine. "Boats *have* gone through," said a pompous man on the bridge as he pointed out the worst places to us, "but even if they got under the arch they have always been sucked in *there!*" He pointed to a white seething circle of water. "You'll never get through that in your cockle-shell, and you'll be arrested even if you do."

"Arrested,—how?" we asked. By way of answer he raised his eyebrows and held up a fat hand in eloquent warning. However, we carefully selected our channel from the bridge, and twenty minutes later were coming down stream towards the arches as cautiously as our speed would permit. People ran along the shore waving their hats and shouting to us to stop. The bridge in front was black with the crowd waiting to see the *verrückte Engländer* upset. We reached the arch and recognised our channel. The water dropped suddenly in front of us and the canoe dipped her nose with it. We were off. The bank and the shouting people flew past us in a black streak. I was just able to recognise one man, our pompous friend, standing below the bridge shading his eyes with his hand, evidently determined to get the best view possible. The roar of voices dwindled behind us into a murmur and a minute later we were out of sight; Ratisbon, bridge, whirlpools, and townsfolk were things of the past. We were not arrested, but perhaps the police are still trying to catch us.

After this came a dull spell as we crossed the great wheat-plain of Bavaria, winding for two days with many curves and little current. Every morning here the workers in the fields woke us early, and praised the boat, and asked us the usual questions, and told us the usual falsehoods about the depth of the river, the distances of the towns, the floods of past years, and all the rest of it. We made no halt at Straubing (Servio Durum of the Romans), or at Deggendorf where the Isar adds its quota of mountain-gathered waters.

Another day was very dismal,—cold showers and storms of wind following one upon another. We crouched under bridges, trees, and anything else that gave cover, paddling fast between the squalls to keep ourselves warm. The plain of Straubing affords little shelter. Towards evening, however, the river made a welcome turn towards the mountains, and we camped on a high bank among clumps of willows with thick woods behind them. New potatoes, dried prunes, and onions in the stew-pot were points of light in a gusty and otherwise dismal meal. We pegged the tent inside and out. All night the wind tore at it, howling; but a gipsy-tent never comes down. The wind sweeps over it, and finding an ever lessening angle of resistance, only drives it more firmly into the ground.

Gradually, now, we were passing out of the lonely portions of the upper river. The country was becoming more populated; larger towns were near; railway-bridges spanned the river; steamers and tugs raced down, and toiled up it.

A few miles above Passau we camped on an island, and were visited by an inquisitive peasant, who saw our fire and came over from the mainland in a punt. "Are we trespassing?" I asked. "No; the island's usually under water." This was all he ever said in our hearing, though he stayed with us, it seemed, for hours. He was a surly-looking fellow in the roughest clothes, with trousers turned up to his knees, and bare feet. His curiosity was immense; with arms crossed and legs wide apart, he stood and stared in silence with expressionless features. We had some villainous Black Forest cigars, bearing on the label the words *la noblesse*, which we sometimes used to get rid of obnoxious people. We gave him two. Knowing nothing about the Greeks and those bearing gifts he nodded his thanks,—and smoked both to the very end! Yet he never stirred, his eyes never left us. It was impossible to prepare our frugal dinner under this merciless scrutiny. At length I prevailed upon him to go over for some eggs, and to bring them to us in the morning for breakfast. He left without a word in his punt, and a sense of oppression seemed to go with him. But, just as dinner was over and we were settling round the fire to our tobacco, he suddenly reappeared. He had brought the eggs in his hat, and he was dressed this time in his Sunday clothes! For an hour he stood beside the fire, answering no questions, volunteering no remarks, till at length my friend went up, shook hands, wished him good-night, and straightway disappeared into the tent. I did likewise, and then the fellow took the hint, and went.

This happened at a place called Pleinling. Another thing also happened there. On the smaller of the arms into which our island divided the river was a weir. With empty canoe, and dressed in shirt and trousers, we practised shooting this weir next morning. The day was hot, and our other things were meanwhile drying on the bank. The silent peasant came over to watch the proceedings, and with him came a picturesque old fellow, most talkative and entertaining, with white hair and a face like Liszt's. When he saw us preparing to shoot the fall he was much excited. "Have you wives and children?" he asked shaking his head warningly. I went over first while my friend took the camera, and got his picture a second before the canoe plunged into the foam and upset. The old fellow, whose name was Jacob Meyer, was not in the least put out. He leaned on his scythe and watched me struggling in the water with the overturned canoe without making any effort to help. Afterwards, when we gave him a *noblesse* he took a lean, dirty little purse out of his pocket, and said, "How much am I to pay for it?" And when we promised to send him the photographs he asked the same question again.

Some hours later we reached Passau, a few miles from the Austrian frontier, and this last glimpse of Bavaria, after traversing its entire breadth, was the sweetest of all. But only from the river itself can you see the quaint old houses leaning over at all imaginable angles; the towers and crooked wooden balconies; gardens hanging from the second storeys; walls with ancient paintings dimmed by wind and weather; and decayed archways showing vistas of tumbling roofs, broken chimneys, and peeps of vivid blue sky at the far ends. The picture it made in my mind as we paddled through it in the late afternoon is uncommonly picturesque,—a jumble of gables, towers, bridges, and the swift muddy Danube rushing past it all in such tremendous hurry.

Half a mile below, the Inn poured in from the Tyrolese Alps and carried us into the finest gorge we had so far seen. The new corner brought cold air with it, and we swept into the gloomy ravine between high mountains with something like a genuine shudder. More and more swiftly ran the river as it compressed itself with an angry roar into a few hundred yards' width and swirled into the hills raging at the indignity thus heaped upon it. It became very difficult now to choose camping-places, as the stream fills the entire gorge, leaving only narrow ledges at the foot of the heights where a tent can stand. Upon one of these ledges, broader than the rest, we managed at length to land. A projecting point of rock sent the water flying out at a tangent into mid-stream and formed a strong backwater below it. Into this we contrived to twist the canoe's nose and on a little promontory, covered with yellow ragwort, we pitched our tent. It commanded a view for two miles up the ravine with the sinking sun at the far end. A boy was tending half a dozen cows among the scanty bushes; a queer little imp with wide-open blue eyes, who watched us land and prepare our camp with no signs of fear or surprise. We gave him cherries and chocolate, and he stuffed his mouth with one and his pockets with the other; then he came and stood over our fire and warmed himself without invitation, as if it had been made for his special benefit. A quaint little figure he cut with his pointed, feathered hat and big eyes. He told us that his name was Josef, that he lived two miles further on, went to bed every night at nine o'clock and got up every morning at four. Then he took off his hat, said good-night, and vanished into the bushes after his cows.

The sun set in a blaze of golden light that filled the whole gorge with fire; but when the glory faded, the strange grandeur of the place began to make itself felt. The ravine was filled with strange noises, the wooded heights looked forbidding, and the great river rolled in a sullen black flood into the night.

Next morning we passed a big rock in midstream with a shrine perched on its summit; and just beyond it we entered Austria and visited the customs at Engelhartzell, a village on the right bank with an old Cistercian monastery behind it. There was no duty to pay, and we raced on past the mountain village of Obermühl, and out of the gorge into a fertile and undulating country basking in the fierce sunshine.

Neuhaus, with a fine castle on a wooded height, and Ashach, with a view of the Styrian Alps, flashed by. The river from here to Linz is full of history, and its muddy waters have more than once borne crimson foam. There were bloody fights here during the revolt of the peasantry of Upper Austria. Ashach, in 1626, was the insurgents' headquarters where (as also at Neuhaus) they barricaded the Danube with immense chains to prevent the Bavarians from assisting Count Herberstein, the Austrian governor, who was shut up in Linz. When in flood the Danube escapes from this narrow prison with untold violence. Everywhere the villages bear witness of its path, though most of them lie far away from the banks. High upon the walls lines show the high-water marks of previous years with the dates. "A single night will often send us into the upper storeys," said a woman who sold us milk and eggs; "but the water falls as quickly as it rises, and then we come down again." She took it as a matter of course.

The shores became lonely again and our camps were rarely disturbed. One morning, however, about six o'clock we heard someone rummaging among our pans. Then something stumbled heavily against the tent, and there was a sound of many feet and an old familiar smell. We rushed out, to find ourselves in the centre of a herd of about fifty cows. One had its nose in the provision-basket; another was drinking the milk standing in the pail of water; a third was scratching its head against the iron prop of the kettle. Their curiosity was insatiable; every time we drove them off they returned. While my friend was frying the bacon and I was performing ablutions lower down on the river bank, a squadron swept down upon us unexpectedly by a clever flank movement, and one of them whipped up my pyjamas near the tent and ran down the shore with them on her horns. My friend dared not leave the bacon—and I was *in nudis!* It was exciting for the next few minutes.

In blazing heat that day we came to Linz, the capital of Upper Austria. Below it the Traun and the Enns flowed in, and the Danube became a magnificent river rolling through broad banks alternately wooded and covered with crops and orchards; and now, too, we begin again to see vineyards, of which Bavaria had seemed bare.

For a long time, strange as it may sound, we had been enforced vegetarians and drinkers of condensed milk. We could rarely get fresh milk, though we trudged many a mile to farmhouses and inns for it; either it was all used for butter, or had already been sent to the towns. Of course it would not keep sweet in our canoe under the blazing heat, and we could only trust to the chance of getting it an hour or so before we needed it. But, when we were lucky enough to get it, how delicious were those messes of boiled bread and milk! Meat, too, was hard to come at, except at certain hours. The butchers in the small towns open their shops at certain times only. Not one of them would ever trouble himself to supply us with merely a pound of meat, and more would not, of course, keep fresh.

We were drawing near Vienna now, but first we passed through another fine gorge. It began at Grein (where the Duke of Coburg's castle, Greinburg, looks down from the heights) and before we emerged breathless at the other end we had come through the famous whirlpools known as the Wirbel and Strudel. The river, narrowed by half its width, plunged with many contortions round sharp corners between high cliffs and past the island-rock of Worth. Rising in long, heaving undulations the water was alive with whirlpools, twisting and sucking, and throwing us here and there, gushing up underneath us with ugly noises and seething on every side. There was no foam, no crests, no waves or spray; it was like a monstrous snake trying to writhe through a hole too small for it. The shore raced by at top speed, and steering was uncomfortable for a time. In former years these whirlpools were a source of great danger to the navigation; but in 1866 the Emperor had certain rocks blown up and now an inscription on the face of the cliff testifies to the thanks of a grateful people. The traveller in a big steamer might think this description exaggerated. He would not think so in a canoe.

It is impossible to mention, as one would like, all the abbeys, churches, monasteries, ruins, islands, and other points of historic interest that throng the banks. The scenery is enchanting as well as enchanted. There were some interesting castles in these mountains, and grim they still look even in their ruins. Aggstein rose in solitary grandeur on a peak that commanded miles of the Danube in both directions. It was built in the twelfth century by the Kuenings, a robber-race which stretched chains across the river, plundered the traffic, and drowned the owners. We could still see the Blashaus Tower from which the sentinel announced the approach of boats. Its was a plundering, murdering family, and was finally destroyed by the great Ulrich von Grafeneck.

Before Ybbs (the Roman Pons Isidis) we saw the wonderful ruins of Dürrenstein where Richard Coeur de Lion was imprisoned. Here, on the very spot, it was interesting to recall how he was recognised when walking through the fields at Erdberg (since merged in Vienna), captured, and handed over to his enemy, Duke Leopold of Austria, who entrusted him in turn to the keeping of the Kuenings. They kept him for fifteen months (1193) in the great castle of Dürrenstein beneath whose grim walls we passed in our canoe. In Austria the story is implicitly believed, whatever we may think of it in England.

The following day we saw the blue hills of the Wiener Wald rising behind Vienna, and before long we were obliged to don our best clothes, and send a porter down from our hotel to fetch the luggage from the bathing-house where the canoe lay below the Reichsbrücke.

We did not stay long in Vienna. Rooms in July seem stuffy after a tent, and a fly-spotted ceiling is a poor substitute for the stars.

The canoe was packed full of provisions ready to start when our first accident occurred. The river had risen a couple of feet and was very swift. My friend had just taken off his shoes and placed them on the top of the other luggage. Several of the crowd, in their misguided fashion, were trying to help us, when I stepped into the little space vacant for me in the stern. How it happened no one knew; someone let go too soon, and she was instantly swept out sideways into the current. The next second I was dropped out neatly into five feet of water, and the canoe, settling till only the tops of the luggage remained in sight, went full tilt down stream. There were fifty yards of clear water, and then came a row of barges tied ten feet from the shore and leaving an inner channel. Into this the canoe luckily was swept; had she careered off into midstream probably we should never have seen her again. With boat-hooks and poles we ran along the banks to catch her before she banged into the barges. My friend ran in his socks. The hotel-porter, the bath-house man, and a dozen idlers all followed shouting different things at once. But the canoe and the mad current had the start of us. Crash! With a sound of rending, splintering wood she banged into the nearest barge and turned completely over. A few seconds later the various articles appeared on the surface again, and there began a sort of obstacle-race that might have been highly comical had it not been so serious. Our beds with the cork mattresses floated high out of the water. Jumbo (a huge kit-bag holding our wardrobe) came next, up to his neck. A smaller waterproof bag, tied at the neck and holding bread and cameras, followed, spinning merrily. The provision-basket (filled with the morning's careful shopping and some tea just arrived from England) showed only its nose above the surface. Coats, hats, socks, maps, tent-poles and tent followed in motley array at the end of an idiotic looking procession. Every time an article banged into a barge it went under for a few seconds, and meanwhile the canoe was crashing on among ropes and poles in the van. The heavy articles defied our efforts, and Jumbo pulled one man bodily into the water when he tried to drag it ashore.

In the end, however, most of the things were saved. The men caught the canoe as she spun past a barge, and held her till help came. All the articles, too, were fished out except those that would not float. Thus, we lost our lantern, the prop of the kettle, a pair of my friend's shoes, an odd one of mine, the ridge-pole of the tent, and my town hat and coat. It was wonderfully little. The bows of the canoe, however, were completely smashed in; and to make it worse, the rain suddenly came down in torrents and a cold wind blew from the north.

Then a carpenter appeared on the scene and said he could mend the canoe and make a new tent-pole. The people of the bath-house took our things in to dry, while we jumped into a closed carriage and drove back into Vienna, my friend with no shoes on his feet, and I without a hat on my head. Yet, such was our good luck, that three hours later we were spinning down the river in the mended canoe; the sun was shining brightly, our things were dried, we had a new tent-pole, Vienna was out of sight below the horizon,—and when we landed for camp the place was so lonely that, on climbing the bank, I looked straight into the eyes of a great stag with branching antlers.

For two days at racing speed we journeyed through wild and lonely country towards the frontiers of Hungary. The river was like a wide lake,—no houses, no boats, no token of man except the daily steamer between Vienna and Budapest. We passed signs of Roman days and Turkish occupancy strangely mingled: Carnuntum, where Marcus Aurelius is said to have written much of his philosophy; Theben on a spur of the little Carpathians, with its rock-perched fortress destroyed by the Turks in 1683 when they swept on to besiege Vienna, and again by the French in 1809. At its very feet the March (the boundary between Austria and Hungary) comes sedately in, and the Danube received a new impetus as we passed below its shadow and into Hungary at last.

The Germans had been kind in a negative fashion, the Bavarians courteous, the Austrians obliging; but the hospitality of the Hungarians was positively aggressive. "Nothing is too much," they used to declare when we expostulated with them on the overwhelming nature of their attentions, "nothing is too good for Englishmen. Everybody will tell you the same in Hungary." Kossuth was the magical word, and hatred of the Austrians the key-note of their emotions. We blessed the generation that had welcomed him in exile and went on our way rejoicing. The crowds no longer stood gaping; they helped without being asked. When we landed for provisions they ran down to hold the canoe, while others went into the village to make our purchases more cheaply for us. Even their questions were intelligent. German is of uncertain value here, and we had carefully learned the Magyar words for the articles we most needed. "Now you begin to learn Magyar when it is too late," laughed the woman in a Pressburg shop where we bought milk and eggs and bacon; "but it's no matter; you can't starve in Hungary." The Hungarian name of the town is Pozsony. It was formerly the capital, where the kings of the Hapsburg race were crowned. Below it the Danube branches into three arms, one of which makes a circuit of fifty miles and comes in again at Komorn. The main river is a couple of miles wide and full of islands, separated by rapids and falls. An officer assured us that we should get lost for days together unless we carefully kept to the main channel. The country is utterly deserted, save for the little black landing-stages of the steamers that appear every twenty miles or so, the villages lying far back and protected by high earthen banks. The loneliness and desolation of these vast reaches of turbulent river and low willow-clad islands were impressive; in flood-time it must be grand.

The water escaped into so many side channels and lagoons that the depth of the river was most variable. Grey shingle-beds appeared often in midstream, and over and over again we were swept into them before we could cross to deeper water. It was difficult to distinguish them in time from the muddy, foam-streaked river, until we learned that the cormorants invariably used them for fishing-grounds; and then we took the black bodies in the distance as warning signals that saved us much dangerous wading. The velocity of the stream is so great that one almost expects to see the islands swept bodily away. Big grey hawks circled ever over head and grey crows by the thousand lined the shores. That evening, after crossing and re-crossing the river, we found a sheltered camp on a sandy island where pollards and willows roared in the wind. As if to show the loneliness of the spot an otter, rolling over and over among the eddies, swam past us as we landed. About sunset the clouds broke up momentarily and let out a flood of crimson light all over the wild country. Against the gorgeous red sky a stream of dark clouds, in all shapes and kinds, hurried over the Carpathian mountains, and when we went to bed a full moon cast the queerest shadows through the tossing branches. We dined,—prosaic detail!—off tongue, onions, potatoes, tea, and dried prunes which we stewed and ate with quantities of beetroot sugar.

Next day the river grew wider, swifter, and even more deserted. At Kortel-jes we landed to buy provisions, though only the watchman's hut was in sight. As we stepped on shore my hat blew off and floated down stream. At once the man (who spoke a little German) went into his hut and produced one of his own which he begged me to wear; it was a greasy wide-brimmed felt, but I could not refuse it, and he seemed delighted. He directed us to a farm a mile inland for milk and eggs, and gave us the correct pronunciation of the necessary words. The farm stood on the broad plain in a grove of acacia trees, with snow-white walls and overhanging thatched roofs, forming a square, within which were oxen, buffaloes, pigs, geese, and romping children in brilliant skirts. The older girls had yellow kerchiefs on their heads; one little girl, in flaming colours, was chasing a chicken in and out among the trees and oxen; all stopped to stare as we approached, swinging an empty milk-can. Through the farmhouse door I got a glimpse into a spotless kitchen, and a most courteous woman with bril-liant dark eyes sold us what we required very cheaply. I took off my new greasy hat to them when we left, and the children followed us to the river, a motley es-cort.

On we went down the great rushing stream, ever flanked by a sea of silvery willows swaying and bending in the wind, reed beds, ten feet high, alternating with stretches of grey shingle. Between the wooded islands vistas opened in all directions; narrow glades where the river sent out new arms in patches of sun-shine with the faint sound of water tumbling over distant shallows; while down some far blue reach, filled with the afternoon shadows, we could see im-mense herds of cattle, swine, and flocks of geese, feeding in meadows lined with poplars and birch trees. Horses in vast quantities roamed along the banks, watched by herdsmen who wore cool white skirts instead of trousers. Often, in the backwaters, oxen, horses, buffalo, pigs, and geese were all crowded together trying to keep cool in the great heat.

At Komorn, rising with its fortress just above the dead level of the plain, we laid in provisions. The grocer was inquisitive: "Where have you come from? Where are you going to? How do you cook? Where do you sleep? Are you not afraid of grasshoppers and snakes? What an awful distance you have come—the source of the Danube, where is it? You are both quite young, aren't you? But you are so enormous,"—and so on, and so on.

From here we saw the blue mountains that encircle Budapest,—not more than forty miles away as a crow would fly it, but a splendid loop of sixty-five miles by the river. Budapest draws one like a magnet. There is a suggestion of deli-cious wildness about it born of I know not what. The very name seems set to some flying fragment of the wild national music,—a bar of the *csardás*, or of the wailing Hungarian songs that thrill with such intense virility. The West, too, sinks lower on the horizon when Budapest is reached, and the Danube sweeps you on through the Iron Gates to Turkey and the Fekete Tengerig (Black Sea).

Willows, reeds, and islands have all vanished now, and there were no sudden whirlpools in mid-stream. With majestic dignity that disguised the real speed, the mass of water, a mile to a mile and a half wide, swept steadily down under that fierce heat towards the mountains. We kept to mid-stream and were never tired of watching the banks slip by with their ever changing pictures: open shore; fields with barley standing in sheaves; vineyards coming down to the water's edge; cottages with thick thatch and white walls; villages full of wild, over-grown gardens, and groves of acacia trees of brilliant washed green. We landed for milk at a farmhouse on the right bank and found that the proprietor spoke English and had travelled in England and Norway and studied in Vienna. "It's only twenty-six kilometers to Budapest," he told us. Later on we overtook some peasants in a boat full of vegetables, and kept pace with them for a little, while we chatted in German. "It's a little over forty kilometers to Pest," they said. Boats became frequent after this, broad, flat-bottomed, laden with farm-produce, and rowed by men and women who took their hats off to us and asked many questions in bad German. All agreed on one thing,—that the Austrians were a poor lot of people compared with the Hungarians; and all differed on another thing,—the distance to Budapest. It varied with every boat, and at length we became so confused with the arguments of the spokesman in German and the mocking chorus of the rest in Hungarian, that we almost expected to hear that we had already passed it, or were perhaps on the wrong river altogether.

To avoid calamities we increased our speed and left the string of boats behind. In the afternoon we came to Gran. The dome of its huge Italian basilica dominates for miles the plain we had just traversed, but looks like a round gleaming pebble beside the mountains that rise behind it. The charms of this quaint little town made us realise that time is after all but a form of thought; in other words, we stayed too long. At half-past six we entered the wide deep valley of these magical mountains hoping to find a camping-place so soon as we were beyond the town. The sun was hidden; the mountains stood outlined in purple against a wonderful sky, with long thin clouds just touching some of the higher peaks; the water glowed as though fires burned beneath the waves. Mile after mile we followed the windings of the valley, the hills folding up behind us, but opening ever in front again into new and darker distances. But no camping-place appeared; one side was too steep, the other treeless. The shadows lengthened and grew deeper; the hills changed from purple to black; the lights of villages twinkled across the river as across a wide lake. They fairly lined the base of the hills, and secluded camping-spots were evidently things of the past; there was not even an island.

Eight, nine o'clock passed; it became too dark to cross or recross with safety. We hugged the left bank, eagerly scanning the shore under the steep hills and waiting for the moon to rise. It was ten o'clock when the moon topped the mountains of the other shore and filled the valley with silver. We found a level yard or two below some vineyards, unpleasantly close to the abode of the proprietor, and there made a small fire and dined late off eggs and cocoa. The scenery was more thrilling than the meal; the dim hills rising through the moonlight; the white river filling the space between as if the whole valley were sliding noiselessly past, the fragrant air, warm and still, shot here and there with fireflies,—and Hungary,—wild, musical, enchanted Hungary! The fire had died down and we were smoking at the mouth of the tent when sounds of music floated to our ears, and presently a barge of peasants towed by three men along the shore came slowly up the stream. Cymbals and violins were playing a national air and a few low voices were singing. The barge floated past as if no one had seen us, and the music died away in the distance.

And on the mere the wailing died away.

Several hours later the returning voices and violins woke us in the tent as the party went down again too far from shore to be visible to the eye.

A man fishing woke us early and asked if the *weinhüter* (watchman of vineyards) had not disturbed us. Luckily he had not. "That's because it's Sunday and he's overslept himself." In spite of this warning we breakfasted leisurely, and then paddling down stream in blazing sunshine landed a mile below at Visegrad on the opposite bank. This little town, with its ruined castle, and fortress destroyed by the Austrians, nestles among the mountains, and here the good folk of Budapest come in summer to their villas among the acacia trees. Everybody spoke to us, helped to pull up the canoe, told us what to see, where to get good coffee or cooling drinks, described (with painful detail) the remaining twenty miles to Budapest, and showed themselves in all ways most courteous and obliging. Gipsy-music sounded everywhere among the trees, and the peasants in bright Sunday costumes lent colour to the scene.

Below Visegrad, which we left with much reluctance, begins an island which stretches the whole twenty miles to Budapest. Taking the inner channel we paddled peacefully all day under blue mountains in a haze of delicious heat, past villages, ferries, churches, castles, private villas, acres of vineyards over the slopes of the hills, and vast herds of horses and oxen standing in the water, till we camped at sunset on a treeless bit of plain at the extreme point of the island, only a mile from Budapest. It was like camping on the Brighton downs. With difficulty we collected scraps of wood enough to make a fire that would boil water. It was a windless night, and our candle stood tied to a stick in the open air with a motionless flame. The moon, rising late, showed rounded curves of bare hills behind us,—and then, two figures approached us cautiously from the river. They came to the outside of the firelight circle and stopped; but at our invitation they came within and smoked the last of our *noblesse* cigars—poor fellows! Night-fishermen they were, short, thick-set, dark-faced Huns. They drank our cocoa and explained their strange-looking nets to us while waiting for the moon to rise higher. All night long they fished, and on their way home to bed at five next morning they looked in to give us a hearty good morning and the information that the cows were coming.

The thunder of hoofs confirmed this, and we got up in time to protect the tent from a herd of several hundred cattle. A herder followed them, a dwarf-like creature with a pole-axe as big as himself, and a badge which proclaimed him Government keeper of the plain (Crownland) where all men's cattle might feed on certain conditions. He spoke no German, but he understood the meaning of a plate of veal, and he finished our meat (two pounds) in about ten minutes. Then he drank some cocoa, asking, with a wry face, if it were paprika (Hungarian pepper).

It was piping hot on the treeless plain, and Budapest lay waiting for us. We shaved and donned our town suits. The herder, grateful for his meal, helped to carry our things to the canoe, and, long after we were off, stood shading his eyes with his hand and staring after us. We drifted lazily down another mile of steaming hot river and landed at the wharf of the Hunnia Rowing Club on the right bank,—nearly a thousand miles from the sleepy little village in the Black Forest where we had embarked six weeks before.

The Psychology of Places

The considerable role played by the Psychology of Places in certain temperaments must produce a noticeable extension of their gamut of feeling—the "note" of pleasure or pain, I mean, they receive from even the common places of the world. For, where many can pass through a given stretch of landscape untouched, these others may receive from the same space a series of impressions varying through every shade of emotion from exaltation to depression. Every "note" produces a reaction. The barrenest mile brings meaning. A tree that to one temperament "brings tears of joy," to another is but "a green thing standing in the way."

Yet, the hidden causes that prompt this perception of the psychology of places rest upon something far more profound and subtle than the mere love of Nature—upon a million delicate decisions, probably, of ancestral and utterly primitive origin. "I do not like thee, Dr. Fell; The reason why I cannot tell," appeals to everyone, of course; but, whereas most of us are quick to get the "note" of a *person*, for like or dislike, it has been my experience that only a few respond vividly to the "note" of a place—appreciate the psychology of places, that is.

With towns and the inhabited spots of the world it is easily traceable to definite causes. Going from one town to another is similar to going from one person to another for conversation in a room. Each in turn draws out a different aspect of the personality and, whether you like it or no, an unconscious readjustment of your inner world and forces takes place automatically. You present instinctively another front, though without any loss necessarily of sincerity in the process. You show new wares to a new customer, pushing others, felt "not wanted," below the counter. Leaving London one kind of man, you find two days later in Paris that you are another kind of man—showing at least a different grouping of emotions to the sun. And, later still, in Vienna and Pesth, a further readjustment has taken place, and the emotional kaleidoscope has shaken into view an aspect of your personality very different from the one that left the murk of heavy London behind a week before. With the towns this is all very obvious and analysable, although it has always seemed to me as significant—the beginning of a simple variant of the amazing phenomenon of multiple personality, and the difficulty sensitive natures find in knowing which is really their true Self.

But with regard to the uninhabited regions of the World, the interest in this question of the psychology of places deepens and complicates at once. I have watched its operation in a thousand cases, yet never found any satisfactory explanation, outside the region of mystical theories, upon which one may not draw to beg the question. In the trackless Canadian forests the backwoodsman, experienced in all the essentials of woodcraft, who acts as your guide, invariably takes the "note" of a new camp before he allows you to settle down, and while a dozen practical details (wood, wind, water, fall of land, &c.) may seem to determine his decision alone, I have always noticed that a dozen unknown and unguessed causes contribute their element as well—things he can only shrug his shoulders over without reply. Almost as though some places grow a crop of big invisible Query Marks like trees, each demanding a satisfactory answer before one can settle for the night in comfort—and safety. And to watch these primitive men choose their resting-place has always suggested to me the actions of a wild animal wandering to and fro before it selects a lair; or the behaviour of a domestic beast, such as a cat or dog, before it curls up in a corner of the room and finally deposits itself in *the* right place.

One man in particular I remember (my companion in more than one of the desolate places of the world) who had this curious instinct unusually developed. He went through a regular ceremonial—unconsciously—before settling down and proclaiming the camp all right. Every essential of a good camp might be present, yet he was not satisfied until he had nosed about, explored and investigated a dozen vague conditions he seemed to "sense" yet could never have named; it almost suggested the survival of some deep atavistic tendency to placate the deities of the place before it was safe to eat and sleep there. Certain innate objections and predilections he had that clamoured to be satisfied before he felt really at home; and one of these—about the only one I ever heard him describe definitely—was "Never pitch your camp on the edge of anything; put the tent in the wood or out of it, but never on the borderland between the two."

And his objection, though laughingly expressed, was deep-seated and genuine; he was invariably consistent; and, while a man of normal modern culture, free from any shadow of superstition, he clung to this particular shibboleth with a tenacity that has often set me thinking since. Instinctively, and by no process logically worked out to a conclusion, I think he said a true thing there. For a threshold is ever the critical frontier that invites adventure and therefore possible disaster. The frontier, the entrance, the gateway, of course, sets the line between two opposing things, and may mean passing towards an attack from the unknown conditions that lie beyond. "On the edge of a wood," he said to me once as we lay round a camp-fire in the wilds, while I pressed him for an explanation of his feeling, "the tent stands on the very line where two sets of forces meet—the forces of the Wood and the forces of the Open. It is not a place of rest, but of activity. I like being right in the wood, or right out in the open."

His words, suggesting the strip of unclaimed ground between the fringes of hostile armies, made us smile, while at the same time every man in the party recognised that he was right, and that what he said about the ethics of pitching a tent was, indeed, true of all frontiers and gateways. The psychical aspect of a threshold is essentially thrilling: the critical character of the very act of Entrance announces itself instantly in any nature not utterly dead to the finer sensibilities. The moment the doorposts are left behind—of a railway carriage, your dentist's house, an afternoon call even!—the adventure has begun. It is the moment of birth, of life, thrill, excitement. The *prelimenaries* are over; you have entered the Unknown. And though a boundary line is, of course, a merely theoretic conception without actual existence, its invention is due to that fundamental need of human nature that seeks some kind of measurement by which to check its retrogression or advance. The feeling which prompted the Roman husband to carry his wife across the *limen* of his house, after which she should tread no more her own *fines* as a separate individual, is a manifestation of the same instinct that forbade my camping friend to pitch his tent upon an imaginary frontier-line; the same again, doubtless, which in the deeper regions of the soul-life has erected another more terrible Gateway between two worlds and crystallised the emotion born of it into that haunting and awesome embodiment of warning—the Dweller on the Threshold.

The Glamour of Strangers

As a youngster, one was always cautioned to beware of strangers and to re-
pel their advance with coldness and disdain. Their motive, it was assured us by
those who knew better, could never be a good one; and I perfectly remember
the time when I believed that if a stranger spoke to me it was because he had de-
signs upon my pocket-money or, when I was a little older, that he sought to
make me an accomplice in crime or convert me to some dreadful new religion.
No stranger addressed one without a sinister object: that at least was certain; and
I shudder now to think of the rudeness I must have shown to more than one
meek individual whose only desire was to pass the time of day or to enquire the
shortest way to museum or post-office. With what superior wisdom, sitting in
my corner of train or omnibus, I used to smile as I watched a couple of strangers
enter gradually into conversation; and, secure in my knowledge that all strangers
were villains, I used to wonder which would first succeed in "doing" the other,
and why on earth the other passengers did not interfere and call the police.

Life in those days must have been full of bogies. They lurked in the dark corners of all roads and came out in swarms, especially after dusk. Chief among
them at that period was certainly the Stranger, the Unknown One; whereas,
now, his whole aspect has marvellously changed, and he delights rather than dis-
mays; he moves in sunshine rather than in shadow; and, instead of following
me stealthily, it is I who am obliged to run after him, for he disappears only too
easily, and requires no little coaxing before he will consent to speak at all. For
it must be admitted, even by those who have not quite got over their fear, that
the Stranger is somewhat of a seductive creature—a "foreigner," as the dic-
tionary calls him, "one of another place; one unknown, or not familiar." To me,
he is frankly fascinating. The very word charms, suggesting a world untried, a
whole zone of new possibilities. There floats in its atmosphere something that
entices and allures. It vibrates with suggestion, and the tiny threads of new hopes
are at once most delicately insinuated into the woof of one's daily life. Beneath
even the shabbiest hats the heads of Strangers may often wear a halo, for they
carry about with them something that *may* be utterly different to all one has ever
known; while, more often than not, their faces proclaim that they possess the
very elements of delight in which one's own life and circumstances are lacking.

The charm, of course, lies in the unknown possibilities locked up in the
mysterious figure; a Stranger may say, do, or look exactly what you wish and
have always longed for, whereas the people you know so not—and never will!
There comes a time when the soul seeks novelty. You are not faithless to old
friends, but you welcome a change and desire it. Repetition has dulled the edge
of what was once absorbing; so, putting on hat and coat, you go forth to seek

the Stranger who, fortunately, is always within reach. And then it becomes at once evident that the art of talking to strangers is not too easily acquired, and the paradox is soon apparent that the more you learn about your stranger, the less interesting he grows. A stranger, ceasing to be such, becomes—there lies the danger—a bore!

And one of the charms, you soon discover, of speaking to strangers is that they accept your statement as true and final. They do not press you for explanations, for itemised accounts. Your words are suddenly important. You begin, perhaps, with a friendly little difference about the temperature, and then pass on to the difficulty of knowing "what to wear" in "this sort of weather." A topic is next suggested by a line on a poster or an incident on the journey, and you say things *à propos* that are listened to with apparent interest and respect. The stranger credits you, as you credit him, with a knowledge and discernment that probably far exceeds your combined possessions. And then, soon after, the conversation terminates with a simple statement of fact: "this is my station and I must leave you here,"—and you go out of each other's lives and there is no harm done.

The glamour of strangers is over everything; it is impossible to escape their influence. Your attitude invites them, and you can never tell when the invitation will be accepted. The call has gone out, and the Stranger is already moving towards you. "He" will be the opposite sex, probably, and may come from the North or from the South, from the land of the sunset or out of the East; or, perhaps, even further, from before the thrones of the pale stars. But one day, when you least expect it, he will poke his nose over the rim of this old world and move swiftly in your direction. No one can intercept him; no one can rob you of your delight; for he comes to you out of the Eternal Distances, mysterious, ideal. He seeks no one but yourself, and cares for none other. And, meanwhile, yours also are the joys of anticipation.

And the joys of anticipation, some say, far exceed those of realisation. Every morning the smoky, lamplit railway carriage holds for you unknown possibilities. You meet there Strangers who suggest a life far larger than your own. You merely exchange a word or two with them, but it is quite obvious that they enjoy privileges, and win from the facts of life sweeter experiences than ever fall to your lot. That tall, dark man who made the slight remark just now about the fog, is assuredly not journeying, as you are, to a mere Office. True, he carries a black bag, and a shabby one too; but, instead of briefs and contracts, it contains a change of raiment in which, soon after arriving at his destination, he will emerge glorious and radiant. The singy black clothing he now wears cannot conceal from your eye the numberless indications that proclaim him a participant in some gorgeous ceremonial. He is on his way to the Temple where censers swing in the light of innumerable tapers, and where music rolls between dim arches.... It is manifestly absurd to think that such eyes and such features have any portion in a modern "office." Those are the gestures, that is the bearing, of a priest, a High Priest, nothing less!

And that slender girl next to him, whose fingers in thin black gloves drum incessantly upon the roll of papers in her lap—no modern instrument, be it typewriter or piano, could ever teach such grace and charm of movement. And those soft coils of hair certainly belong not to the insipid world in which you play your own dull part! You see, instead, the figures that Böcklin knew, moving in white robes among whispering poplars; you catch an echo of the open-air chanting as they approach the altar. Her eyes are difficult to see, and the lines of mouth and chin are lost in that furry thing about the throat, but it is plain her sphere is nearer to the Immortals than yours; and when you open the door for her, and hear that silvery "thank you," you know for certain that she, too, is on her way to the very things in life, or out of it, that you seek for yourself, yet never find....

Yet, it is vain to follow these Strangers too closely; it would be a violation of the rules. You trace them a short distance, perhaps, through dream-streets, but they turn suddenly and are gone, and you look up, amazed to realise that you have been following a shadow—and find the bus horses thundering down upon you, or the cabman shouting in your ear. They slip into the doorway of some dingy building, black with centuries, and leave you with the empty fact that you have again known, and lost, an inhabitant from this fascinating but unknown country. For the doorway is, of course, a mere blind, and they hie them thence by unknown courses to the enchanted regions that lie ever just beyond the horizon of the things that make up your own insignificant life.

After all—to come back to earth for the full stop—it seems that the Stranger (and herein lies the secret of his curious power) is merely a point of departure, a spot, as it were, whence you may leap towards the Infinities. He is, in fact, a spring-board for the imagination and, as such, he is wholly delightful—and utterly misleading.

On Wings

No thinking man can watch the flight of birds, especially of big birds, without grave thoughts of wonder and delight rising in him. Their ease and grace and strength of movement, their light and sure supremacy over the medium which they navigate with such consummate facility, their speed and dropping swiftness, are all so incomparably superior to any mechanical motor skill that we possess ourselves. No other living organism, perhaps, express so well the joy of motion. It is difficult to watch the circling seagulls, the posied and hovering hawk, the darting swallows, or the soaring lark, without feeling that here is life really enjoying itself in the best possible form of free, unimpeded motion. No wonder that the poets give the angels wings, and the symbolism of wings is found in the most vital thoughts of all religions. The wings of the soul, the wings of the imagination, these are more than mere empty phrases!

The choice of the air to illustrate some imagined spiritual region, of course, is obvious enough, for air will most certainly be the last department of Nature men will conquer; and, apart from unwieldy mechanical contrivances, men will never really fly—as birds do. To pass through and across the air is quite another thing to flying as the birds know flying. The religious temperament made a wise, instinctive selection of flying to describe the motion of a "spirit," for nothing could be further from possible corporeal achievement. The weight of men's bodies in proportion to their muscular development for ever blocks the way; whereas the power of the muscles that drive the wings of birds, compared to the weight of their slender, delicate frames, their tiny bones, their hollow quills, is overwhelmingly to their advantage. A drumming partridge can flap its sturdy wings four hundred times to the minute. It is doubtful if the supplest man can "flap" his arms at a quarter of this speed, and a broad wing offers far more resistance to the air than the thin line of a human arm. The eye cannot even follow the beats of a flying pigeon's wings to count their number.

To watch the seagulls from the stern of some steamer is a keen delight. One notes the cunningly contrived arrangement of the feathers, which lie one upon another in such a way that the downward stroke is not exactly counterbalanced by the upward. In the former the air presses them closer together, thus supplying the resistance necessary to rise; whereas in the upward stroke they open out, letting the air slip through. With what minimum effort, too, they compass the maximum of movement; with how tiny a tilting of the body they steer to avoid collision; how rapid, almost instantaneous, is their judgment when to dive, seizing an opening in the flash of an eye, or rising, swerving, swooping for a plunge! There is nothing in all Nature to compare with their consummate skill and lightning ease. The accuracy of a martin's or a swallow's aim in darting through mid-air to snap at a zigzag-flying insect is an exhibition of surpassing skill.

And equally fascinating to watch, perhaps, is the adroit and wonderful balancing a bird displays in hovering with motionless wings outstretched, and the way it uses every current of air to sustain or propel its perfectly adjusted weight. One could almost imagine that there ran through every feather down to the very tips, some exquisite system of nerves more delicate even than those of human beings. They seem to *feel* the wind, to be forewarned of every slightest change, to sense the advance and retreat of every little current.

It was always the sea-birds that, as a boy, I envied most. Their mastery over two elements seemed so unfair. They are free of more of the earth than is their right, as it were. But one never grudged the birds their happiness and powers for long. Childhood always loves the birds—their mystery lies closer to the dreams of imaginative childhood, perhaps, than the mystery of four-footed life, and in proportion to their number they contain fewer fierce and savage, certainly fewer dangerous, species. The air would mean to us so little without them; their song and movement seem to interpret all the vault of the sky. The passion of a single lark can set a whole spring morning to music; and where would be half the beauty of the summer dusk without the whistle of a blackbird across the lawn, the trill of a thrush in the laurels, the glory of the nightingale in the shrubberies and larches?

Scenery for some comes back most vividly to the mind with the memory of the bird-life associated with it. To hear the laughter of the loons, so weirdly human in its note, and see their straight and level flight across wide, lonely lakes, so close that their feet must catch the spray of every wave, recalls for me the Canadian backwoods far more completely than any memory of deer or moose or bear. For me, personally, the birds divide this reconstructive power about equally with the *smells* of trees and flowers or, above all, the odour of wood smoke. A line of dark cormorants, or the storks and herons fishing in the shallows, are more evocative for me of the Hungarian reaches of the Danube, where I once canoed, than any other detail of the banks or landscape I can call to mind. Those circling hawks of giant size above the endless marshes! Those flocks of grey crows rising from some shingled island in mid-stream as our canoe approached! The great white swans of the upper sections in the Black Forest and Bavaria! All the little pictures of the thousand-mile journey that come back to haunt the mind with their separate bits of loveliness have bird life in them somewhere. The rest, even the rapids, dangerous rocks and whirlpools, lie indistinct and rather vague; these with the birds, on the contrary, stand out sharply and well defined.

Last year, while crossing the Black Sea in early May towards the Caucasus, our steamer had from time to time, strange winged visitors who certainly paid no passage-money. Vessels were few and far between, and many birds rested in their long flight from shore to shore upon the rigging. Some accompanied the boat for days together, and one and all were obviously very weary. There were brown birds, like pigeons, only smaller, that rested on the stern rails, flew off for long detours about the ship, then presently returned again to settle; there was a large, dark hawk that perched high up on the cross-trees watching them hungrily (and, happily, in vain); and there were numerous small fry of various kinds, whose names I knew not, for ever dodging the cats and passengers. Swallows, evidently belated, came to join them and would flit up and down in front of rows of occupied deck-chairs after dinner in search of sleeping places. There was one in particular that showed no fear of human kind, but calmly fluttered on to my cap and settled itself down comfortably, after a little preliminary fidgeting, for sleep. Being in the middle of a story that necessitated turning the head to neighbours on either side of me, the attention at first was awkward and the interest in the bird eclipsed all interest in the story. But the compliment, I felt, was greater than that of applause, and I soon found it was possible to turn the head so carefully that the little creature need not be disturbed. At any rate, it stayed for fully half-an-hour, doubtless sound asleep, and fortunately for its feelings no one on deck wore hats with stuffed birds on them!

Several of the brown, pigeon-like birds, however, came to a curious end. Whether in their weariness they dropped into the sea and were drowned or whether waiting and watching fish pulled them under, as the ship's doctor affirmed, was hard to say. One saw them skimming beside the steamer, so close to the waves they almost touched their crests, then suddenly—disappear. They went under at once. There certainly was no struggle of any kind, and no attempt to swim or rise again. Without a flutter of the wings they simply vanished.

Spring Notes in the Jura

When I left the Jura a few weeks ago, snow still held the ridges and the spears of her white scouts shook before the gateways of all the higher valleys; the woods were dead; lumps of ice clattered in the streams, and winds were merciless and keen. But, now that I am back again in the little village that no map knows, I find a curious thing has come to pass, for a great Personage has suddenly arrived, yet no room been found for her in the towns. Geneva, noisy and busy, knew her not; Neuchâtel, picturesque and stately, was bored; and Pontarlier—well, Pontarlier, the little mountain town where the absinthe comes from—was so high and frosty that she heard about it too late and shrugged her bleak shoulders across the miles of peak and plateau to her high sister town, La Chaux de Fonds—as usual.

The result has been—so they tell me—that the entire mountain range has "put up" as best it can the suddenly arrived Personage and her suite. At once, all through these sombre forests the electric message ran, and a flush of soft delight dropped everywhere upon the great network of wooded valleys and hills. Having agreed to take her in, the Range instantly gave up its pretence of playing at being Alps and sent out its great sigh of pleasure, which melted all its million perfumes into one and merged the cries of water, wind and echo into a single word of welcome. The peasants, ever subtly in league with the spirit of the mountains, knew that perfume and heard that word instantly; and now all the châlets in the upper valleys, closed these six months, are opening doors and windows to the sun and wind, sending fragrant peat smoke in blue columns to the sky and, like gigantic beehives, becoming centres of busy teeming life. The cows are on the move again.... Old Père Langel is sharpening his ancient scythe....

For this great Guest of the Mountains stays but a short time, and the preparations for her proper reception are of necessity rapid and concentrated. Suddenly, one morning when the Sun melts the low-lying mist upon the pastures, she is gone, and though her footsteps lie on all sides, radiantly coloured, there is no indication of the direction she has taken, although the fresh sweetness of her presence still lingers in the air. How she came so swiftly, too, none pretend to explain; for some say she stepped across the Lake of Neuchâtel from the south when the mist lay so close that no track upon the surface of the water was visible, while others claimed that she slipped stealthily at night down one of the secret valleys that run so tenderly into France. It is probable, though, that she landed directly from the sky itself, when the South Wind brought softness for the first time and "all the pathways of the birds were thick with rain." For the clouds that let her through changed in a day, turning their faces towards the earth instead of skywards, and dropping shadows of incredible softness to weave a carpet for her feet. But, whatever the method of her approach, the magic of her presence is felt universally, for everywhere flowers have put their little faces up to wonder and to ask, and the wind is so busy tearing to and fro to carry question and reply that the countless insects, come out to see what all the fuss is about, have threatened to retire again, as they dislike being roughly blown about before their wings are stronger. Their pretence, however, only fills the air with laughter, for when *She* comes, no one objects to a little bit of wild dancing.... The curiosity is intense, too. Even the Snow came back to see if it were really true (an excuse she often gives!) and then fled away, convinced, into the caverns of moisture, where she hides invisible until her own mountain apartments are ready for her again.

"Who is it calls?" asked the Wind Flowers.

"Someone with a thousand feet like the rain," laughed the breeze in a whisper among the tree tops.

"And with ten million eyes," added voices soft as perfumes from the thick carpet of moss.

The Anemones opened their starry eyes absurdly wide and stared all about them, and everywhere else, too, eyes opened, eyes with colour dipped in dew and running over—the myriad eyes with which this cloaked and hooded Jura smiles at Spring.

It was the old and heavy-shouldered trees that let out the truth. They nodded solemnly to one another over the heads of the rest, and in their deep and hidden hearts they sighed the secret out. For the Sun streamed on their soaked bark and they loved it, and could no longer keep it to themselves.... Then the gay young beeches that sprinkle these pine woods hurriedly drew on their brilliant lacework of moist green, sifting the blue sky downwards by some magic of their own into the depths of shadow below; and soon afterwards the poplars in the fields beyond the vineyards, catching sight of them, arranged their most delicate underskirts and passed on the rustling sound of woodland frou-frou to the reeds that fringe the lake itself. Word flew thus across the water to the further shore. Among those nurseries that flank the larger woods the scattered silver birches, quick as light, were dressed and ready. "Here we are!" they sang as plainly as children anxious to be noticed. "Here we are, all spick and span"— and not unlike overgrown flowers who are afraid they may not be asked to dance....

But it is the Jura flowers that most prodigally proclaim the change; they swarm and shimmer in crowds right up to the very summits of the range where the snow still hides in crannies on the northern slopes, and where the jonquils on the Tête de Rang gleam before the crocuses are gone. Everywhere the air is crystal.

In the heart of the woods only the hollies remain sulky.... "Are we not always terrible?... Then why change?" And the army of upstanding periwinkles that nod about their roots look up in wonder and open their blue eyes even wider than the Wind Flowers. For in the Jura, the spring is neither flaming nor showy, but simple, tender, swift and exquisitely modest. The lilies of the valley have already pushed their spear-like leaves above the surface of the ground. They have caught two murmurs: the footsteps of Someone leaving and the deep, soft sound of Summer that is even now coming.

From My Caucasus Note-book

It is difficult for anyone with moderate powers of observation and imagination to spend even a week in this land of beauty and marvels without wanting to write at least a volume about it. The impressions are so novel, varied, picturesque, and immense. When my Black Sea steamer landed me at Batoum, for instance, I found its little cobbled streets so fascinating that with great difficulty only did I tear myself away to Tiflis. In Tiflis, again, one felt the desire to settle down for a year or two to watch, study, and absorb. But when, having left this capital of Georgia by a wrench that was like a physical operation almost, I made my way into the big mountains, the spell of their stupendously-scaled scenery and the charm of their many and ancient tribes, of their colossal and quasi-primeval flora, above all of their vast loneliness, somehow made one feel it would be difficult ever to escape at all!

Countries affect and modify the personality just as cities do—you are not the same man in London that you are in Rome, Stockholm, Budapest. A side that the brilliance and rush of Paris win uppermost retires half-ashamed before the picturesque severity of Edinburgh. In one town you feel at your best, in another at your worst. A readjustment of the inner life takes place. In the Caucasus I found new tracts of consciousness, as it were, stirring into life—feelings, points of view, thoughts, desires but dimly, if ever, divined before. There is nothing in this great unstained land to remind you of anything you ever saw or knew before. The modern world drops away in a single leap—silently. You step back, not a few centuries, but into some half-imagined childhood world where anything and everything becomes possible of belief. You forget your age, your past, your stupid little limitations, and run back through this brilliant, coloured atmosphere into a time when the world was young—very young.

There are moments, of course, when you are forced to forget this new-found freedom—such as when, with but a smattering of Russian, you find yourself obliged to bargain in the hotels for linen, pillow, towels and samovar, to say nothing of a mere bedroom; when you fight amid anguished words for a bath, and are told that the bath is in the restaurant full of live trout for the guests to choose their particular fish for dinner; when the police come up and arrest you for aiming your Kodak at some street scene; or when, still worse, you want to leave that day and find you have forgotten to get your passport endorsed, and the hotel-keeper can accordingly keep you for another day of robbery, insects, and wretched matutinal splashings in a basin that has no stopper in its hole…!

But those little things are nothing when your heart is touched—as the Caucasus can touch it. For instance, in Tiflis you can go to the post office and hire an odd little cart for a certain journey—say, the 200-verst trip across the great

Georgian Pass of Darial to Vladikavkaz on the northern side—and after paying an absurdly small price (3os. in this particular case), you can set out at any
hour that suits you, and take as long over the journey as ever you please. At the
numerous stations *en route* fresh horses are supplied, with fresh drivers of all
sorts of nationalities, and behind a team of two, three or four lively Caucasian
animals, you go from point to point—spending a few days, a fortnight, or several months *en route* if you choose. Or you can pick up a Georgian as guide, being careful to tell him you carry a revolver, but no money worth speaking of (and
that little in very small change), and with a small extra sum for a horse to carry
sleeping-bag and blankets, you can wander off into those immense and trackless mountains and see something of the numerous strange races that inhabit
them, sleeping among beech and rhododendron forests, sniffing fields of
azalea, honeysuckle, lilies, and varieties of flowers and towering scented weeds
you never even heard the names of before. The brilliance of the air is remarkable, and the huge peaks that top the Alps easily come close—awfully close
sometimes. The steepness, depth, and scale of the lonely valleys is prodigious.
Their sweep carries with it something of cloud scenery—belongs more to sky
than earth. Up the Asian side of the mountains the verdure is luxuriant and soft,
full of blue shadows, golden and white blossoms, alive with birds and butterflies; then you cross the snows, finding but primitive hospitality in the "stations" or shanties of the rarely placed engineers' quarters, and at length descend
towards Vladikavkaz and the steppes through a wilderness of bleak and desolate precipices, enormous and abrupt, treeless but for a few pines, devoid of life,
silent, dark, and weirdly inspiring. The very word "tourist" escapes your memory. You pass Ossetines and Georgians, clothed in *bashliks* of lambswool, and
with flowing *bourkas* that cloak them from the neck right down over their
horses' haunches, giving them an appearance of centaurs—armed with rifle,
dagger, and rows of silver or bone cartridges across the breast. They are fine,
big, muscular men, but they leave you alone for the most part, unless you mention that you are English, when you may have to answer curious and delightful questions. Legend and poetry go with you; mystery, too. You may believe
anything you please, and no one will whisper "But that's incredible"; rather they
will open their fine eyes a little wider and "tell you another" in return! You find
yourself among the raw material, so to speak, of the "Arabian Nights," and one
reason a town like Tiflis is so fascinating is that a great deal of this leaks down
into its thronged and coloured streets, haunting the bazaars and Mohammedan
quarters, jostling you at every turn on the pavements among the stream of cos-
tumed Persians, Tartars, Georgians, Armenians, Ossetines, and all the rest.

How long this may last is another question. Already dreadful schemes are
afoot. A great motor that carries a dozen passengers, indeed, now runs three
times a week between Tiflis and Vladikavkaz in a dozen hours. To see the
mountain folk crowd round it at the "stations" is a suggestive and pathetic sight.
They approach gingerly, stare curiously, look half-offended, half-angry, and

then spring back as the horn toots and the beast leaps forward. But it is worse
still to watch the expression of injury and insult with which the lonely native
riders in the upper regions urge their horses at full speed up the open slopes to
get out of the way of the approaching monster. How they hate it! One feels almost as if the terrible pyramid of the giant Kasbek—the 16,000-ft. mountain
where Prometheus lay chained for centuries—must rise another half-mile into
the air and send down a thousand tons of rock to crush it. This motor that crosses
the Caucasus—it seems an act of audacious sacrilege that cannot go long un-
punished.

Yet—I must admit it—the thing is uncommonly useful and practical, and one
day when I was in a hurry to get back to Tiflis I did not despise to make use of
the seat beside the chauffeur. What comforted me, perhaps, was the thought
that the Caucasus stretches east and west for leagues and leagues of gorgeous
and lonely splendour where no roads exist at all. This Georgian Pass is, of
course, only its Simplon or St. Gothard. Go further east into Daghestan, or westwards into the heart of Immerethia and Swanetia: there are no motors there!

I found the priests—the priests of the Orthodox Greek Church—always
charming, simple, and delightful beings. Their size, huge shoulders, long,
ragged beards, and, above all, their deep and splendid voices never failed to attract me. Our conversations were restricted, since but one in a dozen knew a
word of my available languages, and my own Russian was confined chiefly to
such phrases as "How much?" "Go to the Devil," "Hurry up," and "It is very
good" (*haracho*) "only *be quick!*" But I always loved "talking" with them.
There was a perfect monster in Tiflis whom I often found standing at the gate
of his little house next the church. His voice boomed like the sea. Another huge
fellow I discovered in Mtzhket—ancient capital of Georgia—and took a photograph of him. He stood in the court of his ancient cathedral and stared at me
on my horse till I got down and tried to chat. We shook hands; he bowed mag-
nificently, smiled a little, looked approvingly at my stature of 6 feet 3 inches, because his own was the same, and then finally, when language failed us at length,
pointed to my camera. I asked to be allowed the pleasure. He bowed and vanished into his wretched little wooden house, throwing me a dark look over his
shoulder. My fear that I had offended him was soon dissipated by his return—
fully robed. He was a majestic figure, yet I felt all the time I was dealing with
a great overgrown boy—a child.

In the Lesser Caucasus, the chain that runs parallel with the main one and included the mighty Ararat, further south, one finds again quite a different
world of people—Turks and Mohammedan Georgians, smiling, luxuriant
valleys full of fruit and nut trees, Caucasian walnut in particular being a precious article of export. Here the azaleas and rhododendrons were in full bloom
at the time of my visit, and I shall never forget going up a 10,000-ft. peak to see
the sunrise burst over the Black Sea that lay at my feet like a vast lake. Mist filled
a dozen purple valleys, whose slopes were covered by forests of beautiful beech

trees. Snow summits shone white towards the Turkish frontier. And at a level of three thousand feet below us stretched the world of rhododendron bushes like an immense park or garden scattered prodigally all over the mountain sides, the crimsons, mauves, and pinks gleaming like fire as the sun caught them. We had some good glissading down the snow-slopes on the way home, but the two Turks, who insisted on accompanying me for my safety, looked on with disapproval. They would not venture. I think they were afraid their rifles might go off halfway down. At noon in the snow they both knelt down and prayed. The devotions of these people come to interrupt one's journey at many odd and awkward moments, and nothing can stop them. They found the big nails of my heavy Alpine climbing boots very wonderful; they climbed themselves in soft leather top boots, with soles as smooth as silk. Yet they climbed like cats, and never made a false step.

A real danger in the upper mountain valleys, though it may sound a trifle ludicrous, is—the dogs. The sheep-dogs are savage to a degree. They are biggish, thick-set brutes, with long muzzles and ugly teeth, very useful to keep off the bears, but very awkward when a couple come bounding towards yourself over the grass slopes. You find them everywhere. *Sabarka* (dog) was one of the first words I learnt. You are especially warned to use neither stick nor stones in self-defence, but to sit down quietly and stare at them. It takes some courage to do this, and I must plead ignorance of the precise effect of such tactics. I invariably made for a tree, or a wall, or whatever shelter seemed handy; but the shepherds assure you that if you sit thus quietly on the ground the dogs will not touch you. They may keep you there, however, in this uncomfortably established truce for the length of time necessary for their owner to arrive and release you. And how you are to stare steadily at two or three dogs without contracting a squint that may prove permanent I never heard satisfactorily explained. In any case, one thing is certain—if you do an injury to the creatures the shepherds will not spare you in return, and a very serious difficulty might be the result.

I was sorry, indeed, to leave the Caucasus. Everything about it is big, and queer, and vast—new thrills and emotions at every turn. I caught one of the excellent little Paquet steamers at Batoum that carry you to Marseilles for a £10 note. Coasting leisurely along the wooded and mountainous southern shore of the Black Sea, however, had its compensations. The sea was blue as the Mediterranean, and the people who came on board, bound from one little port to another, repaid attention. At Trebizond and Ineboli a hundred peasant folk from the interior of Asia Minor came as third-class passengers bound for Marseilles and—America. Emigrants! What these dark-skinned, wild-eyed, dirty, ragged people actually were I never properly ascertained, but they were wonderfully entertaining and picturesque. They lived on the after-deck, mostly cooking their own food, and the women and children sleeping beneath a large tarpaulin the sailors stretched for them the entire width of the deck. At night they played their pipes and danced, singing, shouting, and waving their arms—always the same tune played over and over again. They brought with them their own peculiar odour, and—well, other things besides. From the upper deck we watched them sometimes in the morning sunshine, poking heads and shoulders over the rail from beneath the tarpaulin, and casually dropping unmentionable living freight—carefully selected with finger and thumb—into the sea. In the middle of the dreadful operation they would glance up at us, then continue the process, nothing abashed! In the heat of the day they slept like logs on ropes, canvas, boards—anything they could find. And one brilliant July afternoon, just after we had left Ineboli, everybody dozing in the blaze of the day, there was a sudden splash, followed by a rushing of feet down the decks. One of the men, insecurely asleep upon a pile of boards against the bulwarks, had toppled over into the sea.

The ship began to turn instantly, and three white lifebuoys dropped into the water without many seconds' delay; but the man was far astern before a boat could be lowered. It was impossible to help him. In his thick clothing, with the bulging, baggy trousers and heavy boots, he only kept afloat for a few minutes. Instead of swimming towards the buoys he swam away from them; and his companions declared he did not even know what they were, for most of these people had never seen the sea before, much less been afloat on it. It was a painful sight. Before we quite realised that the man was deliberately avoiding the buoys, we saw his fez bobbing on the calm blue surface, the face below it gone. For two hours the boat searched, but the body never came again to the top, and in due course the steamer continued her slow course towards Constantinople.

The brother and father of the victim seemed to take less interest in the misfortune than anyone else. There was a Turkish officer on board, who drew up an official account of the affair, but they answered his questions without emotion or distress. They were Mohammedans; it was Kismet. All that afternoon they sat apart by themselves, however, on the deck, rolling endless cigarettes and making coffee. And from time to time, down the expressionless countenance of the older man, I saw a tear fall and drop to the ground. They did not speak to each other. They simply sat there—waiting.

Egypt: An Impression

A considerable amount of nonsense has been written about the spell of Egypt. Cheapened by exaggeration, vulgarised by familiarity, it has become for many a picture post-card spell, pinned against the mind like the posters at a railway terminus. The moment Alexandria is reached, this huge post-card hangs across the heavens, blazing in an over-coloured sunset, composed theatrically of temple, pyramid, palm trees by the shining Nile, and the inevitable Sphinx. And the monstrosity of it paralyses the mind. Its strident shout deafens the imagination. Memory escapes with difficulty from the insistent gross advertisement. The post-card and the poster smother sight.

Behind this glare and glitter there hides, however, another delicate yet potent thing that is somehow nameless, not acknowledged by all, perhaps because so curiously elusive, yet surely felt by all because it is so true: intensely vital, certainly, since it thus survives the suffocation of its vile exaggeration. For the ordinary tourist yields to it, and not alone the excavator and archaeologist; the latter, indeed, who live long in the country, cease to be aware of it as an outside influence, having changed insensibly in thought and feeling till they have become it; it is in their blood. An effect is wrought subtly on the mind that does not pass away. Having once "gone down into Egypt," you are never quite the same again. Certain values have curiously changed, perspective has altered, emotions have shifted their specific gravity, some attitude to life, in a word, been emphasised and another, as it were, obliterated. The spell works underground and, being not properly comprehensible, *is* nameless. Moreover, it is the casual visitor, unburdened by antiquarian and historical knowledge, who may best estimate its power—the tourist who knows merely what he has gleaned, for instance, from reading over Baedeker's general synopsis on the voyage. He is aware of this floating power everywhere, yet unable to fix it to a definite cause. It remains at large, evasive, singularly fascinating.

All countries, of course, colour thought and memory, and work a spell upon the imagination of any but the hopelessly inanimate. Greece, India, Japan, Ireland, or the Channel Islands, leave their mark and imprint—whence the educational value of travel-psychology—but from these the traveller brings back feelings and memories he can evoke at will and label. He returns from Egypt with a marvellous blur. All, in differing terms, report a similar thing. From the first few months in Egypt, saturated maybe with overmuch, the mind recalls with definiteness—nothing. There comes to its summons a colossal medley that half stupefies; vast reaches of yellow sand drenched in a sunlight that stings; dim, solemn aisles of granite silence; stupendous monoliths that stare unblinking at the sun; the shining river, licking softly at the lips of a murderous desert; and an enormous night-sky literally drowned in stars. A score of temples melt down into a single monster; the Nile spreads everywhere; great pyramids float across the sky like clouds; palms rustle in mid-air; and from caverned leagues of subterranean gloom there issues a roar of voices, thunderous yet muffled, that seem to utter the hieroglyphics of a forgotten tongue. The entire mental horizon, oddly lifted, brims with this procession of gigantic things, then empties again without a word of explanation, leaving a litter of big adjectives chasing one another chaotically—chief among them "mysterious," "unchanging," "Formidable," "Terrific."

But the single, bigger memory that should link all these together intelligibly hides from sight the emotion too deep for specific recognition, too vast, somehow, for articulate recovery. The Acropolis, the wonders of Japan and India, the mind can grasp—or thinks so; but this composite enormity of Ramesseum, Serapeum, Karnak, Cheops, Sphinx, with a hundred temples and a thousand miles of sand, it *knows* it cannot. The mind is a blank. Egypt, it seems, has faded. Memory certainly fails, and description wilts. There seems nothing precisely to report, no interesting, clear, intelligible thing. "What did you see in Egypt? What did you like best? What impression did Egypt make upon you?" seem questions impossible to answer. Imagination flickers, stammers and goes out. Thought hesitates and stops. A little shudder, probably, makes itself felt. There is an impotent attempt to describe a temple or two, an expedition on donkey-back into the desert; but it sounds unreal, the language wrong, foolish, even affected. That dreadful Post-card rises like a wall. "Oh, I liked it all immensely. The delightful dry heat, you know—and one can always count upon the weather for picnics arranged ahead, and—" until the conversation can be changed to theatres or the crops at home.

Yet behind the words, behind the Post-card, one is aware all the time of some huge, alluring thing, alive with a pageantry of ages, strangely brilliant, dignified, magnificent, appealing almost to tears—something that drifts past like a ghostly full-rigged vessel with crowded decks and sails painted in an underworld, and yet the whole too close before the eyes for proper sight. The spell has become operative! Having been warned to expect this I, personally, had yet remained sceptical—until I experienced its truth.... And it was undeniably disappointing. After time and money spent, one had apparently brought back so little.

I remember asking myself point blank in solitude, what I had gained, and I remember the fruitless result. Nothing came but that abominable, shouting Post-card, endlessly extended. Its very endlessness, however, was a clue. Egypt *is* endless and inexhaustible; some hint of eternity lies there, an awareness of immortality almost. To-day, after a doze of four or five thousand years, subterranean Egypt peeps up again at the sun. The vast Memphian cemetery that stretches from Sakkhâra to the Mena House has begun to whisper in the daylight. The Theban worship of the sun is being reconstructed. There is a sense of deathlessness about the ancient Nile, about the grim Sphinx and Pyramids, in the very colonnades of Karnak, whose pylons now once more stand upright after a sleep of forty centuries on their backs; above all, in the appealing strength of the floating, rustling sand—something that defies time and repudiates change in death. Out of that flat, undifferentiated landscape which is Egypt, still stand the unconquerable finger-posts of stone, pointing, like symbols of eternity, to the equally unchanging skies. The spell is laid upon you once you have looked into the battered visages of those Memnon terrors, which reveal, yet hide, far better than the Sphinx. They have neither eyes, nor lips, nor nose; their features, as their message, inscrutable. Yet they tell this nameless thing plainly *because* they have no words. Out of the green fields of millet they stand like portions of the Theban mountains that have slid down into the plain, then stopped for a few more centuries to stare across the Nile and watch the sunrise. From them, as partly from the opened tombs of priest and Pharaoh, comes some ingredient of this singular spell.

But the mind has to escape first from the picture post-card influence before the genuine effect emerges. For the mind has in reality suffered a bludgeoning that is partly stunning. Then, with the passing of the weeks amid surroundings of lesser scale, the glamour asserts its magical accomplishment. Slowly it stirred to life in me; and its grip may be, with some, tremendous. It has attacked unseen, and few escape it altogether, while yet it can neither be told nor painted, nor quite explained. Unguessed at first, because sought for in some crude, tangible form it never, never assumes, it flames up unexpectedly—perhaps in a London street when fog shrouds the chimneys; perhaps at a concert; perhaps in a tearoom among perfumed, gossiping women; in church, at the club, even in bed when falling sleep just after a commonplace evening at a commonplace play. A sound recalls the street cry of the Arabs, with its haunting sing-song melody, a breath of air brings back the heated sand, a rustle of the curtain whispers as the palms and acacia whisper—and the truth is realised. Up steals the immense Egyptian glamour. It pours, it rushes up. It is over you in a moment. All this time it has lain coiled in deep recesses of the inner being—recesses where there is silence because they are inaccessible amid the clamour of daily life. There is awe in it, a hint of cold eternity, a glimpse of something unchanging and terrific, yet, at the same time, soft and very tender too. The pictures unroll and spread. You feel again the untold melancholy of the Nile. The grandeur of a hundred battered temples beats upon the heart. There is a sense of unutterable beauty. Something in you bows to the procession that includes great figures of non-human lineage. Up sweeps the electric desert air, the alive wind, the wild and delicate perfume of the sand; the luminous grey shadows brush you; you feel the enormous scale of naked desolation which yet brims with strange vitality. An Arab on a donkey flits in colour across the mind, melting off into tiny perspective. A string of camels stands against the sky, swaying forwards the same moment as though it never ceased. A dozen pyramids cleave the air with monstrous wedges, pointing holes in space. In peace and silence, belonging to a loneliness of ages, rise heads and shoulders of towering gods of stone, little jackals silhouetted, perhaps, an instant against thighs half buried in sand. Great winds, great blazing spaces, great days and nights of shining wonder float past from the pavement or the theatre stall, and London, dim-lit England, the whole of modern life indeed, are reduced sharply to a miniature of trifling ugliness that seems the unreality. Egypt rolls through the heart for a second, and is gone. You remember resignedly that you have an appointment to play golf tomorrow with Jones, or you are to lunch with Lady X., and that it may probably rain, and you must go in tubes and taxis, be crowded, jostled, pressed upon by ugly details of time and space. Conventions drive you; your top-hat has to be blocked before you can wear it. You have calls to pay. But out there, the days swam past in a flood of golden light and, caught in a procession of ancient splendours, changeless as the leisured Nile, majestic as the tameless desert, and fresh still with the wonder that first created them, you moved with the tide as of some unconditioned world. Egypt steals out and whispers to you in your dreams. Once more you float in an atmosphere of passionate mirages. The spell is upon you heavily. And this is not mere spinning of words in an attempt to conjure up an atmosphere. The thing is really there. You feel it always, and it always evades analysis. The mind is aware of something that is unmanageable. The idea suggests itself that, while some countries give, others may take away.

Egypt, with a power of seduction almost uncanny, has robbed the mind of a faculty best described perhaps as the faculty of measurement. Its scale has stupefied the ability to measure, appraise, estimate; and this balance once destroyed, wonder and awe capture the heart, going what pace they please. Size works half the miracle, for it is size including a quality of terror—monstrous; and, but for the glorious beauty that thunders through it, this sheer size might easily work a very different spell—dismay. The modern mind, no longer terrified by Speed, to which it has grown contemptuously accustomed, yet shrinks a little before this display of titanic and bewildering size. Egypt makes it realise that it has no handy standard of measurement. It listens to words that are meaningless. The vast proportions uplift, then stupefy. The girth of the pyramids, the height of the Colossi, the cubic content of the granite columns and the visage of the Sphinx expressed in yards—these convey as little truth as the numbered leagues of the frightening desert or the length of that weary and interminable Nile. You draw a deep breath of astonishment—then give up the vain attempt to grapple with a thing you cannot readily assimilate. A dizziness of star-distances steals over you; there is a breathlessness of astronomical scale in it that exhilarates while it stuns. What mind can gain by the information that our sun, with all its retinue of planets, sweeps annually thirty-five million miles nearer to a certain star in Hercules—yet that Hercules *looks* no closer than it did thousands of years ago? Such distance lies beyond comprehension. Similarly, in Egypt, there is something that continually evades capture in the monstrous details of sheer size, beautiful with majesty, that day and night tower above the shrinking reason. You believe because you see, but though you know you see, you are not sure what you quite believe. Herein lies one letter, at least, of the spell of Egypt. The mind is forever aware of something that haunts from the further side of experience.

But assuredly it is only one letter in a sentence that no one hears complete, for there seems an other-worldly element in this strange land that is acknowledged by every type, its presence detected in the most ordinary remarks. At a Cairo dance or a Heliopolis gymkhana you may hear a thoughtless woman observe: "But, you know, there *is* something queer in Egypt, isn't there? One simply can't deny it!" while the man, half puzzled and half contemptuous, laughs it off, falling back for explanation upon historical associations, vanished civilisations, mummies, temples and the rest. The "queer thing" however, is not so easily denied, for it is more than any of these. Just as in good conversation there is present among the talkers something that is greater than any one of them separately, so, when your mind meets Egypt and communes with it, there rises up this odd other-worldly presence, equally real, equally undecipherable.

A party of us—to quote an instance of its effect upon an ordinary wholesome mind, called usually "level-headed"—were on our way one night to see the Sphinx by moonlight under the guidance of a distinguished Egyptologist. We were on donkey-back. The night was very still, the sky thick with stars, moonlight flooding everything. As we skirted the huge flanks of the Great Pyramid, half in silver, half in black, its soaring edges lit by stars as by stationary lanterns, the business man asked a question of our learned leader. And in daily life he was a man of acute intelligence, guided by logic and reason, successful, rich. "Did they build the pyramid from within outwards?" was his question, as he gazed up at the towering mystery of the colossal outline. The question seemed quite natural, its utter absurdity not at first apparent. A second afterwards one realised the nonsense of it, and longs to hear the grave reply: "No, they hung the apex in mid-air and then built downwards from it." But, though the Egyptologist resisted the temptation to be funny at the questioner's expense, one somehow felt that had he answered thus, the man would have accepted the explanation without demur. It would have caused him no surprise, for *credo quia incredible* does actually represent one's attitude to things in this ancient and mysterious country. "Ah, I see," was all he said, with a sigh, when told that a pyramid was merely a king's mausoleum and that a layer of stone was added for each year he lived; "a big job for a contractor, wasn't it?" He was no whit ashamed of his idiotic question. "A hundred thousand men working for twenty years built this one," added the other, as we turned its corner and saw the dark head of the monster guarding its approach through all the centuries.

So everywhere—one hears this kind of question, as though the mind grew childish before an incomprehensible thing. Some shadowy magic pervades the faculties; their natural alertness fails; talk is in whispers, almost as if someone were listening; unreality broods over mood and speech and action. The Impossible, dressed in colours of strange, unfading brilliance, stoops down from some tremendous height, steals close past the windows of the mind, halts a moment, peers in—and vanishes. But the mind has seen the outline, has felt the eerie fascination. What it would instantly reject in the Midlands, on a Scotch moor, on a Rhine steamer, or on Brighton Pier, it harbours here with semi-acceptance and belief. The land exhales a steam of enchantment that lulls the senses. You move through this almost visible glamour. All about you is a high, transparent screen, built by the centuries, and left standing; and here and there are gaps in it; modern life, cast like a cinema picture upon this screen, becomes the unreality; but, behind it, a vast audience gathered by the ages watches and looks on—at *us*. And occasionally, aware of being watched, the mind sees through a gap—and asks a wild question, as the businessman at the pyramid asked one. Anything is possible, and anything may happen.

There are some who claim things *do* happen. Imagination constructs swiftly in Egypt, with small opposition from the reason. The creative instinct fairly strides. "I always expect something unusual to happen when I'm out here," is a sentence repeatedly heard. "Last time I came out there was disaster. Something unexpected will happen this year, too." As though in this coaxing heat of climate, in this rich glory of a past now being unearthed from day to day, and in this brilliant, vivid quality of its present personality, so oddly stimulating, there lies some quality that acts with the effect of a forcing-house upon the character, bringing out latent possibilities, hurrying on events, developing a rush of life too swift for comfort or full understanding. Certainly no one can see Egypt and remain quite what they were before, however much interpretation of its haunting effect may vary for individuals.

For some, a rather dominant impression is undoubtedly "the monstrous." A splendour of awful dream, yet never quite of nightmare, stalks everywhere, suggesting an atmosphere of Kubla Khan. There is nothing lyrical. Even the silvery river, the slender palms, the fields of clover and barley and the acres of flashing poppies convey no lyrical sweetness, as elsewhere they might. All moves to a statelier measure. Stern issues of life and death are in the air, and in the grandeur of the tombs and temples there is a solemnity of genuine awe that makes the blood run slow a little. Those Theban Hills, where the kings and queens lay buried, are forbidding to the point of discomfort almost. The listening silence in the grim Valley of the Tombs of the Kings, the intolerable glare of sunshine on the stones, the naked absence of any sign of animal or vegetable life, the slow approach to the secret hiding-place where the mummy of a once powerful monarch lies ghastly now beneath the glitter of an electric light, the implacable desert, deadly with heat and distance on every side—this picture, once seen, rather colours one's memory of the rest of Egypt with its sombre and funereal character.

And with the great deific monoliths, the effect is similar. Proportions and sheer size strike blow after blow upon the mind. Stupendous figures, shrouded to the eyes, shoulder their way slowly through the shifting sands, deathless themselves and half-appalling. Their attitudes and gestures express the hieroglyphic drawings come to life. Their towering heads, coiffed with zodiacal signs, or grotesque with animal or bird, bend down to watch you everywhere. There is no hurry in them; they move with the leisure of the moon, with the stateliness of the sun, with the slow silence of the constellations. But they move. There *is*, between you and them, this effect of a screen, erected by the ages, yet that any moment may turn thin and let them through upon you. A hand of shadow, but with granite grip, may steal forth and draw you away into some region where they dwell among changeless symbols like themselves, a region vast, ancient and undifferentiated as the desert that has produced them. Their effect in the end is weird, difficult to describe, but real. Talk with a mind that has been steeped for years in their atmosphere and presence and you will appreciate this odd reality. The spell of Egypt is an other-worldly spell, its vagueness, its elusiveness, its undeniable reality are ingredients, at any rate, in a total result whose detailed analysis lies hidden in mystery and silence—inscrutable.

SECTION 4: CONFLICTS OF THE SOUL

This final section looks at how Blackwood coped with the First World War. The essay "The Old World Beauty," written over a year into the conflict, showed how Blackwood despaired at the damage the War was inflicting on those places of beauty that he had visited and how we needed to cling to that memory of beauty to maintain our spirits.

Blackwood had sought to help in the War by working in the Field Ambulance Service but delays led to him becoming involved in writing propaganda. Blackwood's approach was to try and lift people's spirits as evident in "The Miracle" and "The Soldier's Visitor." "The Paper Man" shows a different mood, however. On one level it works to show the low morale of those who wanted to contribute to the war effort but could not, but on a deeper level it gives some idea of how shallow Blackwood regarded they way most newspapers sought to disseminate propaganda. To him, sending thousands of young men into the killing fields and trenches was achieving nothing and he believed that many of those guiding the war were weak and lacked vision. He was particularly affected by the disastrous Gallipoli Campaign of 1915/16 and in order to get some sense of proportion from the scale of death and carnage he wrote "Proportion" during the summer of 1916.

Soon after this, following a brief period working for the Field Ambulance Service, Blackwood was recruited as an Intelligence Agent because of his knowledge of French and German and his familiarity with Switzerland. Blackwood could only sustain this work for six months before the consequences of his actions haunted him. Not only did he fear for his own safety, but also for those of the agents whom he helped recruit and despatched on their dangerous ventures. The trauma of this work laid heavily with him and eventually emerged in a bizarrely surreal story "Onanonanon."

Blackwood subsequently worked as a Searcher for the Red Cross trying to trace the lost and missing. It was another job that drained his soul and spirit and laid him low. He had to draw upon all his reserves and spiritual strength to psychologically survive the War and cope with post-war life. Inevitably he drew upon his love of nature and his memory of wonders past, and towards the end of the War he incorporated these into the short story "The Memory of Beauty."

—*Mike Ashley*

The Old-World Beauty

It is the fact, probably, that a large number of people are dazed at the present time, and have been dazed for many months. To grasp so vast a situation is a painful effort beyond the reach of the majority. The scale, the magnitude, bewilders. No ordinary mind can retain a picture of so many fronts at once, let alone obtain a general, or what is called a bird's-eye, view of all the Empire's scattered operations. The Flanders front can be managed, perhaps the Russian line, even the French front in Artois, Champagne, the Vosges; but to obtain a steady mental picture even of these is a distinct effort, the Belgian piece in the puzzle coming in as best it can. The shower of daily maps, set to various scales in one's favourite newspaper, confuses the memory. Nine persons out of ten have little notion where the British Army's front links on respectively to the French and Belgian fronts, and "somewhere in Flanders" describes (with an accuracy the Censor never intended) the picture most of us succeed in visualising.

But when it comes to the Balkans, the Caucasus, Greece, to say nothing of Persia and the Tigris, not five in a hundred, at a generous canvass, would acquit themselves with anything approaching honour. How many know where the magic Tigris flows? How many could dot Bagdad within one clear degree? Is there any one of ordinary education who could indicate within a hundred miles where Bessarabia, Rumania, Bulgaria take the Black Sea waters? The lie of the ancient Danube, once it curves away sharply below Budapest, is nothing but an ingenious snare for any memory, and as for Thrace and Macedonia, except for those who have travelled there on foot or mule-back, it is surely as vague as our dear old lady's Mesopotamia. We are learning something of geography at last, though at a price that is cruelly prohibitive. Our new-learned maps are drawn, alas! in crimson. We know the heroic outline of little Serbia, at any rate; nor are we likely ever to forget it.

In a Canadian canoe, I once paddled down the Danube from its source in the shadows of the Black Forest as far as Budapest—something like 1000 miles, perhaps; but before studying the map for the journey I confess I had little notion what course the mighty river took, and that it rose in the Schwarzwald, near Donauieschingen (which has several times been bombed from the air by French aeroplanes since 1914), was a distinct shock to me. I had imagined it so much more remote. To paddle along its little stream between the flowered meadows of Bavaria offended somehow the memory of my schooldays. It seemed too near home—though the Austrian and Hungarian reaches soon restored my cherished perspective. Again with the haunted Caucasus, the old longing to see the dim Prometheus peak and precipice, to land on the shores of

Colchis, where the ghostly Argonauts would watch me lest I see the gleaming fleece among the walnut woods—this keen desire yet left me wholly uninformed of where the frosted mountains actually stood upon the map. By sea, however, the approach to the Caucasus is adequate. From Marseilles the leisurely steamer stopped at Naples, skirted old smoking Stromboli, left on one side the deep caves where Æolus stored the winds, then slipped past Messina and Reggio, and paused for some hours in the shadow of towering Etna. It was all so gradual that the remoteness and grandeur of the Titans' mountains increased with every stage in the voyage. Then Crete and the Isles of Greece came floating on that mythical blue sea, and the birth of Aphrodite seemed no less distant in time than the dark gorges where Demogorgon ruled. And from Smyrna to Brussa, and Brussa to Constantinople, and thence across the Black Sea to Batum, were no longer intervals upon the map, but dim, vanished centuries within the mind. The gleaming summit of Elbruz in the blue, seen first from the steamer deck at an incredible height of air, was the true vision of the ancient Caucasus. Those astounding mountains where Turks and Russians fight in the twentieth century descended upon me from the very heavens. Even to-day that perfect vision I first had of them seems to shine behind every communiqué the papers print.

It was early in the war that the Turks and Russians battled for the copper mines at Artvin, and I vainly try to remember now who eventually obtained possession. But I recall vividly my own journey there, before losing myself in the bigger mountains. Artvin lies some fifty miles south-east of Batum, and the copper is so thick that it can almost be struck loose with a pick-axe. In past ages the Phœnicians worked these mines, but when I was there, some five years ago, an American syndicate, including Mr. Pierpont Morgan, had control. The labour employed was Persian, Georgian, Russian—that is, Mahometan and Christian. The higher posts of responsibility were held by Armenians, by far the most alert and intelligent element of the Caucasian (Georgian) population— and hated accordingly. The mixture of creeds produced confusion, sometimes disaster too, as when, instead of emptying the huge cauldron of molten copper, the devout Mahometan prostrated himself in prayer. The American engineer told me many a tale of his troubles. An aerial trolley carried the ore in trucks to the smelting works a thousand feet below. These trucks never halted, only paus- ing a fraction of a minute to empty themselves. A live pig, sent up as food one day to the upper quarries, went round and round for hours—the man who ought to have "emptied" it out being a Persian, who refused to touch the un- clean thing at any price. The country here (6000 ft. up) was very wonderful— miles of azalea and rhododendron all in blossom; the air too strongly per- fumed to be comfortable. Accompanied by three armed Turks as escort—the Yankee engineer insisted—I climbed a ten-thousand-feet peak to see the sun rise over the far Black Sea. A land of magical beauty lay below; but warships, black and grim, rush to and fro where the high-curved prow of the Argonaut vessel once cut the waves, while the woods where the Golden Fleece hung shining now bristle, presumably, with barbed wire and machine guns!

Among the lesser losses caused by this war is certainly a loss of beauty and poetical association that for many will be poignant. The Isles of Greece, for instance! The lofty ideal of heroic days, the grandeur of Marathon and Salamis! In their place (*timao Dañaos*) rises the sordid picture of a frightened monarch, treachery, and cynical double-dealing in every word and act. The glory that was Greece, of course, safe in the keeping of the past, can never die, and Marathon still looks on the sea; but "Hellas" for most of us is now become a synonym for honour purchased by an alien gold, and of a mean and spiritless scramble for safety. The Caucasus, too, has changed significantly in certain ways. True, we shall ever associate the name with the splendid fighting of the Russian armies in the cause of liberty, but at the same time those grim heights overlook the plains where an entire nation has been exterminated in cold blood like so many stampeded cattle. What once was the prison of the hero who stole heaven's fire to benefit the human race has witnessed the systematic annihilation of the Armenian nation—the ghastliest crime of the entire war. These names of beauty, instead of causing a thrill of happiness and yearning in future for most of us, will waken sighs and shuddering.

And, nearer home, the loss is poignant too. Where, now, is the haunting wonder of the fabled Hartz? The gentle beauty of the old German forests, where fay and cobbold danced and sang, sweet with the associations of our childhood? The castles on the Rhine, the Lorelei, the water-maidens, and the fair princesses of that old-world atmosphere of blue and gold? One and all obliterated by blood, by the blackest cruelty the world has ever known, by a spirit that has proved itself literally non-human!

There are numerous other instances where peculiarly devilish horror of the Prussian ideal has stripped beauty from the minds of men. Yet the spirit of this old-world beauty will not die, but only find a safer and more lasting home. Already Belgium has enshrined it afresh for all of us. Italy, true to the great legends in her soul, keeps it alive and flaming. With Allies like France and Russia the vision will not leave the world. For the world has need of it, the simple old-time beauty; and the ideal we are fighting for contains this, too.

The Miracle

Beauty has crept into our darkened streets again, and the soul of London is aware of it. The phenomenon is strictly wonderful. London herself, in the blue gloom of the Parks, along the shadowy streets, and at the upper windows of a million houses—London, as an entity, is aware. For behind and through this veil of unaccustomed shadow stirs something that is deathless. Unnoticed during easy and luxurious days, too obvious in hours of sunshine to be detected, it now steals forth, claims recognition, draws attention to itself. It is a marvellous and delicate thing, yet of incalculable potentiality. It is that which scientists are supposed to ignore and biologists to deny. It is the soul. But it is not individual. It is corporate.

With the dipping of the flashing lights it now comes forth into its own. And it is passing strange. We see the stars again. We are witnessing a religious and mystical phenomenon of ultimate significance, that which the Churches insist must happen in a regenerated heart, that which religions of all climes and ages affirm as of paramount importance—sign and proof of spiritual awakening. And this mystical occurrence is already accomplished in our midst—the midst of a practical, hard-headed business nation of the twentieth century. It is essentially divine. It is the loss of self.

It was effected in a moment, in the twinkling of an eye. Out of that night in early August when the wireless and cables flashed round the world the news that England had gone to war it emerged. By morning it was an accomplished fact. The inner and outer reconciliation of all conflict and disagreement in every corner of the Empire was its evidence. It was a miracle. And the miracle was conversion, regeneration. The result, attained so simply, was strictly wonderful.

Separate, smaller entities, groups of opponents, bodies at war with other bodies, all merged at that significant bugle-call into a corporate and indivisible whole. The Empire became, psychologically, a crowd: one Being. The ease, the simplicity, the instantaneous character of the result—these are of the spiritual order. The individual passed away, sunk his differences, forgot his personal ambitions, lost and merged in something greater than himself. There was no effort, there was no resistance. A group-consciousness came into existence spontaneously and of its own accord.

The thing is happening still on every side; rather, the evidence that it has happened is to be seen all day long in street and park and courtyard: drilling. Men, to whom such an event had never once appeared as even a possible eventuality, are drilling by the thousand; are being drilled as naturally as they formerly ate their breakfast or went to golf and tennis. What has taken place as a whole is taking place in every smaller portion of that Whole. The object, more-over, is not to kill, but to keep alive—truth, justice, mercy, Liberty. Awkward Squads are visible on every hand, nobility the word of command. Next to you stands a scholar, beyond him an artist famous in two hemispheres, behind you a singer whose voice brings joy to thousands. In July the notion that these men could ever drill in an Earl's Court building would have seemed ridiculous. Now it is right, reasonable, and beautiful as well. They have lost themselves and found themselves: they are part of a Whole, their Company. Proud, willing, happy, they just let themselves be drilled, and have no questions to ask, even of them-selves. They are scolded, shouted at, rebuked and praised alternately, by a lad who happens to have learned the words of command and technique they are ig-norant of. In July he sold behind a counter the twelve-and-six-penny volumes that the scholar wrote, or through a narrow window took in guineas from members of the public who wished to hear the singer ten days later—but now he has these great men obedient to his will and orders, hanging intently upon his lightest word, because these are the word and orders of the larger Being whose servant he likewise is. He and that awkward squad are one. The items composing it no longer are individuals. All are merged into a harmonious, cor-porate body that is a group-soul.

And those who cannot drill in an Earl's Court or Post Office quadrangle, who for the best reasons continue the daily round, the common task as usual, these are none the less equally involved in the loss of the personal which is due to ab-sorption in the thing that is greater than themselves. They drill invisibly, but they are drilled. The religious, mystical phenomenon is consummated in them also. For even—and especially—the Saint, worthy of the name, still does his daily duties, but does them unto an ideal larger, higher than himself, an ideal he styles variously, perhaps, but usually styles God.

The Paper Man

Dimble was not too proud to fight, but he was too old, too stiff, too blind; he could not drill properly, because he really had to think a moment before he knew which was his left and which his right. There are some men who can positively do nothing; he was one of them. With the best intentions in the world, burning, zealous intentions too, he was yet useless. Unable to help, he lost that comfort which comes the moment one's smaller burden is merged in the collective burden of the nation. That peace being denied him, his interest in the war, on the other hand being intense, he merely—*read*. Morning, noon and night, he read. He read all the papers, but on Sunday he read only four, not counting "extras." Sunday was his day off.

He plunged with the ease of a bird from the heights of optimism to the depths of pessimism. It wore him out. He believed everything he read. Every move made on the great chess-board was a clever trap into which either the enemy or the Allies would march blind-eyed. He yearned to warn the latter. In time, however, the "trap" idea collapsed; it never came off; the lure was non-existent. A certain paper declared that the enemy would never be caught without its glasses... he gave up buying it for a week, then surreptitiously went back to it because it *proved* that the Germans were using their last reserves. A bad communiqué could keep him awake at night—so could a very good one....

From the Eastern and Western fronts, at length, he switched off upon the Balkans, till he became so entangled that he—well, though his walls were covered with maps, he never could remember whether Roumania was north of Bulgaria, or vice versa; nor which country claimed Bucharest or Sofia as its capital. Invariably he had to inspect his maps. Bucharest, since it began with B, ought to belong to Bulgaria; sometimes judging by the articles, it didn't. The Balkans became a gigantic jig-saw puzzle, all corners and curves and points and angles that would not fit. The coloured flags pricked his fingers, the maps got stained, the strip of carpet below them grew threadbare.

For a time he confined himself to picture-papers, till he read that most of the scenes were made somewhere in Surrey or taken from manoeuvres of five years ago. He flung himself next upon strategy and diagrams of positions, till the chintzes on his chairs expressed surprise and peril, and the very blood in his strained eye-balls mapped the empty air with danger; reality faded from the world. He himself "advanced" up the street or "retired" to his bedroom. On the way to his bath he muttered left, right, left, left, left—halt!—then had to "retreat in perfect order" for his forgotten sponge and towel.

He confined himself in the last resort to "official news." This called for grim restraint, but the truth was he was getting a little frightened. His speech showed

signs of trouble and sounds became audible in his head occasionally—z...
sz... scz... czs... and pmj or mjp... and the like. He became aware of showers
of them sprinkling almost visibly through the air—in the darkness, explosive,
spitting sparks. They even pricked him. His tongue and throat grew sore. And
there were other symptoms that alarmed him. The worst, perhaps, was the mute
j. He had somehow got full of them without knowing it, either swallowed
them or breathed them in, he knew not which; but in any case he was interiorly
somewhat crowded with soft heaps of these mute js. They were akin to microbes
of a suppressed illness; for any moment—it was horrible to think of—they
might emerge, appear, express themselves, become not mute!

"And what are *you* doing, Dimble?" asked Spriggins at the Club one day,
good-naturedly. Spriggins, though bald and crooked, wore "G. R." and a big
red armlet every Sunday on route marches that nearly killed him. Dimble
looked up helplessly into his face. He answered. Speech of a kind, at least, came
twanging, buzzing from his lips:

"Czskz... kivitch... ski... kzs... z... z... z... jjjjjj!" he replied. His voice
cracked oddly; tiny explosions were audible inside his chest; his throat held
soda-water.

He did not notice how Spriggins got away; he "retreated," apparently in good
order. It was certainly a rapid movement. Spriggins was not surrounded, at all
events. And he left Dimble standing there as though he had been burned, destroyed, utterly devastated till nothing of any value remained inside his outer
physical frame.

Matters had grown so serious by this time that he made a prodigious effort
and renounced all papers whatsoever—for an entire day. For twenty-four
hours he read no news, no expert articles, no forecasts, no résumés, no analy-
ses of the Balkan soul, nor one single report from a neutral traveller just returned
from everywhere. He did not even look at a line from an official or diplomatic
source whose authority it is impossible to doubt. He moved no single pin
upon his many maps. He lay in darkness—he also lay in bed. He starved. A
strange hunger woke in him. He knew an intolerable emptiness. He slept a little, however, and murmured in his sleep—for it was troubled—"Official news,
official news... csz... ksz... j.j.j...!"

Dimble recovered a bit and lived his life as best he could. He was careful now,
not to say cautious. He reconnoitred before every single act; also he deployed. But
things went rather quickly after that. He slept by day in a darkened room, and
went out only in the night. He could not see the posters thus; the paper man at
the corner, who now cut him dead instead of smiling cheerfully, could be avoided.
This was the serious stage for Dimble. By the candlelight in his bedroom he noticed curious marks upon his arm; the skin seemed mottled. He said, "Bites, by
Nicholas!" and thought of queer, invisible insects. Yet the marks apparently traced
a pattern; they had design, meaning, almost rhythm. They were horribly familiar. And then he knew—they were js. The mute js were coming out!

"Spies!" he cried in terror. "I'm betrayed! I've harboured spies! All this time they've been in my very midst."

He knew he was done for then, but he did not realise his ghastly position until the following night he detected further marks. They were quite distinct. He easily made them out in the dark. He saw "Official...."

It was a dreadful business. He could not tell a soul, because his communications were all cut. He faced the worst with courage; no one should say he was a coward or a slacker. He ordered all the papers again, and sat reading them by daylight in his room. He went boldly to the Club and read them openly, brazenly, with true defiance. He agreed with everything he read, he understood it all, but he had no feelings now, he was neither optimistic nor the reverse. He simply read....

It was odd, but no one noticed him. In his room one day the landlady came in to brush and sweep—she ignored his presence, tidying the papers up all round him as though he were not there at all. The same thing happened at the Club. A waiter even tried to smooth him out and hang him on the file, and once he was nearly—oh, it was wicked—nearly picked up and offered to another member—Spriggins! Only, luckily, Spriggins had the decency to refuse him. He did it so nicely, too: "No thanks," he said, with a little smile. "I've read it. There's nothing in it, anyhow!"

It was that very night when Dimble woke towards the early hours and heard a crackling as he turned in bed. Terror gripped him. He lay quite still and listened. It was at the end of the bed, apparently—a faint swishing, crackling noise with tiny reports accompanying it. He moved his foot; the sound was repeated. Something glimmered dimly. He moved the other foot, his arm as well; he sat up, briskly. There was a leaping rush of the vague white form across the air; with a tap and slither it fell upon the floor beside him. He stooped over to pick it up and his hand came into contact with something smooth and warm that was in the act of settling on the floor. He felt the little wind it made. It was, of course, a newspaper.

But the same instant, and before he removed his hand, he knew by the warmth of it that it was something more besides. It was not different from himself. What in the world had happened to him? It *was* himself. His hand was on the skin of his bare chest. He was crackling all over... but very nicely, very crisply. He settled back into bed with a kind of rush and slither. His terror passed. He felt well pleased with himself. "It's all right," he murmured as he fell asleep. "For a moment I thought it was a halfpenny one! I must be more careful. Near shave, that! I must mention it to Spriggins... when I'm out!" There was an odd smell of printer's ink in the air.

Next morning he came out duly, and Spriggins bought him for a penny, right enough, and took him in his pocket on a long route march. While resting for lunch with his company, out by the Welsh Harp, which is Endon Wy', he lit his pipe with him. Dimble tried to utter a protest, but he stammered horribly.

He could not get his words at all. He made a fizzy, crackling noise instead—of which Spriggins, puffing the smoke at him, took no slightest notice.

Then Dimble curled up, turned slowly black, and passed away into the wind, and fell into a stubble-field near by, and lay there quite happily until the dew that night came down softly and dissolved him into nothing—nothing visible or of value, at any rate.

The Soldier's Visitor

I sit in my room and dream.... Autumn steals across the slanting sunlight on the lawn, for the year stands at the keen, and the smells of childhood float beneath the thinning branches. In my long chair by the open window I sit and dream.... I played upon that lawn, I took the hawks' eggs from the dizzy, topmost branches; it was on turf like that I won the hundred yards. Sure of myself, I moved swiftly, easily, a few weeks, a few months—or was it years?—ago.... I have forgotten. It is past. I sit and dream....

The little room is narrow, but autumn, entering softly, brings in distance as of the open sky, with misty places that are immense. Once they seemed endless. The whole world enters; there are two magnificent horizons, where the sun sets and where it rises: both I could reach easily, without toil or pain, without the help of anyone. Birds pass from one horizon to the other, singing, high above all obstacles; I loved free space as they do; the sails are flashing white on blue, blue seas; there is the plash of mountain streams, the rustle of foliage... and the autumn wind goes past my window, picking the crisp, dying leaves from every bough.

"He will recover. At least, he will not lose the other," are the words I remember dimly, each syllable a century, each word an age. It was so long ago. And I try to rise and see the folded daisies as they take the sunset by the grey thatched summer-house. But my body stops—I cannot move without assistance.... I remember how it happened. I remember a pause, then saying aloud as quietly as if I were playing tennis, "Now, old chap, it's your turn! Go it!" There was a blank, but no terror, and no pain. I heard no noise, the explosion was quite soundless; my last cartridge was gone, my bayonet was in... then came the stretcher.... God bless those fellows, those brave and tireless bearers.... A dirty job! He'll bless them for me. I can't even go across the field to find them.

The sunlight dies; the leaves are down; the chill air cloaks the laurel shrubberies in white and gauze; the soaking dew begins to fall. I am in England. England! She was in danger, so they said. That's why I'm here, I suppose. She's taking care of me. I did my bit, my best. Nine months of weary training, three days of glorious fighting. Then this....

I am carried back into the bed, the lamp is lit, the figures, speaking low and with marvellous tenderness, are gone. I am alone, my pals are out there... where there is singing, stories, action. There is no singing here, no stories. I am in a hothouse—damn...!

I glance at my little table by the pillow, at the small white jug of liquid food, at the little silver bell, the glass with the sleeping draught... and I turn the lamp out and watch through the open window the faces of the peeping stars. A bat flies past; I hear a moth's big wings; a corncrake whirrs and rattles far away—I used to chase all three.... No other sound is in the world. The hours are asleep. Autumn sits in her lonely wood, weaving her red and yellow leaves into a net to hold me lest I fall! When I wake in the morning, I shall see her tears upon the crimson leaves, upon the grass, upon the iron railing, big, big drops as clear as crystal, holding all the sky. I shall see the few lost stitches that she dropped, floating on cobwebs in the yellow sunlight. I shall hear her cloak sweep trailing through the beech-wood on the hill. And that is the cloak I ask to cover me—below the knees. I shall also smell the perfume of her lustrous hair—but that hair, that perfume I shall take to wrap my thoughts in, and my dreams, through years to come....

For I shall recover. But I shall not—no, I shall never again in this world—I cannot say it—below both knees—I know it—I am nothing.

There came a knock quite suddenly at the door... and I shut my eyes, because I had no liking for my night-nurse. I left my hand outside upon the coverlet, that she might take my pulse, then leave me without that meeting of the eye, that intimate gesture, that exchange of little words that were distasteful to me. It was, no doubt, a sick man's whim, and yet to me just then it was intolerable. To meet the eye is an intimacy that draws the other person near, too near, unless she be desired and desirable. I feel the soul in contact. It is only one degree more intimate than to hear the mention of my name, my little name.... And yet, before my mind could question—it works slowly, thickly in this pain—who it was for certain my voice had answered, I had said, "Come in...."

I closed my eyes, however, none the less. But, through my lids, I felt the searching glance that saw me—more—that met my own. And I heard my name, my little name. A strange and marvellous thrill went through me. The very intimacies I had dreaded I now claimed eagerly. I opened my eyes and looked.

No especial revelation of beauty have I ever claimed in life, but I have known ideals, I have had my dreams like other men. The figure I now saw before me was surely not of this earth. The stars, the moon, sunlight, and wild flowers had made her, perhaps.... I was speechless.

"I have come like this," said the woman in the soft brown garment, "because there are things that I can give you now. Before—when you could seek them—you could not find them. Now that you cannot go to them they may come to you. They are all within your reach."

And then I saw that, while more beautiful and desirable than anyone I had ever known, she was yet strangely familiar to me. Where, how, under what conditions, I could not recall. She was some Grandeur, surely. Queens and the like, I knew, were visiting chaps like me, and yet she was not dressed as such folks dress, and her robe of russet-brown spread in some kind of imperial way behind her. It trailed, I fancied, through the open window, joining the mist above the lawn. The stars shone in it very faintly. But it was her incomparable beauty that made it difficult to speak, for my heart became suddenly so large it choked me.

"I must have dreamed of you," I murmured at length. A feeling of endless life rose in me—the life people so glibly call eternal. It was beyond description.

"Dreamed!" she echoed gently, shaking her head and smiling. "Oh no; not dreamed! I called you and you came." There was a touch of sternness in her smile that stirred the blood in me. But I did not understand.

"You *called* me?" I asked faintly, for such beauty put confusion in me.

"And you came," she answered. "It was no dream. You gave me all you had to give." She paused an instant; there was moisture in her eyes. "It is now my turn to give all you desire, all you ask or dream."

The feeling of familiarity was afflicting; but still I could not understand. As she spoke I saw burning love in the great clear eyes. But there was more than love; there was sympathy, understanding—a woman who could understand everything in the world—there was admiration, gratitude, and more than these—I swear it—there was worship.

"I have asked for nothing," I faltered, an unbelievable happiness rising. "I did not call—I had no thought—at least I only—"

"It is yours—all, all," she answered, "because of that. You did not ask, you did not think of self."

My face, of course, betrayed me hopelessly. The strange joy found utterance in a somewhat trembling voice, humbly, perhaps a little awed.

"I meant your Beauty…!" I whispered it in my inmost heart. For there was a shyness in me I could not understand.

And then a strange thing happened, for, as she stood between me and the open window, a light air stirred her dress, and I caught the gleam of something bright beneath, almost as though she wore a breastplate of some kind—like shining armour.

"Who are you, then?" I murmured, trying to raise myself, but sinking back again before the painful effort. I had the feeling that for such love as hers, such beauty, splendour, strength, no loss, no pain was of the least account. I forgot my conditions, almost my identity. I was just—a man like other men.

"I am rich," she answered, "I am true, and I am faithful unto death and after it. All that you ask is mine to give. And I am here to give it you."

"Me—?" I could not believe my ears. Something broke within me, bathing my soul in light. I repeated my astonished questions. I mentioned my name. I thought swiftly. Everything, by heaven, was worth it, if this were true.

She looked down at me for a long time without speaking. Then her lips moved a little; the wonderful eyes brimmed over; she said two perfect words as she gazed at me: "Thank you…." It was followed by my name, my little name.

What happened exactly I cannot tell. I remember thinking it must be somewhere a miserable mistake, that it was too impossible for truth, when in the midst of my anguish she again repeated my name with such pride and gratitude in her voice, such love and admiration in her eyes, that my doubts were gone and I felt re-made in joy. "It is written here," she said, pointing to where her heart lay beating behind the gleaming metal.

She then bent over me and kissed me... she took me in her comforting arms... I fell asleep. And in my sleep I dreamed of a new and glorious movement, light as air, and easy, swift as wind. Everything in the world was mine, for everything came to me of its own accord. All space lay within my reach. I was no longer walking, running, climbing. I had wings.... But also I remembered where it was that I had seen her, and consequently why I loved her so. I understood at last, God bless her, and I loved her all the more.

Hitherto, indeed, I had asked nothing of her knowingly, yet I had taken all she had to give. I suppose, unconsciously as it were, I knew this well enough. That, apparently, was why I fought.... At any rate, I remembered clearly where I had seen her, and why she seemed so curiously familiar, yet unrealized; for her face, now stamped upon my soul, is also stamped upon every copper penny of the Realm.

Proportion

I've been looking at the stars and thinking what an immense distance
they are away. What an insignificant thing the loss of, say, forty years
of life is compared with them! It seems scarcely worth talking
about....

(*From letter written home by a young officer on June 30. He was killed
on July 1.*)

Tired out with business by day and special-constabling by night, Heber
contrived a day or two at sea—what people called before the war, a week-end.
The town was full of soldiers, nurses, countless figures in blue with crutches,
bandages, armslings, eye-shades, and the rest. An extraordinarily cheerful lot;
he watched them with deep admiration. "If I were younger," he thought, "I
should be doing their job and, if they were older, they would be doing mine."
Self seemed eliminated before two mighty symbols—England and the Empire.

He pictured the little island on the map, so insignificant in size, so unconquerable in spirit. He saw in his mind huge India and the distant Colonies flock-
ing in to help. His thoughts, inspired by the khaki and blue on all sides, ran in
this groove, and his mind was crammed with detail he wanted to discuss. But
he had no companion, so had to keep his thoughts to himself.

He strolled out after the early hotel dinner, and walked idly along the front.
A few convalescents were about. Not a light was visible anywhere. The big stone
houses stood in rows with sightless windows—a desolate, deserted town,
empty and shuttered. No gleam, no single ray escaped; the blinds were down,
the curtains closely drawn, even the hotel front-doors were thickly shaded. The
inhabitants, it seemed, had fled. From a mile at sea no one could have known
there was anything but a lonely strip of undulating shore.

It was warm. A moon, somewhere between the half and quarter, sank on her
side into the quiet sea beyond a headland. Heber sat down in one of the shel-
ters and began to smoke; and just as he neared the end of his cigarette a figure
came shuffling in and sat down a few feet away—a convalescent soldier; even
in the dimness the outline was unmistakable, and the broad band of white where
the long trousers turned up above the boots gleamed faintly. It was a Tommy,
but the voice was cultivated. A Tommy in these days may be anybody.

Heber wondered. "Pretty dark, isn't it?" he ventured.

"Oh, you get used to that," was the reply. "It's right. In these sheltered coves
the submarines are apt to slip up for a breather and to get their bearings. And
the smallest light may help them."

There was something in the voice that made Heber interested. It stirred imagination in him. He thought of the stealthy, prowling under-water life, sneaking to and fro past wrecks and deep-sea fish, striking swift blows that seemed treacherous compared to fighting in the open. He wondered about the psychology of the men who did it. But these thoughts he did not utter. He offered a cigarette instead.

"Oh, that's kind of you. I'd like one. No—better not strike matches here. I'll take a light from yours, if I may."

The man, he saw, had one arm in a sling. The face he could not see, beyond that the eyes were shaded with dark glasses. "Flanders or the East?" he allowed himself to ask sympathetically.

"Gallipoli. A bit of shrapnel," was the brief reply.

"Bad luck."

"Might have been much worse. The eyes are nearly well now. I'd rather lose two legs than one eye." And he laughed slightly. "Sight means a lot to me."

The moon went down, the stars shone thickly, making little tremulous golden pathways on the sea. Heber fell to wondering who the man was, and what he did. He seemed about thirty or thereabouts. Somehow he did not make the impression of a soldier only. "You joined for this war, I suppose?" Heber ventured presently.

"That's right." And then he added, "New Zealand. My father's in sheep." Yet the man himself did not quite sound like "sheep." They smoked in silence for some minutes. Then came: "First time I'd seen these stars." And he began to talk about them. They were familiar to him as if he had lived beneath them all his life. He pointed out Jupiter and Venus, described the position of Sirius, mentioned Orion, just rising, and referred to the great nebula in his Belt; he knew their various magnitudes, indicated coloured Vega, and another brilliant star that he said was two stars actually, revolving round each other. Stranger still, he spoke of Jupiter's eight moons as though he knew accurately how many would be visible from the earth just now. While he did not say very much, his words were suggestive in some way that made Heber forget the details of the war he had wanted to discuss, and respond involuntarily to this less personal note.

"You know quite a lot about the stars," he remarked. "It's fascinating. I'd like to be an astronomer."

"Never tried it, have you?" said the other.

Heber laughed. "Costs too much for one thing—telescopes and so on."

"Telescopes, yes; they do cost a bit. I had one." He mentioned the power and Heber knew it was not procurable under many thousand pounds. "It was up at my father's place in the hills. Hobby of mine. In fact, I did nothing else. I gave it up, though—after a bit." He paused. There was a note of longing in his voice. "The strain was too much, I found."

"Health?" inquired his companion.

The soldier laughed. "Never had a day's illness in my life till Gallipoli knocked me out." A note of passion crept in somehow. "It was another kind of strain," he went on quietly. He seemed to hesitate. "A kind of strain—on the soul," he finished abruptly.

Heber was not a stupid man; he had an inkling of what the other meant. "Distance and that kind of thing?" he said understandingly. "Immensity, eh?"

"That's right. I had to give it up. Went back to sheep instead."

"But how did it affect you exactly?" Heber asked presently, with real interest.

"It's not easy to explain, perhaps," said the soldier who had once been an amateur astronomer by choice, "but—well, once you get into it as deep as I did, you—forget the earth a bit, that's all. It's all right, no doubt, if it's your regular job, paid by Government, I mean, and for a useful purpose. Because then imagination hardly comes into it, does it? But for a hobby   as I did it—imaginatively—trying to *realise*—well, it was too much. Distance, space, number, they're all too vast to mean anything. You're always on the edge of infinity—the mind's always trying to conceive something far beyond its powers. The unit of measurement, you see, is a bit staggering to start with—the distance light travels in a second. And then so many stars whose light takes four or five thousand years to reach us even at that rate—may have gone out when the Sphinx was being carved—yet we still see them—" He stopped abruptly and puffed his cigarette a moment. "It's a bit unsettling," he went on. "Yet that's only a beginning—"

"No words for it, are there?" put in Heber.

"That's where the strain comes in," continued the Tommy from New Zealand damaged by Turkish shrapnel. "You get dizzy—unfit for daily life. You get the feeling that nothing matters. You move and think all day against that stupendous background." He turned in the gloom and peered at Heber. "It gets terrifying," he said in a lower voice with conviction. "And I'll tell you why: the intellect knows it can't bridge that gulf, but the soul knows it can. And the soul goes on trying."

"The touch of the infinite, I suppose."

"That's why I went back to sheep."

"Sanity!"

"Why, think of it!—even the biggest telescope can't bring one star near enough to show it as a disc. It is still nothing but a point in space. D'you know how they measure distance, too? Take a triangle with the star you want at the apex. Then measure the two base angles. Only most of the stars are so distant that the earth isn't broad enough to give a base line. So they take the position of the earth in June, then again in December—the length it's travelled in those six months provides a base line *just* long enough, perhaps, for the angles to be measurable. Whew! It's appalling, eh? With *that* scale in your mind for six weeks you're apt to forget that you can't drop out of a second-floor window without breaking something."

"Proportion," said Heber, feeling that the earth beneath his feet was not of the importance he had always believed.

"Yes, everything's proportion. But that's just where the mind gets unhappy—with such a scale. There's horror in magnitude of that kind. You feel scared, and think of a paternal deity—it comforts. Not a sparrow falleth, you see, and all that. But that's if you've got belief. If you haven't, you just—shiver. The mind shrinks. You feel so insignificant, it doesn't seem to matter if you live or die, or what you do. You lose proportion, as you said just now—get out of relation with the rest of life. Why, there's not one man in a hundred who knows what you mean when you tell him that our sun is actually in the Milky Way, and if you mention that our own System travels thirty-five million miles every year nearer to a certain star in Hercules, yet Hercules looks the same today as it did to Rameses—looks no nearer—well, he just says, 'Oh,' or 'Really,' and wonders what you mean—luckily for him!"

"And, of course, there are dozens of other suns and other solar systems," put in Heber, knowing himself classed with the men who would say "oh," or "really."

"Scores upon scores, enormous, endless, prodigious! It's an awful word—*endless!* A big telescope simply frightens you. The Coal-Sack, for instance, where you peep through into outer space, so called, the only spot in the heavens where it's empty of any stars at all—! Why, our solar system's nothing but a few marbles placed at intervals round a football on some endless prairie compare to—"

"And our earth we think so important," broke in Heber, "one of the smallest planets in it—"

"Covered with a few million two-legged creatures who—are squabbling—and killing each other—"

A man came in at that moment and sat down to smoke on the same bench. A band shone faintly on his sleeve. He was a special constable. The *War*—!

"—having a rough-and-tumble fight on a comparatively small section of it—" the soldier finished his sentence, then hesitated.

For the arrival of the stranger made it difficult to continue talking freely. Heber felt as though he had just dropped from some gigantic height—upon the front of the little English sea-coast town. They got up to go. Heber gave his arm to the wounded soldier. They walked along together beside the quiet sea, beneath the brilliant stars.

"It's a good thing," remarked the latter presently, "men's senses are so nicely limited. Still, with bigger powers—say the sight of a million miles or so—the mind would be different too, I suppose. Better as it is, though, isn't it?"

They talked a little about the war.

"I almost wonder," ventured Heber, before they parted, "that a fellow with thoughts like yours—enlisted."

"That's just it. That's where proportion comes in. I wouldn't fight for anything less than—*this!*" He turned his shaded eyes towards the sky. "What I'm fighting for, personally, is to keep all this beautiful and fit to live in—"

And he added "Good night," and shuffled off past the Pier towards his convalescent home.

Onanonanon

Certain things had made a deep impression in his childhood days; among these was the incident of the barking dog.

It barked during his convalesence from something that involved scarlet and a peeling skin; his early mind associated bright colour and peeling skin with the distress of illness. The tiresome barking of a dog accompanied it. In later years this sound always brought back the childhood visualization: across his mind would flit a streak of vivid colour, a peeling skin, a noisy dog, all set against a background of emotional discomfort and physical distress.

"It's barking at me!" he complained to his old nurse, whose explanation that it was "Carlo with his rheumatics in the stables" brought no relief. He spoke to his mother later: "It never, never stops. It goes on and on and on on purpose—onanonanon!"

How queer the words sounded! He had got them wrong somewhere—onanonanon. Or was it a name, the name of the barking animal—Onan Onan Onanonanon?

His mother's words were more comforting: "Carlo's barking because you're ill, darling; he wants you to get well." And she added: "Soon I'll bring him in to see you. You shall ride on his back again."

"Would he peel if I stroked him?" he enquired, a trifle frightened. "Is the skin shiny like mine?"

She shook her head and smiled. "I'll explain to him," she went on, "and then he'll understand. He won't bark any more." She brought the picture-book of natural history that included all creatures in Ark and Zoo and Jungle. He picked out the brightly coloured tiger.

"A *tiger* doesn't bark, does it?" he asked, and her reply added slightly to his knowledge, but much to his imagination. "But does it ever *bark?*" he persisted. "That's really what I asked."

"Growls and snarls," said a deep voice from the doorway. He started; but it was only his father, who then came in and amused him by imitating the sound a tiger makes, until Carlo's naughtiness was forgotten, and the world went on turning smoothly as before.

After that the barking ceased; the rheumatic creature sniffed the air and nosed the metal biscuit tray in silence. He understood apparently. It had been rather dreadful, this noise he made. The sharp sound had broken the morning stillness for many days; no one but the boy was awake at that early hour; the boy and the dog had the dawn entirely to themselves. He used to lie in bed, counting the number of barks. They seemed endless, they jarred, they never stopped. They came singly, then in groups of three and four at a time, then in a longer series, then singly again. These single barks often had a sound of finality about them, the creature's breath was giving out, it was tired; it was the full-stop sound. But the true full-stop, the final bark, never came—and the boy had complained.

He loved old Carlo, loved riding on his burly back that wobbled from side to side, as they moved forward very slowly; in particular he loved stroking the thick curly hair; it tickled his fingers and felt nice on his palm. He was relieved to know it would not peel. Yet he wondered impatiently why the creature he loved to play with should go on making such a dreadful noise. "Doesn't he know? Can't he wait till I'm ready?" There were moments when he doubted if it really was Carlo, when he almost hated the beast, when he asked himself, "Is this Carlo, or is it Onanonanon...?" The idea alarmed him rather. Onanonanon was not quite friendly, not quite safe.

At the age of fifty he found himself serving his King during the Great War—in a neutral country whose police regarded him with disfavour, and would have instantly arrested and clapped him into gaol, had he made a slip. He did not make this slip, though incessant caution had to be his watchword. He belonged to that service which runs risks yet dares claim no credit. He passed under another name than his own, and his alias sometimes did things his true self would not do. This alter ego developed oddly. He projected temporarily, as it were, a secondary personality—which he disliked, often despised, and sometimes even feared. His sense of humour, however, made light of the split involved. When he was followed, he used to chuckle: "I wonder if the sleuths know which of the two they're tracking down—myself or my alias?"

It was in the melancholy season between autumn and winter, snow on the heights and fog upon the lower levels, when he was suddenly laid low by the plague that milked the world. The Spanish influenza caught him. He went to bed; he had a doctor and a nurse; no one else in the hotel came near his room; the police forgot him, and he forgot the police. His hated alias, Baker, also was forgotten, or perhaps merged back into the parent self.... Outside his quarters on the first floor the plane trees shed their heavy, rain-soaked leaves, letting them fall with an audible plop upon the gravel path; he heard the waves of the sullen lake in the distance; the crunching of passing feet he heard much closer. The heating was indifferent, the light too weak to read by. It was a lonely, dismal time. On the floor above two people died, three on the one below, the French officer next door was carried out. The hotel, like many others, became a hospital.

In due course, the fever passed, the intolerable aching ceased, he forgot the times when he had thought he was going to die. He lay, half convalescent, remembering the recent past, then the remoter past, and so slipped back to dim childhood scenes when the cross but faithful old nurse had tended him. He smelt the burning leaves in the kitchen-garden, and heard the blackbird whistle beyond the summer-house. The odour of moist earth in the toolhouse stole back, with the fragrance of sweet apples in the forbidden loft. These earliest layers of memory fluttered their ghostly pictures like a cinema before his receptive mind. There were eyes long closed, voices long silent, the touch of hands long dead and gone. The rose-garden on a sultry August afternoon was vivid, with the smell of the rain-washed petals, as the sun blazed over them after a heavy shower. The soaked lawn emitted warm little bubbles like a soft squeezed sponge, audibly; even the gravel steamed. He remembered Carlo, with his rheumatism, his awkward gambol, his squashy dog-biscuit beside the kennel and—his bark.

In the state of semi-unconsciousness he lay, weary, weak, depressed, and very lonely. The nurse, on her rare visits, afflicted him, the hotel guests did not ask after him. To the Service at home he was on the sick-list, useless. The morning newspaper and the hurried, perfunctory visits of the doctor were his only interest. It seemed a pity he had not died. The mental depression after influenza can be extremely devastating. He looked forward to nothing.

Then, suddenly, the dog began its barking.

He heard it first at six o'clock when, waking, hot and thirsty in a bed that had lost its comfort, he wondered vaguely if the day was going to be fine or wet. His window opened on to the lake. He watched the shadows melt across the dreary room. The late dawn came softly, its hint of beauty ever unfulfilled. Would it be gold or grey behind the mountains? The dog went on barking.

He dozed, counting the barks without being aware that he did so. He felt hot and uncomfortable, and turned over in bed, counting automatically as he did so: "fifteen, sixteen, seventeen"—pause—"eighteen, nineteen"—another pause, then with great rapidity, "twenty, twenty-one, twenty-two, twenty-three—" He opened his eyes wide and cursed aloud. The barking stopped.

The wind came softly off the lake, entering the room. He heard the last big leaf of the plane trees rattle to the gravel path. As it touched the ground the barking began again, his counting—now conscious counting—began with it.

"Curse the brute!" he muttered, and turned over once more to try and sleep. The rasping, harsh staccato sound reached his ears piercingly through sheets and blankets; not even the thick duvet could muffle it. Would no one stop it? Did no one care? He felt furious, but helpless, dreadfully helpless.

It barked, stopped, then barked again. There were solitary, isolated barks, followed by a rapid series, short and hurried. A shower of barks came next. Pauses were frequent, but they were worse than the actual sound. It continued, it went on, the dog barked without ceasing. It barked and barked. He had lost all count. It barked and barked and barked. It stopped.

"At last!" he groaned. "My God! Another minute, and I—!"

His whole body, as he turned over, knew an immense, deep relaxation. His jangled nerves were utterly exhausted. A great sigh of relief escaped him. The silence was delicious. He rested at last. Sleep, warm and intoxicating, stole gently back. He dozed. Forgetfulness swam over him. He lay in down, in cotton-wool. Police, alias, nurse and loneliness were all obliterated, when, suddenly, across the blissful peace, cracked out that sharp, explosive sound again—the bark.

But the dog barked differently this time; the sound was much nearer. At first this puzzled him. Then he guessed the truth; the animal had come into the hotel and up the stairs; it was outside in the passage. He opened his eyes and sat up in bed. The door, to his surprise, was being cautiously pushed ajar. He was just in time to see who pushed it with such gentle, careful pressure. Standing on the landing in the early twilight was Baker, his other self, his alias, the personality he disliked and sometimes dreaded. Baker put his head round the corner, glanced at him, nodded familiarly, and withdrew, closing the door instantly, making no slightest sound. But, before it closed, and before he had time even to feel astonishment, the dog had been let in. And the dog, he saw at once was old Carlo!

Having expected a little stranger dog, this big, shaggy, familiar beast caused him to feel a sense of curious wonder and bewilderment.

"But were *you* the dog down there that barked?" he asked aloud, as the friendly creature came waddling to the bedside. "And have you come to say you're sorry?"

It blinked its rheumy eyes and wagged its stumpy tail. He put out his hand and stroked its familiar, wobbly back. His fingers buried themselves in the stiff crinkly hair. Its dim old eyes turned affectionately up at him. It smiled its silly, happy smile. He went on rubbing. "Carlo, good old Carlo!" he mumbled; "well, I'm blessed! I'll get on your back in a minute and ride—"

He stopped rubbing. "*Why* did you come in?" he asked abruptly, and repeated the question, a touch of anxiety in his voice. "How did you manage it, really? Tell me, Carlo?"

The old beast shifted its position a little, making a sideways motion that he did not like. It seemed to move its hind legs only. Its muzzle now rested on the bed. Its eyes, seen full, looked not quite so kind and friendly. They cleared a little. But its tail still wagged. Only, now that he saw it better, the tail seemed longer than it ought to have been. There was something unpleasant about the dog—a faint inexplicable shade of difference. He stared a moment straight into its face. It no longer blinked in the silly, affectionate way as at first. The rheum was less. There was a light, a gleam, in the eyes, almost a flash.

"*Are* you—Carlo?" he asked sharply, uneasily, "or are you—Onanonanon?"

It rose abruptly on its hind legs, laying the front paws on the counterpane of faded yellow. The legs made dark streaks against this yellow.

He had begun stroking the old back again. He now stopped. He withdrew his hand. The hair was coming out. It came off beneath his fingers, and each stroke he made left a line of lighter skin behind it. This skin was yellowish, with a slight tinge, he thought, of scarlet.

The dog—he could almost swear to it—had altered; it was still altering. Before his very eyes, it grew, became curiously enlarged. It now towered over him. It was longer, thinner, leaner than before, its tail came lashing round its hollow, yellowing flanks, the eyes shone brilliantly, its tongue was a horrid red. The brute straightened its front paws. It was huge. Its open mouth grinned down at him.

He was petrified with terror. He tried to scream, but the only sound that came were little innocent words of childhood days. He almost lisped them, simpering with horror: "I'd get on your back—if I was allowed out of bed. You'd carry me. I'd ride."

It was a desperate attempt to pacify the beast, to persuade it, even in this terrible moment, to be friendly, a feeble, hopeless attempt to convince *himself* that it was—Carlo. The Monster was twelve feet from head to tail, of dull yellow striped with black. The great jaws, wide open, dripped upon his face. He saw the pointed teeth, the stiff, quivering whiskers of white wire. He felt the hot breath upon his cheeks and lips. It was fetid. He tasted it.

He was on the point of fainting when a step sounded outside the door. Someone was coming.

"Saved!" he gasped.

The suspense and relief were almost intolerable. The touch of a hand feeling cautiously, stealthily, over the door was audible. The handle rattled faintly.

"Saved!" his heart repeated, as the great brute turned its giant head to listen.

He knew that touch. It was Baker, his hated alias, come in the nick of time to rescue him. Yet the door did not open. Instead, the monster lashed its tail, it stiffened horribly, it turned its head back from watching the door, and lowered itself appallingly. The key turned in the lock, a bolt was shot. He was locked in alone with a tiger. He closed his eyes.

His recurrent nightmare had ruined his sleep again, and outside, in the dreary autumn dawn, a little dog was yapping fiendishly on and on and on and on.

The Memory of Beauty

It began almost imperceptibly—about half-past three o'clock in the afternoon, to be exact—and Lennart, with his curiously sharpened faculties, noticed it at once. Before anyone else, he thinks, was aware of it, this delicate change in his surroundings made itself known to these senses of his, said now to be unreliable, yet so intensely receptive and alert for all their unreliability. No one else, at any rate, gave the smallest sign that something had begun to happen. The throng of people moving about him remained uninformed apparently.

He turned to his companion, who was also his nurse. "Hullo!" he said to her, "There's something up. What in the world is it?"

Obedient to her careful instructions, she made, as a hundred times before, some soothing reply, while her patient—"Jack," she called him—aware that she had not shared his own keen observation, was disappointed, and let the matter drop. He said no more. He went back into his shell, smiling quietly to himself, peaceful in mind, and only vaguely aware that something, he knew not exactly what, was wrong with him, and that his companion humoured him for his own good. She did the humouring tenderly, and very sweetly, so that he liked it, his occasional disappointment in her rousing no shadow of resentment or impatience.

This was his first day in the open air, the first day for weeks that he had left a carefully shaded room, where the blinds seemed always down, and looked round him upon a world spread in gracious light. Physically, he had recovered health and strength; nursing and good food, rest and sleep, had made him as fit as when he first went out with his draft months ago. Only he did not know that he had gone out, nor what had happened to him when he was out, nor why he was the object now of such ceaseless care, attention, and loving tenderness. He remembered nothing; memory, temporarily, had been sponged clean as a new slate. That his nurse was also his sister was unrecognized by his mind. He had forgotten his own name, as well as hers. He had forgotten—everything.

The October day had been overcast, high, uniform clouds obscuring the sun, and moving westwards before a wind that had not come lower. No breeze now stirred the yellow foliage, as he sat with his companion upon a bench by Hampstead Heath, and took the air that helped to make him whole. In spite of the clouds, however, the day was warm, and calm, as with a touch of lingering summer. He watched the sea of roofs and spires in blue haze below him; he heard the muffled roar of countless distant streets.

"Big place, that," he mentioned, pointing with his stick. There was an assumed carelessness that did not altogether hide a certain shyness. "*Some* town—eh?"

"London, yes. It's huge, isn't it?"

"London..." he repeated, turning to look at her quickly. He said no more. The word sounded strange; the way he said it—new. He looked away again. No, he decided she was not inventing just to humour him; that was the real name, right enough. She wasn't "pulling his leg." But the name amused him somehow; he rather liked it.

"Mary," he said, "now, that's a nice name too."

"And so is Jack," she answered, whereupon the shyness again descended over him, and he said no more. Besides, the change he had noticed a moment ago, was becoming more marked, he thought, and he wished to observe it closely. For in some odd way it thrilled him.

It began, so far as he could judge, somewhere in the air above him, very high indeed, while yet its effect did not stay there, but spread gently downwards, including everything about him. From the sky, at any rate, it first stole downwards; and it was his extreme sensitiveness which made him realize next that it came from a particular quarter of the sky; in the eastern heavens it had its origin. He was sure of this; and the thrill of wonder, faint but marvellously sweet, stirred through his expectant being. He waited and watched in silence for a long time. Since Mary showed no interest, he must enjoy it alone. Indeed, she had not even noticed it at all.

Yet none of these people about him had noticed it either. Some of them were walking a little faster than before, hurrying almost, but no one looked up to see what was happening; there were no signs of surprise anywhere. "Everybody must have forgotten!" he thought to himself, when his mind gave a sudden twitch. Forgotten! Forgotten what? He moved abruptly, and the girl's hand stole into his, though she said no word. He was aware that she was watching him closely but a trifle surreptitiously he fancied.

He did not speak, but his wonder deepened. This "something" from the eastern sky descended slowly, yet so slowly that the change from one minute to another was not measurable. It was soft as a dream and very subtle; it was full of mystery. Comfort, and a sense of peace stole over him, his sight was eased, he had mild thoughts of sleep. Like a whisper the imperceptible change came drifting through the air. It was exquisite. But it was the wonder that woke the thrill in him.

"Something is up, you know," he repeated, though more to himself than to his companion. "You can't mistake it. It's all over the place!" He drew a deeper breath, pointing again with his stick over the blue haze where tall chimneys and needle spires pierced. "By Jove," he added, "it's like a veil—gauze, I mean— or something—eh?" And the light drawing itself behind the veil, grew less, while his pulses quickened as he watched it fade.

Her gentle reply that it was time to go home to tea, and something else about the cooling air, again failed to satisfy him, but he was pleased that she slipped her arm into his and made a gesture uncommonly like a caress. She was so pretty, he thought, as he glanced down at her. Only it amazed him more and more that no thrill stirred her blood as it stirred his own, that there was no surprise, and that the stream of passing people hurrying homewards showed no single sign of having noticed what *he* noticed. For his heart swelled within him as he watched, and the change was so magical that it troubled his breath a little. Hard outlines everywhere melted softly against a pale blue sea that held tints of mother-of-pearl; there was a flush of gold, subdued to amber, a haze, a glow, a burning.

This strange thing stealing out of the east brought a wonder that he could not name, a wonder that was new and fresh and sweet as though experienced for the first time. For his mind qualified the beauty that possessed him, qualified it in this way, because—this puzzled him—it was not *quite* "experienced for the first time." It was old, old as himself; it was familiar....

"Good Lord!" he thought, "I've got that rummy feeling that I've been through all this before—somewhere," and his mind gave another sudden twitch, which, again, he did not recognize as a memory. A spot was touched, a string was twanged, now here, now there, while Beauty, playing softly on his soul, communicated to his being gradually her secret rhythm, old as the world, but young ever in each heart that answers to it. Below, behind, the thrill, these deeply buried strings began to vibrate....

"The dusk is falling, see," the girl said quietly. "It's time we were going back."

"Dusk," he repeated, vaguely, "the dusk... falling...." It was half a question. A new expression flashed into his eyes, then vanished instantly. Tears, he saw, were standing in her own. She had felt, had noticed, after all, then! The disappointment, and with it the shyness, left him; he was no more ashamed of the depth and strength of this feeling that thrilled through him so imperiously.

But it was after tea that the mysterious change took hold upon his being with a power that could build a throne anew, then set its rightful occupant thereon. By his special wish the lights were not turned on. Before the great windows, opened to the mild autumn air, he sat in his big overcoat and watched.

The change, meanwhile, had ripened. It lay now fullblown upon the earth and heavens. Towards the sky he turned his eyes. The change, whose first delicate advent he had noticed, sat now enthroned above the world. The tops of trees were level with his window-sill, and below lay the countless distant streets, not slumbering, he felt surely, but gazing upwards with him into this deep sea of blackness that had purple for its lining and wore ten thousand candles blazing in mid-air. *Those* lights were not turned out; and this time he wondered why he had thought they might be, ought to be, turned out. This question definitely occurred to him a moment, while he watched the great footsteps of the searchlights passing over space....

The amazing shafts of white moved liked angels lighting up one group of golden points upon another. They lit them and swerved on again. In sheer delight, he lay in his chair and watched them, these rushing footsteps, these lit groups of gold. They, the golden points, were motionless, steady; *they* did not move or change. And his eyes fastened upon one, then, that seemed to burn more brightly than the rest. Though differing from the others in size alone, he thought it more beautiful than all. Below it far, far down in the west, lay a streak of faded fire, as though a curtain with one edge upturned hung above distant furnaces. But this trail of the sunset his mind did not recognize. His eye returned to the point of light that seemed every minute increasingly familiar, and more than familiar—most kindly and well-loved. He yearned towards it, he trembled. Sitting forward in his chair, he leaned upon the window-sill, staring with an intensity as if he would rise through the purple dark and touch it. Then, suddenly, it—twinkled.

"By Jove!" he exclaimed aloud. "I know that chap. It's—it's— Now, where the devil did I see it before? Wherever was it...?"

He sank back, as a scene rose before his inner eye. It must have been, apparently, his "inner" eye, for both his outer eyes were tightly closed as if he slept. But he did not sleep; it was merely that he saw something that was even more familiar though not less wonderful, than these other sights.

Upon a dewy lawn at twilight two children played together, while a white-capped figure, from the window of a big house in the background, called loudly to them that it was time to come indoors and make themselves ready for bed. He saw two Lebanon cedars, the kitchen-garden wall beyond, the elms and haystacks further still, looming out of the summer dusk. He smelt pinks, sweet-william, roses. He ran full speed to catch his companion, a girl in a short tumbled frock, and knew that he was dressed as a soldier, with a wooden sword and a triangular paper hat that fell off, much to his annoyance, as he ran. But he caught his prisoner. Leading her by the hair towards the house, his GHQ, he saw the evening star "simply shining like anything" in the pale glow of the western sky. But in the hall, when reached, the butler's long wax taper, as he slowly lit the big candles, threw a gleam upon his prisoner's laughing face, and it was, he saw, his sister's face.

He opened his eyes again and saw the point of light against the purple curtain that hung above the world. It twinkled. The wonder and the thrill coursed through his heart again, but this time another thing had come to join them, and was rising to his brain. "By Jove, I know that chap!" he repeated. "It's old Venus, or I'm a dug-out!"

And when, a moment later, the door opened and his companion entered, saying something about its being time for bed, because the "night has come"—he looked into her face with a smile: "I'm quite ready, Mary," he said, "but where in the world have you been to all this time?"

THE END

A CHRONOLOGY OF ALGERNON BLACKWOOD'S PUBLISHED WORKS

The following lists all of Blackwood's short fiction, novels, plays and essays in the order in which they were first published. It cites the original source of publication, where known, and the volume of Blackwood's books in which the work was first collected. For radio broadcasts I list both the original broadcast date and its first appearance in print. The list excludes poetry, reviews and general reportage. All items are presumed fiction unless followed in parentheses by (essay) or some other descriptive form. Novels and other book and magazine titles are in *italics*. Short stories and essays are in "quotes." It will be seen that quite a few of the stories appeared some years before inclusion in a collection and this list will thus allow Blackwood devotees to explore his work in the order in which it first appeared. It is possible that some stories had a prior publication other than that noted. If anyone discovers such details, or indeed knows of any published material not listed here, I would be delighted to hear from you.

—*Mike Ashley*

1889-1899

"A Mysterious House," *Belgravia*, July 1889; *The Magic Mirror* (1989).

"A Strange Adventure in the Black Forest," *Blackfriar's Magazine*, November 1889; *The Face of the Earth* (2015).

"Christmas in England" (essay), *The Methodist Magazine*, December 1890.

"Thoughts on Nature" (essay), *Lucifer*, 15 December 1890; *The Face of the Earth* (2015).

"Memories of the Black Forest" (essay), *The Methodist Magazine*, January 1891.

"About the Moravians" (essay), *The Methodist Magazine*, February 1891.

"Notes on Theosophy" (essay), *Lucifer*, 15 March 1891.

"In the Jura—Neuchatel" (essay), *The Methodist Magazine*, June 1891.

"The Mount Pilatus Railway" (essay), *The Methodist Magazine*, November 1891.

"From a Theosophist's Diary" (essay), *Lucifer*, 15 January 1892.

"Over the Splügen" (essay), *The Methodist Magazine*, June 1893.

"The Story of Karl Ott," *Pall Mall Magazine*, October 1896.

"Some of the True Ones . . ." (essay), *New York Times Saturday Review*, 10 September 1898.

"Some of the Real Ones . . ." (essay), *New York Times Saturday Review*, 17 September 1898.

"Emerson, Macauley, Hazlitt and Coleridge—Reading That is Merely Tippling" (essay), *New York Times Saturday Review*, 15 October 1898.

"Wordsworth and Bryant" (essay), *New York Times Saturday Review*, 7 January 1899.

"A Haunted Island." *Pall Mall Magazine*, April 1899; *The Empty House* (1906).

1900-1905

"Kirkcaldy—Some Literary Associations of That Old Scottish Town" (essay), *New York Time Saturday Review*, 14 April 1900.

"A Spiritualist Camp in New England" (essay), *Macmillan's Magazine*, May 1900.

"'Mid the Haunts of the Moose" (essay), *Blackwood's Magazine*, July 1900; *The Face of the Earth* (2015).

"Matthew Arnold: His Relation to America" (essay), *New York Time Saturday Review*, 18 August 1900.

"A Case of Eavesdropping," *Pall Mall Magazine*, December 1900; *The Empty House* (1906).

"Summering in Canadian Backwoods" (essay), *Longman's Magazine*, January 1901.

"Down the Danube in a Canadian Canoe" (essay), in 2 parts, *Macmillan's Magazine*, September 1901 to October 1901; *The Face of the Earth* (2015).

"In Hungary With Tent and Canoe" (essay), *Boy's Own Paper*, 23 November 1901.

"The Last Egg in the Nest" (essay), *Boy's Own Paper*, 23 August 1902.

"The House of the Past," *The Theosophical Review*, 15 April 1904; *Ten Minute Stories* (1914).

"Testing His Courage," *Pearson's Magazine*, September 1904.

"How Garnier Broke the Log-Jam," *Boy's Own Paper*, 31 December 1904.

"At School in the Black Forest" (essay), in 3 parts, *Boy's Own Paper*, 7 to 21 January 1905.

1906

"My Adventure with a Lion" (essay), *Boy's Own Paper*, 2 June 1906.

"About Moose and Moose Hunting" (essay), *Boy's Own Paper*, 11 August 1906.

"A Holiday Down the Danube with Punt and Tent" (essay), *Boy's Own Paper*, 1 September 1906.

"The Empty House," *The Empty House* (1906).

"Keeping His Promise," *The Empty House* (1906).

"With Intent to Steal," *The Empty House* (1906).

"The Wood of the Dead," *The Empty House* (1906).

"Smith: An Episode in a Lodging House," *The Empty House* (1906).

"A Suspicious Gift," *The Empty House* (1906).

"The Strange Adventures of a Private Secretary in New York," *The Empty House* (1906).

"Skeleton Lake: An Episode in Camp," *The Empty House* (1906).

1907

"The Vanishing Redskins" (essay), *Boy's Own Paper*, 10 August 1907

"Kuloskap the Master" (essay) in 2 parts, *Boy's Own Paper*, 24 to 31 August 1907

"The Listener," *The Listener* (1907).

"Max Hensig—Bacteriologist and Murderer," *The Listener* (1907).

"The Willows," *The Listener* (1907).

"The Insanity of Jones," *The Listener* (1907).

"The Dance of Death," *The Listener* (1907).

"The Old Man of Visions," *The Listener* (1907).

"May Day Eve," *The Listener* (1907).

"Miss Slumbubble—and Claustrophobia," *The Listener* (1907).

"The Woman's Ghost Story," *The Listener* (1907).

"The Farmhouse on the Hill," *Adelaide Chronicle*, 21 December 1907; *Ten Minute Stories/Day and Night Stories* omnibus (2013).

1908

"A Psychical Invasion," *John Silence—Physician Extraordinary* (1908).

"Ancient Sorceries," *John Silence—Physician Extraordinary* (1908).

"The Nemesis of Fire," *John Silence—Physician Extraordinary* (1908).

"Secret Worship," *John Silence—Physician Extraordinary* (1908).

"The Camp of the Dog," *John Silence—Physician Extraordinary* (1908).

"The Secret," *Westminster Gazette*, 7 November 1908; *Ten Minute Stories* (1914).

"The Kit-Bag," *Pall Mall Magazine*, December 1908; *The Magic Mirror* (1989).

"Stodgman's Opportunity," *Westminster Gazette*, 5 December 1908; *The Face of the Earth* (2015).

"The Boy Messenger," *Nottinghamshire Weekly Guardian*, week commencing 7 December 1908; *The Face of the Earth* (2015).

"The Story Mr. Popkiss Told," *Westminster Gazette*, 24 December 1908; *The Face of the Earth* (2015).

1909

"Our Adventure with the Danube River Police" (essay), *Boy's Own Paper*, 9 January 1909.

Jimbo, Macmillan, 1909 (February).

"Entrance and Exit," *Westminster Gazette*, 13 February 1909; *Ten Minute Stories* (1914).

"A 'Trunk Call'," *Westminster Gazette*, 27 February 1909; *Ten Minute Stories* (1914, as "You May Telephone From Here").

"The Invitation," *Westminster Gazette*, 3 April 1909; *Ten Minute Stories* (1914).

"The Lease," *Westminster Gazette*, 22 May 1909; *Ten Minute Stories* (1914).

"Pines" (essay), *Country Life*, 29 May 1909; *Ten Minute Stories* (1914).

"Spring Days in the Oberland" (essay), *Westminster Gazette*, 29 May 1909.

"The Man Who Found Out," *The Lady's Realm*, June 1909; *The Wolves of God* (1921).

"Clouds and Mountains" (essay), *Country Life*, 5 June 1909.

"Faith Cure on the Channel," *Westminster Gazette*, 19 June 1909; *Ten Minute Stories* (1914).

"Summer Camps on the Danube" (essay), *Fry's Magazine*, July 1909.

"Carlton's Drive," *Westminster Gazette*, 17 July 1909; *The Lost Valley* (1910).

"Wind" (essay), *Country Life*, 21 August 1909; *Ten Minute Stories* (1914).

"The Laying of a Red-Haired Ghost," *The Lady's Realm*, September 1909; *The Magic Mirror* (1909).

"Up and Down," *Westminster Gazette*, 9 October 1909; *Ten Minute Stories* (1914).

"The Face of the Earth," *Weekly Scotsman*, 11 October 1909; *The Face of the Earth* (2015).

"The Man Who Played Upon the Leaf," *Country Life*, 30 October-6 November 1909; *The Lost Valley* (1910).

The Education of Uncle Paul, Macmillan, 1909 (November).

"The Terror of the Twins," *Westminster Gazette*, 6 November 1909; *The Lost Valley* (1910).

"The Strange Disappearance of a Baronet," *Westminster Gazette*, 27 November 1909; *Ten Minute Stories* (1914).

"The Occupant of the Room," *Nash's Magazine*, December 1909; *Day and Night Stories* (1917).

1910

"A Game Park in the Jura" (essay), *Country Life*, 15 January 1910.

"An Impromptu Valais Pageant" (essay), *Westminster Gazette*, 15 January 1910.

"The Messenger at Midnight," *Westminster Gazette*, 29 January 1910; *Pan's Garden* (1912, as "The South Wind").

"If the Cap Fits—," *Westminster Gazette*, 12 February 1910; *Ten Minute Stories* (1914).

"The Poetry of Ski-Running" (essay), *Country Life*, 26 February 1910.

"The Glamour of Strangers" (essay), *Country Life*, 26 February 1910; *The Face of the Earth* (2015).

"The Strange Experience of the Reverend Phillip Ambleside," *Pall Mall Magazine*, March 1910; *The Lost Valley* (1910, as "Perspective").

"From the Swiss Lakes" (essay), *Country Life*, 19 March 1910.

"The Psychology of Places" (essay), *Westminster Gazette*, 30 April 1910; *The Face of the Earth* (2015).

"Special Delivery," *Pall Mall Magazine*, May 1910; *Pan's Garden* (1910).

"The Lost Valley," *The Lost Valley* (1910).

"The Wendigo," *The Lost Valley* (1910).

"Old Clothes," *The Lost Valley* (1910).

"The Man from the 'Gods'," *The Lost Valley* (1910).

"The Price of Wiggins's Orgy," *The Lost Valley* (1910).

"The Eccentricity of Simon Parnacute," *The Lost Valley* (1910).

"The Message of the Clock," *Nash's Magazine*, June 1910; *The Magic Mirror* (1989).

"Towards the Caucasus" (essay), *Westminster Gazette*, 11 June 1910.

"Impressions at Batoum" (essay), *Westminster Gazette*, 18 June 1910.

"In a Caucasian Train" (essay), *Westminster Gazette*, 21 June 1910.

"The Sea Fit," *Country Life*, 25 June 1910; *Pan's Garden* (1912).

"In a Telega" (essay), *Westminster Gazette*, 22 July 1910.

"In Tiflis" (essay), *Westminster Gazette*, 27 July 1910.

"Among the Rhododendrons of the Caucasus" (essay), *Westminster Gazette*, 13 August 1910.

"Across the Caucasus in a Bus" (essay), *Westminster Gazette*, 27 August 1910.

The Human Chord, Macmillan, 1910 (October).

"The Singular Death of Morton," *The Tramp*, December 1910; *The Magic Mirror* (1989).

"Imagination," *Westminster Gazette*, 17 December 1910; *Ten Minute Stories* (1914).

"Winter Alps" (essay), *Country Life*, 24 December 1910; *Ten Minute Stories* (1914).

1911

"The Empty Sleeve," *The London Magazine*, January 1911; *The Wolves of God* (1921).

"From My Caucasus Notebook" (essay), *The Tramp*, January 1911; *The Face of the Earth* (2015).

"The Deferred Appointment," *Westminster Gazette*, 21 January 1911; *Ten Minute Stories* (1914).

"The Jura in February" (essay), *Country Life*, 25 February 1911.

"The Impulse," *Westminster Gazette*, 8 April 1911; *Ten Minute Stories* (1914).

"Spring and the Mountaineer" (essay), *Country Life*, 22 April 1911.

"Spring Notes in the Jura" (essay), *Country Life*, 6 May 1911; *The Face of the Earth* (2015).

"On Wings" (essay), *Country Life*, 13 May 1911; *The Face of the Earth* (2015).

"The Prayer," *Westminster Gazette*, 17 June 1911; *Ten Minute Stories* (1914).

"The Return," *The Eye-Witness*, 22 June 1911; *Pan's Garden* (1912).

"Two in One," *The Eye-Witness*, 20 July 1911; *Ten Minute Stories* (1914).

"Accessory Before the Fact," *Westminster Gazette*, 2 September 1911; *Ten Minute Stories* (1914).

"Clairvoyance," *The Eye-Witness*, 22 June 1911; *Pan's Garden* (1912).

"Dream Trespass," *The Morning Post*, 24 October 1911; *Ten Minute Stories* (1914).

The Centaur, Macmillan, 1911 (November).

"News vs Nourishment," *Westminster Gazette*, 4 November 1911; *Ten Minute Stories* (1914).

"'Monsieur Joseph' of the Ski" (essay), *Country Life*, 11 November 1911.

"The Glamour of the Snow," *Pall Mall Magazine*, December 1911; *Pan's Garden* (1912).

"The Ski Season" (essay), *Country Life*, 2 December 1911.

"The Transfer," *Country Life*, 9 December 1911; *Pan's Garden* (1912).

"That Distant Eye," *Westminster Gazette*, 9 December 1911; *Pan's Garden* (1912, as "The Messenger").

"In a Jura Village," *The Morning Post*, 26 December 1911; revised as part of Chapter 12 of *A Prisoner in Fairyland* (1913).

"The Golden Fly," *The Eye-Witness*, 29 December 1911; *Pan's Garden* (1912).

1912

"The Heath Fire," *Country Life*, 20 January 1912; *Pan's Garden* (1912).

"Failure of the Swiss Winter Season" (essay), *Country Life*, 27 January 1912.

"The Biter Bit," *Saturday Westminster Gazette*, 17 February 1912.

"The Destruction of Smith," *The Eye-Witness*, 29 February 1912; *Pan's Garden* (1912).

"The Man Whom the Trees Loved," *The London Magazine*, March 1912; *Pan's Garden* (1912).

"The Egyptian Desert from Heluan" (essay) in 2 parts, *Country Life*, 16 March and 13 April 1912.

"Helouan in the Desert" (essay), *The Morning Post*, 30 April 1912.

"Egyptian Antiquities," *The Morning Post*, 9 April 1912.

"The Attic," *Westminster Gazette*, 20 April 1912; *Pan's Garden* (1912).

"Summering in Switzerland" (essay), *Country Life*, 18 May 1912.

"The Empty Room," *The Eye-Witness*, 23 May 1912; *Ten Minute Stories* (1914, as "The Whisperers").

"The Unconquerable Charm of Sussex" (essay), *Country Life*, 6 July 1912.

"The Second Generation," *Westminster Gazette*, 6 July 1912; *Ten Minute Stories* (1914).

"Ancient Lights," *The Eye-Witness*, 11 July 1912; *Ten Minute Stories* (1914).

"Animal Life in the Egyptian Desert" (essay), *Country Life*, 13 July 1912.

"Sand," *Pan's Garden* (1912).

"The Temptation of the Clay," *Pan's Garden* (1912).

"The Goblin's Collection," *Westminster Gazette*, 5 October 1912; *Ten Minute Stories* (1914).

"An Arab Pilgrimage" (essay), *Country Life*, 26 October 1912.

"Algonquin Songs and Legends" (essay) in 2 parts, *Country Life*, 2 and 23 November 1912.

"Let Not the Sun—," *The Morning Post*, 19 November 1912; *Ten Minute Stories* (1914).

"La Mauvaise Riche," *Westminster Gazette*, 30 November 1912; *The Magic Mirror* (1989).

"Wayfarers," *The English Review*, December 1912; *Incredible Adventures* (1914).

1913

"Value" (essay), *Westminster Gazette*, 4 January 1913.

"The Sacrifice," *The Quest*, April 1913; *Incredible Adventures* (1914).

A Prisoner in Fairyland, Macmillan, 1913 (May).

"Her Birthday," *Westminster Gazette*, 3 May 1913; *Ten Minute Stories* (1914).

"Violence," *The New Witness*, 22 May 1913; *Ten Minute Stories* (1914).

"Jimbo's Longest Day," *The Morning Post*, 24 June 1913; *Ten Minute Stories* (1914).

"Who Was She?," *The New Witness*, 26 June, 17 July, 28 August 1913; heavily revised to form chapters 3-5 of *The Promise of Air* (1918); original version, *The Face of the Earth* (2015).

"A Barmecide Feast," *Country Life*, 19 July 1913.

"The Kiss of a Psychologist," *Country Life*, 13 September 1913.

"H. S. H.," *The British Review*, October 1913; *Day and Night Stories* (1917).

"Egypt: An Impression" (essay), *Country Life*, 8 November 1913; *The Face of the Earth* (2015).

"The Story Hour," *The Morning Post*, 18 November 1913; revised as chapter 2 of *The Extra Day* (1915).

"Learning to Ski" (essay), *Country Life*, 22 November 1913.

"The Tradition," *Westminster Gazette*, 29 November 1913; *Day and Night Stories* (1917).

"Mudbury's Xmas Adventure," *The New Witness*, 11 December 1913;

Day and Night Stories (1917, as
"Transition").

"Before the Season" (essay), *Country
Life*, 27 December 1913.

1914

"An Episode in the Desert," *Coun-
try Life*, 10 January 1914; *Day and
Night Stories* (1917, as "A Desert
Episode").

"What Nobody Understands," *The
Morning Post*, 17 February 1914;
incorporated into chapter 5 of *The
Extra Day* (1915).

"Maria," *The Morning Post*, 28
March 1914; incorporated into
chapter 3 of *The Extra Day* (1915).

"By Water," *Westminster Gazette*,
18 April 1914; *Day and Night Stories* (1917).

"A Bit of Wood," *The Morning Post*,
28 April 1914; *Day and Night Stories* (1917).

"The Night-Wind," *Country Life*, 9
May 1914; revised as chapter 7,
"Imagination Wakes" in *The Ex-
tra Day* (1915); original version,
The Face of the Earth (2015).

"The Falling Glass," *Country Life*,
23 May 1914; *Tongues of Fire*
(1924).

"Breakfast Honey," *The Morning
Post*, 9 June 1914.

"The Philosopher," *Westminster
Gazette*, 13 June 1914.

"An Egyptian Hornet," *New
Weekly*, 27 June 1914; *Day and
Night Stories* (1917).

"A Man of Earth," *New Weekly*, 27
June 1914; *Tongues of Fire* (1924).

"The Daisy World," *The Quest*, July
1914; revised as chapter 11,
"Judy's Particular Adventure," in
The Extra Day (1915).

"The Miracle" (essay), *Westminster
Gazette*, 31 October 1914; *The
Face of the Earth* (2015).

"The Wings of Horus," *Century
Magazine*, November 1914; *Day
and Night Stories* (1917).

"The Regeneration of Lord Ernie,"
Incredible Adventures (1914).

"The Damned," *Incredible Adventures* (1914).

"A Descent Into Egypt," *Incredible
Adventures* (1914).

"A Victim of Higher Space," *Occult
Review*, December 1914; *Day and
Night Stories* (1917).

"Non-Human," *The New Witness*,
10 December 1914.

1915

"The God," *Saturday Westminster
Gazette*, 7 August 1915.

The Extra Day, Macmillan, 1915
(October).

"After the War" (essay), *The Standard*, 7 October 1915.

"The Soldier's Visitor," *Land and
Water*, 9 October 1915; *The Magic
Mirror* (1989).

"The Higher Command" (essay),
New Days, 9 October 1915.

"The Paper Man," *Saturday Westminster Gazette*, 9 October 1915;
The Face of the Earth (2015).

"From a Correspondent," *The
Times*, 12 October 1915; *Tongues
of Fire* (1924, as "Laughter of
Courage").

"Coming Changes" (essay), *The
Standard*, 29 October 1915.

"The Other Wing," *McBride's Magazine*, November 1915; *Day and Night Stories* (1917).

"Cain's Atonement," *Land and Water*, 20 November 1915; *Day and Night Stories* (1917).

"Think Victory" (essay), *The Standard*, 25 November 1915.

"The Lying Jade" (essay), *New Days*, 4 December 1915.

"The Old World Beauty" (essay), *The Standard*, 17 December 1915; *The Face of the Earth* (2015).

"The Celestial Motor- bus," *Saturday Westminster Gazette*, 18 December 1915.

"The Starlight Express" (stage play with Violet Pearn), performed Kingsway Theatre, London, 29 December 1915 to 29 January 1916 [unpublished].

1916

"Tenacity" (essay), *The Standard*, 25 February 1916.

"The Snake," *Saturday Westminster Gazette*, 18 March 1916.

Julius Le Vallon, Cassell, 1916 (May).

"The Exiled Gods," *The Quest*, July 1916; *Day and Night Stories* (1917, as "Initiation").

"Proportion," *Saturday Westminster Gazette*, 5 August 1916; *The Face of the Earth* (2015).

The Wave, Macmillan, 1916 (October).

"Camping Out," *Blackie's Children's Annual* (1916).

1917

"The Tryst," *Day and Night Stories* (1917).

"The Touch of Pan," *Day and Night Stories* (1917).

"A Vanishing Race" (essay), *Saturday Westminster Gazette*, 10 November 1917.

1918

"The Memory of Beauty," *Land and Water*, 3 January 1918; *The Magic Mirror* (1989).

"The Winter Nightingale" (essay), *Country Life*, 26 January 1918.

"Psychology in Air Raids" (essay), *Saturday Westminster Gazette*, 2 February 1918.

"S. O. S.," *The Story-Teller*, March 1918; *Tongues of Fire* (1924).

The Promise of Air, Macmillan, 1918 (April).

Karma (with Violet Pearn), Macmillan, 1918 (May).

The Garden of Survival, Macmillan, 1918 (May).

"Missing" (essay), *Red Cross Magazine*, December 1918.

1919

"The Little Beggar," *Saturday Westminster Gazette*, 10 May 1919; *Tongues of Fire* (1924).

"Making Plans" (essay), *The New Witness*, 23 May 1919.

"Picking Fir-Cones," *The English Review*, July 1919; *Tongues of Fire* (1924).

"Points of View" (essay) in 2 parts, *Saturday Westminster Gazette*, 7 June and 19 July 1919.

"The Perfect Poseur," *Saturday Westminster Gazette*, 16 August 1919.

"The World-Dream of McCallister," *Vision*, September 1919;

Tongues of Fire (1924).

"Alexander Alexander," *Saturday Westminster Gazette*, 6 September 1919; *Tongues of Fire* (1924).

"Wireless Confusion," *The Quest*, October 1919; *The Wolves of God* (1921).

"The Other Woman," *Saturday Westminster Gazette*, 8 November 1919; *Tongues of Fire* (1924).

"The Substitute," *Lloyd's Magazine*, December 1919; *The Wolves of God* (1921, as "The Decoy").

"The Call," *Nash's Illustrated Weekly*, 6 December 1919; *The Wolves of God* (1921).

1920

"First Hate," *McClure's Magazine*, February 1920; *The Wolves of God* (1921).

"Chinese Magic," *Romance*, June 1920; *The Wolves of God* (1921).

"Running Wolf." *Century Magazine*, August 1920; *The Wolves of God* (1921).

"The Crossing" (stage play, with Bertram Forsyth), performed The Comedy Theatre, London, 29 September to 9 October 1920 [unpublished].

"Through the Crack" (stage play, with Violet Pearn), performed Everyman Theatre, London, 27 December 1920 to 15 January 1921; *Through the Crack* (1925).

1921

"Onanonanon," *The English Review*, March 1921; *The Magic Mirror* (1989).

"Confession," *Century Magazine*, March 1921; *The Wolves of God*

(1921). Rewritten as "King's Evidence," broadcast BBC National Programme 27 June 1936; *London Calling*, 9 January 1941; *The Magic Mirror* (1989).

"The Tarn of Sacrifice," *The Wolves of God* (1921).

"The Valley of the Beasts," *The Wolves of God* (1921).

"The Wolves of God," *The Wolves of God* (1921).

"Egyptian Sorcery," *The Wolves of God* (1921).

"The Lane That Ran East and West," *The Wolves of God* (1921).

"'Vengeance is Mine'," *The Wolves of God* (1921).

"The Olive," *Pearson's Magazine*, July 1921; *Tongues of Fire* (1924).

The Bright Messenger, Cassell, 1921 (October).

"White Magic" (stage play, with Bertram Forsyth), performed Hart House Theatre, Toronto, 21 November to 5 December 1921 [unpublished].

"Nephelé," *Pears Annual* [Christmas] 1921; *Tongues of Fire* (1924).

"The Halfway House" (stage play, with Elaine Ainley), performed The Victoria Palace, London, 5 December 1921 [unpublished].

"Changing Ats," *Time and Tide*, 16 December 1921.

1922

"Genius," *Weekly Westminster Gazette*, 15 July 1922; *The Face of the Earth* (2015).

"Lost!," *The Morning Post*, 8 September 1922; *Tongues of Fire* (1924).

1923

"Tongues of Fire," *The English Review*, April 1923; *Tongues of Fire* (1924).

"On Ightham Hill" (essay), *Time and Tide*, 18 May 1923.

"The Literary Traveler in Egypt" (essay), *The Literary Digest*, June 1923; *Tongues of Fire* (1924, as "The Spell of Egypt").

"Adventurous Memories" (essay), 5 parts, *Cassell's Magazine*, July to November 1923; extracted and abridged from *Episodes Before Thirty*, Cassell, 1923 (October).

"The Man Who Was Milligan," *Pearson's Magazine*, November 1923; *Tongues of Fire* (1924).

"A Night in the Temple of the Sphinx," *Collins's Schoolboys' Annual*, 1923.

"The Lure of the Unknown, I: In Earth's Secret Places" (essay), *Time and Tide*, 7 December 1923.

"The Ghost That I Like Best" (essay), *T.P.'s-Cassell's Weekly*, 8 December 1923.

1924

"The Lure of the Unknown, II: In the World of Spirit" (essay), *Time and Tide*, 11 January 1924.

"The Lure of the Unknown, III: In the Starry Firmament" (essay), *Time and Tide*, 25 Januaryr 1924.

"Why Ski-ers Ski" (essay), *Time and Tide*, 8 February 1924.

"The Pikestaffe Case," *Tongues of Fire* (1924).

"The Open Window," *Tongues of Fire* (1924).

"Malahide and Forden," *Tongues of Fire* (1924).

"Playing Catch," *Tongues of Fire* (1924).

"A Continuous Performance," *Tongues of Fire* (1924).

"Petershin and Mr. Snide," *Tongues of Fire* (1924).

"The Impulse," *T.P.'s and Cassell's Weekly*, 6 December 1924.

1925

"Full Circle," *The English Review*, May 1925; *Full Circle*, 1929.

"Explorers' Ghost Stories" (essay), *The Occult Review*, July 1925.

"Hands of Death," *Bolton Evening News*, 5 December 1925; *Shocks* (1935)

1926

"Sambo and Snitch," 14 parts, *The Merry-Go-Round*, April 1936 to May 1927; *Sambo and Snitch* (1927).

"Toby's Birthday Presents," *The Treasure Ship*, edited by Cynthia Asquith (1926).

"Chemical," *The Ghost Book*, edited by Cynthia Asquith (1926); *Shocks* (1935).

1927

"The Crossword Alien," *Time and Tide*, 7 January 1927.

"Ski-ing in Switzerland" (essay), *The Spectator*, 19 February 1927.

"Spring in Switzerland" (essay), *The Spectator*, 2 April 1927.

"Have I Lived Before?" (essay), *Weekly Despatch*, April 1927.

"The Stranger," *Fortnightly Review*, June 1927; *Short Stories of To-day and Yesterday* (1930).

"Mr. Cupboard, or the Furniture's

Holiday," *Number Five Joy Street*, 1927; *Mr. Cupboard* (1928).

"The Water Performance," *Sails of Gold* edited by Cynthia Asquith (1927).

"Travelling Light" (essay), *McClure's Magazine*, December 1927.

"The Land of Green Ginger," *Radio Times*, 23 December 1927; *Short Stories of To-day and Yesterday* (1930).

1928

"Dr. Feldman," *The Strand Magazine*, May 1928; *Shocks* (1935).

"When Nick Dressed Up," *The Treasure Cave*, edited by Cynthia Asquith (1928).

"The Chocolate Cigarettes," *Number Six Joy Street*, 1928.

1929

Dudley & Gilderoy, Ernest Benn, 1929 (September).

"By Underground," *Number Seven Joy Street*, 1929; *By Underground* (1930).

"Max Hensig" (stage play, with Kinsey Peile), performed The Gate Theatre, London, 18 September to 5 October 1929 [unpublished].

"Dreams and Fairies" (essay), *The Bookman*, December 1929.

"The Adventure of Tornado Smith," *Country Life*, 7 December 1929; *Shocks* (1935).

"Have We Lived Before?" (essay), *Daily Mail*, 10 December 1929.

1930

"On Reincarnation" (essay), *The Aryan Path*, March 1930.

"The Graceless Pair," 6 parts, *The Sketch*, 23 April to 28 May 1930.

"Mr. Bunciman at the Zoo," *The Children's Cargo*, edited by Cynthia Asquith (1930).

"Shocks," *The Strand Magazine*, May 1928; *Shocks* (1935).

"The Parrot and the–Cat!," *Number Eight Joy Street*, 1930; *The Parrot and the—Cat!* (1931).

"The Survivors," *The Occult Review*, December 1930; *Shocks* (1935).

"The Man Who Lived Backwards," *World Radio*, 12 December 1930; *Shocks* (1935).

"Revenge," *Radio Times*, 19 December 1930; *Shocks* (1935).

"The Colonel's Ring," *The Morning Post*, 31 December 1930; *Shocks* (1935).

1931

"The Fire Body," *North American Review*, September 1931.

"The Italian Conjuror," *Number Nine Joy Street*, 1931; *The Italian Conjuror* (1932).

"A Threefold Cord. . .," *When Churchyards Yawn*, edited by Cynthia Asquith, 1931; *Shocks* (1935).

1932

"Maria (of England) in the Rain," *Number Ten Joy Street*, 1932; *Maria (of England) in the Rain* (1933).

1933

"Sergeant Poppett and Policeman James," *Number Eleven Joy Street*, 1933; *Sergeant Poppett and Policeman James* (1934).

"What the Black Chow Saw," *The Princess Elizabeth Gift Book*, edited by Cynthia Asquith and Eileen Bigland, 1933.

1934

"The Blackmailers," broadcast on BBC London Regional Service, 11 July 1934; *My Grimmest Nightmare*, edited by Cecil Madden (1935); *The Magic Mirror* (1989).

"Queer Stories" (radio talk), broadcast BBC National Programme, 28 August 1934; *The Listener*, 12 September 1934.

"The Fruit Stoners," *Number Twelve Joy Street*, 1934; *The Fruit Stoners* (1935).

The Fruit Stoners, Grayson & Grayson, 1934 (October) [not the same as above].

1935

"How the Circus Came to Tea," *Number 12 Joy Street*, 1935; *How the Circus Came to Tea* (1936).

"Elsewhere and Otherwise," *Shocks* (1935).

"Adventure of Miss de Fontenay," *Shocks* (1935).

"The Train Ghost" (radio talk), broadcast BBC National Programme, 4 October 1935 [unpublished].

"Come With Me" (radio talk), broadcast BBC National Programme, 11 October 1935 [unpublished].

"The Wig" (radio talk), broadcast BBC National Programme, 18 October 1935; *The Magic Mirror* (1989).

"Lion in New York City" (radio talk), broadcast BBC National Programme, 1 November 1935 [unpublished].

"A Backwoods Adventure" (radio talk), broadcast BBC National Programme, 29 November 1935 [unpublished].

1936

"At a Mayfair Luncheon," *The Windsor Magazine*, March 1936; *The Magic Mirror* (1989).

"That Mrs. Winslow," *Pearson's Magazine*, October 1936.

"You Can't Tell Ghost Stories on the Radio" (essay), *Radio Times*, 11 December 1936.

1937

"The Genesis of Ideas" (essay), *The Writer*, February 1937; rewritten for radio, broadcast BBC Home Service, 3 March 1948; *London Mystery Magazine*, October/November 1950 (as "The Birth of an Idea").

"The Man-Eater," *Thrilling Mystery*, March 1937; *The Magic Mirror* (1989).

"By Proxy," *The Bystander*, 17 November 1937; *The Magic Mirror* (1989).

"The Reformation of St. Jules," *The Bystander*, 29 December 1937; *The Magic Mirror* (1989, as "The Voice").

1938
"The Magic Mirror," *The By-stander*, 16 March 1938; *The Magic Mirror* (1989).

1942
"Told in a Mountain Cabin" (radio play), broadcast BBC Home Service, 13 April 1942 [unpublished].

1944
"Running Wolf" (radio play), broadcast BBC General Forces Progamme, 12 October 1944 [unpublished].

"The Castlebridge Cat," broadcast BBC Home Service, 25 October 1944 [unpublished].

1945
"It's About Time" (radio play), broadcast BBC General Forces Programme, 26 February 1945 [unpublished].

"In a Glass Darkly" (radio play), broadcast BBC General Overseas Service, 23 July 1945 [unpublished].

1946
"The Doll," *The Doll, and One Other* (1946).

"The Trod," *The Doll, and One Other* (1946).

"The Russian Dentist" (radio talk), broadcast BBC Home Service, 7 April 1946 [unpublished].

"Lock Your Door," broadcast BBC Home Service, 6 May 1946; *The Magic Mirror* (1989).

1947
"Our Former Lives" (essay), *Prediction*, May 1947.

"The Secret Society" (radio play), broadcast BBC Home Service, 22 October 1947 [unpublished].

"The Fear of Heights" (radio talk), broadcast BBC Home Service, 29 October 1947; *The Listener*, 6 November 1947.

1948
"Roman Remains," *Weird Tales*, March 1948; *The Magic Mirror* (1989).

"Passport to the Next Dimension" (essay), *Prediction*, March 1948.

"Texas Farm Disappearance" (radio talk), broadcast BBC Light Programme, 10 May 1948; *The Listener*, 13 May 1948; *The Magic Mirror* (1989).

"The Holy Man" (radio talk), broadcast BBC Light Programme, 11 May 1948; *The Magic Mirror* (1989).

"Pistol Against a Ghost" (radio talk), broadcast BBC Light Programme, 12 May 1948; *The Magic Mirror* (1989).

"Japanese Literary Cocktail" (radio talk), broadcast BBC Light Programme, 13 May 1948; *The Magic Mirror* (1989).

"The Curate and the Stockbroker" (radio talk), broadcast BBC Light Programme, 14 May 1948; *The Magic Mirror* (1989).

"It's Good English" (radio talk), broadcast BBC Far Eastern Service, 31 August 1948 [unpublished].

"Oddities" (radio talk), broadcast BBC Home Service, 31 August 1948; *The Listener*, 9 September 1948.

"The Midnight Hour" (essay), *The Queen*, 24 November 1948.

"My Strangest Christmas" (essay), *Radio Times*, 24 December 1948.

"Looking Back at Christmas" (essay), *The Leader*, 25 December 1948.

"Little People and Co." (radio talk), broadcast BBC Third Programme, 25 December 1948 [unpublished].

"Flash of Bells" (radio talk), broadcast BBC Far Eastern Service, 25 December 1948; *London Calling*, 24 November 1949 (as "The Festive Season—Then and Now").

1949

"Is Monday Black and the Rest of the Week Uphill?" (radio talk), broadcast BBC Light Programme, 30 May 1949 [unpublished].

"Two Holidays" (radio talk), broadcast BBC Home Service, 13 July 1949 [unpublished].

"The Little Puzzles" (radio talk), broadcast BBC Light Programme, 29 August 1949 [unpublished].

"Minor Memories" (radio talk), broadcast BBC Third Progamme, 8 September 1949 [unpublished].

"On Being Eighty" (radio talk), broadcast BBC Home Service, 25 September 1949 [unpublished].

"Adventures in Thought-Transference," *Prediction*, December 1949.

1950

"Spiders and Such" (radio talk), broadcast BBC Home Service 10 June 1950; *London Mystery Magazine*, February/March 1951.

"The Human Touch" (radio talk), broadcast BBC Light Programme, 12 September 1950 [unpublished].

"Jewel Thieves at Albert Hall" (TV talk), broadcast BBC Television, 30 September 1950 [unpublished].

"Eliza Among the Chimney Sweeps," *The Children's Ship* edited by Cynthia Asquith (1950).

"How I Became Interested in Ghosts" (TV Talk), broadcast BBC Television, 13 October 1951 [unpublished].

1989

"Wishful Thinking," *The Magic Mirror* (1989).

Other Stark House books you may enjoy...

Stark House Press, 1315 H Street, Eureka, CA 95501
707-498-3135 www.StarkHousePress.com

Retail customers: freight-free   holesale: 40%, freight-free on
10 mixed copies or more, re   3 1901 03905 5589   er or Baker & Taylor Books.